Where Would Jesus Go to Church?

Gerald Roe

With Foreword by Ken Hemphill

innovo
PUBLISHING

Table of Contents

Acknowledgments

It was Sir Isaac Newton who, in a 1676 letter to his rival Robert Hooke, wrote the oft-quoted phrase, "If I have seen a little further it is by standing on the shoulders of giants." Interestingly, it appears that this insightful line did not originate with the venerable Newton. In 1159, theologian and author John of Salisbury used a version of the phrase in a treatise on logic called *Metalogicon.* He wrote:

> We are like dwarfs sitting on the shoulders of giants. We see more, and things that are more distant, than they did, not because our sight is superior or because we are taller than they, but because they raise us up, and by their great stature add to ours.

That is exactly how I feel—like a dwarf sitting on the shoulders of giants. The significance of my personal "giants" is largely known only to me. Such anonymity, however, is not fair to them, for they all have made inestimable contributions to my life and thought. The short list includes my early school teachers (such as Mrs. Richardson and Mr. Mustacio), longsuffering deacons (like Larry Jones and Richard Colyer), patient secretaries and assistants (notably Ann Colyer and Arnetta Hart), pastoral mentors (such as Earl Dousay and Wally Tilleman), college and seminary instructors (like Dianne Hom and Dr. Mark Terry), and academic colleagues (most significantly the North Greenville University College of Christian Studies "guys on the hall" faculty: Drs. Walter Johnson, Bill Murray, Adrian Pater, Pete Wilbanks, David Haynie, Jeff Rankin, Donny Mathis, and Curt Horn). With these people in mind, allow me to make Salisbury's words a bit more personal: *they raised me up, and by their great stature added to mine.*

Beyond these important people, several others have had a very direct hand in the writing and production of this book, and who deserve recognition. My sweet wife, Cheryl, is foremost among these. For over a year, she basically gave me up. During this period, I spent most hours at home sequestered in my study, writing. I was in the house, but far away. Cheryl managed this long process without complaint and with full, prayerful support. It is by no means an overstatement to say that without her sacrifice this book would never have come to life. I thank God for a life partner of such spiritual depth and selfless support.

My mother, Mattie, certainly deserves acknowledgment. From day one of my life, she has been my biggest—and most persistent—fan. While others may believe in me as much, no one ever believed in me more. She has provided constant motivation to think, read, and write. Numerous were the times during the writing of the manuscript when writer's block and self-doubt threatened to stymie the process. Her calls and emails of support—and, often, stern prodding—provided needed motivation to stay with it. Thanks, Mom, I love and appreciate you.

Additionally, I will forever be grateful to Bart, Darya, Terry, and all the team at Innovo Publishing. While each played an important role in transforming *Where Would Jesus Go to Church?* from a rough manuscript into a quality book, I am most grateful for the fact that they were willing to take a chance on an unknown author. All who have ever tried to secure a publisher for a first effort understand just how difficult the process is. Most new authors can testify to receiving enough rejection letters to paper a large wall. I am no different. The enthusiasm with which these individuals embraced my work will never be forgotten and will always be appreciated.

I would be remiss to overlook one of the most important and deserving groups in my life. In 2003, I joined the Christian Studies faculty at North Greenville University in Tigerville, South Carolina. Since that time, I have served as associate professor and chair of the intercultural studies/missions department. I can honestly say that for almost ten years I have not gone to work one day. Nothing in over forty years of ministry has equaled the joy I find in showing up on campus each day. This is due in no small part to the students with whom I work. My mission students are some of the best and most committed kids at the university. Their spiritual depth and academic accomplishments are a source of constant inspiration to me. In fact, they challenge me daily to be at my best. Most of them knew I was writing this book. I shared ideas and thoughts with them as the writing proceeded. They offered feedback and insights that were amazing. Often, they played an important role in pushing me forward, never letting me forget that what I had started; I had to finish.

Two of the most remarkable and bright of these students are Zack Melton and Kirk Morris. I consider both these young men as my sons in the ministry.

Zack, who has now graduated, was known by NGU's students and faculty alike as a "Turabian nerd," (always said in love) because of his extensive command of Kate Turabian's infamous style guide. Zack often reviewed whole portions of my developing manuscript. In addition to boldly challenging my citation errors, he shared several textual insights that I openly admit influenced my thinking on certain points and were incorporated in the message of the book. Thanks, Zack. (I've turned up the pressure; now go get your Ph.D.!)

Kirk was (and is) something of my special case. God brought him into my life when he was a senior in high school. Then, during his entire college career, I was Kirk's mentor and faculty advisor. It became obvious to me that God had His hand on this young man. During the writing process, Kirk was often my sounding board for concepts explored in the book. I grew to trust and enjoy his insight and input as representative wisdom from the younger generation of developing ministers. Thanks, Kirk, for helping an old guy see things with fresh eyes.

If I may be so bold and sentimental, I wish to add a very special acknowledgment. You will recall that I spoke of being "sequestered" in my home study while writing. The truth is, however, I was never completely alone. Usually, laying somewhere near my chair, was my friend and constant companion, Lincoln, a large, purebred Golden Retriever. Lincoln refused to be shut out of the study. He wanted to be where I was, and that's where I wanted him. Many times, I would read fresh portions of the manuscript to him. Often, when stumped by how I wanted to say what I intended, I would talk it out with him. He would raise a drowsy head and listen, then drop back to sleep when the words had been worked out, content to wait on his remuneration—a long walk in the nearby woods.

As I write this acknowledgment, the place beside my chair is vacant. A short time ago, Lincoln succumbed to canine cancer. He was eleven years and one month of age. Our life together spanned that entire period. I simply cannot imagine excluding him from my list of gratitude. He heard it all, saw it all, and remained faithful without condition. Lincoln did not care if I ever published a book. All I ever had to do to be his hero was just show up every day after work and let him stay close by. Thanks, "buddy dog."

Finally and most importantly, I humbly acknowledge the Lord God in His precious Son, my Savior, Jesus Christ. His grace and mercy have sustained me throughout the writing of this book. Without the faithful undergirding of God this book would never have been written. Not only would my energy have waned several times, but apart from lifting up Jesus and encouraging His church, I simply would have had nothing of real value to say. I join Jude in declaring, "Now to Him who is able to keep you from stumbling, and to make you stand in the presence of His glory blameless with great joy, to the only God our Savior, through Jesus Christ our Lord, be glory, majesty, dominion and authority, before all time and now and forever. Amen" (Jude 1:24–25).

Foreword

I have struggled to write a foreword to this book. My struggle is not because I can't find anything good to say about the book. It has been because this book has spoken to me in so many ways, I can't figure out how to limit what I should say to encourage you to read and heed this book.

My good friend and colleague, Gerald Roe, asked me to read this manuscript some time ago. As soon as I read it, I knew it needed to be published and read widely. I immediately asked him to lecture from it to several of my master's level classes at North Greenville University. The students were equally enthusiastic about the content.

I will warn you that this is not an "easy" book to read. Please understand that I do not mean that it is too complicated, too theological, or not well written. It is, in fact, very well written. It is actually an entertaining and enlightening read. It is not "easy" to read because it will challenge you to think about your own life and your church in the light of God's design for His church. This book is balanced, biblical, and constructive. Gerald Roe speaks not as a critic but as a lover of the church.

Let me caution you as you begin reading the first pages of this book—don't assume that you already know where this book is headed. This book will keep you reading, thinking, and evaluating your own life and church. I believe this book has the potential of leading to personal and corporate transformation. I am excited to recommend it to you, because I know it contains a message we must hear and heed.

It will lead to change but not simply for the sake of change. In fact, he challenges the current trend to change for the sake of being contemporary. He is calling for real and substantial change not "stylish, repackaged, recycled methods and programs, produced in a rushed effort to do something that gives the appearance of doing something—anything—that demonstrates connectedness with the surrounding culture."

Dr. Roe asserts that we must first ask "what is" in terms of the church before we can know "what to do." This lost sense of identity is a key issue that keeps the church from being transformational. He affirms that "what works" in the church is not a "what" but a "who." It is not a new plan or program that we need but a new connection to the Head, for it is Christ who works through His church. Church is not something we do but something we are because of who He is!

You will be challenged by the look at the early church. Dr. Roe proves to be not only a good theologian but an accomplished church historian. His section on "Lives as Tools" will cause you to think about how you are investing your life. As he looks at the stunning, world-transforming impact of the early church, you will find yourself longing to be part of a church like that. He provides a simple answer as to the "how to" of the early church. "In the fullest sense then, the astounding accomplishments of the early church had little to do with the question, 'what to do?' According to their actions, the answer to that question was self-evident to the early church: *do what Jesus commanded.* In the minds of the first-century believers, Jesus' commands were simple, clear, and consistent; all that remained was to obey Him energetically."

Dr. Roe's discussion of the marks of a true disciple is worth the price of the book. These are not simply to be read and written in the flyleaf of your Bible; they are to be embraced and practiced.

- A true disciple follows in genuine repentance.
- A true disciple follows in an ongoing lifestyle.
- A true disciple follows by living the normality of a sacrificed life.
- A true disciple is intentional about sacrifice.
- A true disciple follows Christ by living a refocused life.

While this book does offer a biblical critique about some of the trends of the modern church growth movement, it is not a negative book. It is both positive and practical in its approach. It not only challenges the reader and the church to allow what it does to naturally emerge from what it is and Who it serves. Chapter six will provide practical steps that will help a church become more missional in its thinking and behavior. This book should be read, discussed, and acted upon by leaders and laity alike.

Dr. Roe does answer his own question concerning the question of where Jesus might go to church if he were to visit your town. "The great truth overarching all of this is—Jesus is supreme as Lord of His church. He is 'Lord-basis' for order; He is the 'Lord-designer' of structure. Because He is a sovereign Lord and fully deserving of the honors of royalty, Jesus feels most at home among people who realize His supremacy, not only by celebrating His deity but by submitting to His full control over every detail of the church's life and function. Such a church would certainly be a place Jesus would attend."

Kenneth Hemphill, Ph.D.
Past President, Southwestern Baptist Theological Seminary
Director, Center for Church Growth and Revitalization
North Greenville University

Preface

This book has been in process for over sixty years. The thoughts and ideas in it are based upon my personal experiences, observations, and reflections spanning a lifetime. All that is within its pages reflect what has been growing within me through the years. Several times in the past, I considered putting my thoughts to paper. Until now, however, the time did not seem right. Perhaps I needed to see more, experience more, or simply grow more. While I am certainly not at the proverbial point of being "there" yet, it seems enough of time's water has gone under the bridge to share my heart with you.

Let me tell you a bit of my journey. I grew up in a pastor's home, viewing life from the perspective of a pew. While church folk in general refer to their particular place of worship as their "church home," they usually mean that place where they periodically gather with other church members for Bible study, worship, and fellowship. For me, church was actually an extension of my physical residence, and all the church members seemed like additional relatives. Consequently, my childhood was colored in very personal ways by all the ups and downs of a pastor's engagement with his congregation. From this vantage point, I saw, heard, and experienced most of what went on, and I felt the mixture of emotions that arise when God's man invests his life in the lives of others.

Further, I was also a front-row observer of church life as it regards an entire local community of worship, witnessing the full range of experiences that both bless and break a pastor's heart. For example, on numerous Sunday nights (actually early Monday mornings) I was awakened by the voice of my father praying in the next room. You see, on the other side of the wall against which the head of my bed was placed was the living room in our small house. The wall was thin and allowed every sound from either side to penetrate. I cannot count the times through the years when I was awakened by the sound of my father praying through the church Rolodex he kept at home. Sometimes, the prayers were joyful and filled with gratitude. On other occasions, I heard Dad weeping over the actions and attitudes of different individuals in the church. Often, his pain was over general problems affecting the entire congregation. All in all, it was quite an education, from the inside out.

The years since my childhood have proved likewise eventful and educational. You see, in the main, the total of my years since leaving home in 1969 have been spent engaged in my own ministry. Most of these years were spent in pastoral ministry, including senior pastorates in Texas, Hawaii, and Kentucky. Additionally, I have been privileged to serve as a vocational evangelist, missionary, mission administrator, and university educator. However, my heart and greatest attention have remained firmly attached to the local church. In fact, even in my current role as professor at a private Christian university, I continue to work with churches as an interim, or transitional, pastor. I can't seem to help it. When it comes to the church and me, old habits are hard to break; old loves are even more difficult to overcome.

I suppose that's the key motivation for my continued working relationship with the church—abiding love. One of the traits of possessing an abiding love is that, for the lover, the thing loved becomes something of an ongoing project. For instance, when two people are truly in love, they will focus an extraordinary amount of attention on one another. They will seek to know all they can about the other person. Everything will be studied; every characteristic will be observed and cataloged. All the experiences the two share will be remembered, not just for the sake of memories, but as a means to better know the individual loved. Said another way, the lover will become a passionate, astute observer, always looking, always thinking. This analogy can be applied to anyone who truly loves the church, as well.

Building on this analogy, one advantage of shared true love is that it allows for honesty without the object of one's affection being diminished or lost. There is no threat of loss, because true love seeks to maintain and build up, never to destroy. In the case of the church, this is a good thing precisely because there are issues affecting the life and effectiveness of the modern church, which need to be honestly addressed. But they must only be addressed in love by people who truly love the church—people who recognize the sacred value of the church and are willing to do the biblically necessary things for change and health, without abandoning the Body altogether. You see, the last thing the church needs are naysaying, "doomsdayers," whose agendas are motivated by personal discontent gone amuck. There are too many of these people as it is.

Sadly, many of these naysaying individuals are not just to be found outside the church; many of them are within the church, right now. In some cases, they even purport themselves as leaders whose call, they claim, is not to restore the timeless, authentic church but rather to remake the church into an image more in keeping with "the times." In far too many cases, these individuals treat the precious Bride of Christ with loveless disdain, regard essential doctrine as a divisive enemy to be stricken down, and approach sound ecclesiology as an impediment to be destroyed.

To anyone of this ilk, I say, there are two deaths necessary for the church, neither of which involves the destruction of the Body. The first of these two has already been accomplished by the sacrificial death of Jesus Christ to bring the church to life. The second is the biblically required death to self of every member of the Body of Christ. Therefore, all naysayers be on notice: the death that needs to occur within the church is very likely your own death to self and all that comprises any agenda of your own design.

However, it is not so much the activities of the more overt naysayers that have precipitated a very real crisis in the evangelical church of North America. The church has always been under fire from those who would destroy it. The greatest peril is for those who truly love the church and are rightly connected with Scripture, but find themselves at a loss as to how to deal with the frustration caused by the church's declining numbers and the loss of authentic discipleship. These are people wearied of the constant infighting over minor issues and who truly desire to experience vibrancy and passion among God's people—people who know that God has a holy "more" for His church, and who are tired of settling for less. Perhaps you are one of these folk. Let's check to be sure.

- You love the historical church of Scripture.
- You love God's people enough to be honest in every respect, even if that honesty points its finger at you.
- You trust the Bible above all else and know that within its pages are the only answers God will ever give or honor as definitive for the church.
- You join with other believers in declaring your wish to be faithful to the teachings of God's Word in every respect, especially with regard to the church.

If you answered yes to these questions, I welcome you. We have much in common. Now, there are two more questions to be asked before we move forward.

- Do you recognize that there is a disparity—a gap— between the church's claim to biblical fidelity in its growth and ministry methods and how it actually operates in practice?
- Do you also understand that it is this *gap* that has created the church's present crisis of identity and definition on one hand, and uncertainty as to correct methodology on the other?

Said another way, in more cases than we might like to admit there seems to be a very real disconnect (gap) between what the true church *is* and what the modern church is *doing*. And it is not enough to bridge this gap; this gap must be closed! It is this gap I seek to address in the following pages.

To the end that love motivates and the needs within the church are addressed, the ideas and thoughts within this book are shared. More than a textbook or a "how to" work, this is a think piece. It is meant to share ideas based upon my own experiences and observations with the goal of stimulating thinking and, hopefully, discussion. I challenge each of us to be like Abraham Lincoln, who once said that when he "locked onto an idea," he would "worry the thing until he had worn it threadbare." The church is worth the time and effort.

Gerald B. Roe
Greer, SC
February 2013

Chapter 1

If Jesus Were "Church Shopping"

Where would Jesus go to church? A strange question? Perhaps. A presumptuous question? Maybe. A foolish question? Not at all, as the following bit of background and context will make clear.

Every other year I teach a church-planting course at North Greenville University in Tigerville, South Carolina. A few years ago, as I was doing my "preps" for the upcoming semester, I endeavored to think of several leading questions I might use to stimulate thinking and enhance student participation. My preparations to that point had brought me to a section of lectures on worship styles and church life after a congregation has been planted. Trying to think like a university student, I set out to list questions I thought would be the kinds of things a student would ask in response to my lectures. One question kept reoccurring: where would Jesus go to church? No matter how hard I tried to think of others, that one persistent question refused to go away. I worked to restate it in some fashion that would sound more academic and less assumptive. None of my efforts were successful and the question would not go away; so, I decided to leave it as is and listen for the replies.

Instead of asking the question as part of the summary of my lectures, I chose to ask it at the beginning of the lecture series, urging students to keep it in mind while I spoke. Then I began. I had been teaching for only a few minutes when, without a raised hand or any other sign that he was about to speak, I was interrupted by a normally quiet student: "That's a good question. Where *do you* think Jesus would go to church?" The questioner was a young man seated near the back of the room. He was not looking at me or anyone else in particular. He just stared ahead as if looking at something far away, with a look of deep contemplation.

Because I had no intention of allowing myself to be led into a rabbit-chasing exercise, I was about to give my cursory response of "that's a good question; we'll get back to that in a minute," then move on with my remarks. However, the class immediately took hold of the question. From around the room came responses like, "yeah," "cool question," and "what *do* you think?" The truth is, I was somewhat intrigued, as well. After all, by this time the question had been so mentally persistent in me that I really did want to explore it.

Before I had a chance to respond, however, the questioner continued. "I mean, what if Jesus came back right now to live on earth like He did in Bible days? Wouldn't He go to church the same way He went to the synagogue back then? Which church would he choose? I mean, like, if the true church is all about Jesus, wouldn't it be a good idea to consider what Jesus would look for in a church and make that part of our church-planting methodology?"

Suddenly, what had earlier seemed a strange even presumptuous question became an inquiry worthy of invest-igation, especially when the question was considered in light of the way the student had framed it. First, it does make sense to believe that if Jesus walked the earth in human form today He would be as conscious of the need for corporate assembly and worship as He was two thousand years ago. Luke's Gospel says, "And He came to Nazareth, where He had been brought up; and *as was His custom, He entered the synagogue on the Sabbath*, and stood up to read" (Luke 4:16, italics added). A key word in this passage is the word *ethō*, the Greek word translated as "custom." The word can also be translated "habit" or "manner." Luke's point seems clear enough: Jesus made a habit of regularly going to the synagogue and engaging in worship. Obviously, the habit of synagogue attendance and worship was so important to Jesus that it became customary, or routine, for Him. It certainly seems sensible to conclude that Jesus would maintain the same priority of custom, habit, or manner today.

Second, what of the student's observation that the church is all about Jesus? That's a vital point. To underscore the fact that church is indeed all about Jesus, it is necessary to review only a couple of key biblical texts. For example, the apostle Paul wrote in Ephesians 1:22–23, "And He put all things in subjection under His feet, and gave Him as head over all things to the church, which is His body, the fullness of Him who fills all in all." Of course, the single "He" under whom God has put all things, *especially the church*, is Jesus. Thus, Jesus, by God's own choice, is the undisputed, divinely appointed, singular head of the church.

Further, these verses identify the church as the God-defined *body* of Christ. Paul's assertion that the church is the *body* of Christ is a point that should not be too quickly passed over. For a variety of reasons, the body metaphor well suits the composition of the church, not the least of which is the fact that human form imagery makes it easy to gain one very important bit of information about the *life* of the church. As the great pastor, Adrian Rogers, once said, "Jesus is the head of the church. Everyone knows that a body with no head is dead, and a body with two heads is a freak." Rogers' words, declared vividly in the charged moments of preaching, are absolutely true. To have no head is certain death; to have multiple heads is to have little hope of survival. The church apart from proper connection to its single head is little more than a lifeless group of dead people trying desperately to appear alive.

Writing to the church at Colossae, Paul was equally explicit about Christ's headship over the church saying, "He is also head of the body, the church; and He is the beginning, the firstborn from the dead, so that He Himself will come to have first place in everything" (Colossians 1:18). Look at what is affirmed in this single, powerful passage: (1) the church is the Body of Christ; (2) Jesus is the single head of that Body (both literally and metaphorically); and (3) in everything related to the Body, Jesus alone has—and is always to have—the preeminence. Recalling Rogers' words, to avoid outright death or deathlike freakishness, it is imperative that the church acknowledge itself as a body with a single head, understand with absolute conviction that the head is Jesus Christ, and assume a posture of submissiveness as a body under the full control of His headship.

Considering the biblical evidence that the church in its multifaceted body composition is all about Jesus—the head—one cannot help but reason that the qualities Jesus might look for in a particular congregation are worthy of being emulated, in both initial church planting and long-term church life. Thus, asking where Jesus would go to church is not at all foolish; it is expedient. Further, if as suggested it is expedient that the question be asked and considered, it makes sense that the question deserves a reasoned answer.

Giving the Question the Attention It Deserves

Think about it for just a moment: Where *would* Jesus go to church? Perhaps one of these adjective-based church names would attract Him: Revolution Church, Generation Church, Journey Church, Liquid Church. Of course, if we assume that church is primarily about the value of the Head, and not the intentions of the Body, one must ask which of these adjectives best describes the character and integrity of the Head.

Maybe Jesus would prefer a church that shares the values expressed in the following church purpose statements:

- ". . . a church that exists for the Unconvinced, the Unconnected, and the Unfinished." (One is left to wonder in which of those categories would Jesus fit?)

- "Church Like You've Never Seen It Before! Outstanding Music . . . No choirs or pipe organs here. Our music is crisp, contemporary, professional, and yes, even hot!" (Perhaps working to make Jesus "hot" is an attempt to keep Isaiah 53:3 from being repeated.)
- "We believe church should be inviting, powerful, transformational, and religion-free." (But didn't the apostle James acknowledge and speak of practices that define true religion?)

Perhaps Jesus would be drawn to a church whose public relations outreach—perhaps even its programming—accepts the counsel of the following church marketing firm.

1. People get saved only for selfish reasons.

If people only get saved because they have a need, a want, some problem, or some fear, then you should show them, right in your ad, how you and your church can help them get what they want.

2. Understand the "Buyer's Box" principle.

At any given time in a large group of people, a certain number of those people will be ready to make a buying decision for whatever product it is you wish to sell. God and the Holy Spirit are continually at work softening people up and making them receptive to His calling. That's why savvy churches continually promote various "felt needs" message series with great success. They know there always is going to be a certain number of people in a "spiritual buyer's box" looking for help with their marriage or their kids or their careers.

3. Use the type of words direct response advertisers use.

There are a few dozen key words and phrases that, when used, will simply cause an ad to work better, words like: You, New,

Proven, Breakthrough, Special, Guaranteed, Discover, Introducing, Miracle, Forever, How To, Easy, At Last, Free, Secrets.

Maybe Jesus would seek out one of the electrifying sight and sound services so readily available on Sunday mornings across North America. Yet I wonder, how impressed would He who created the sun, moon, and stars be with even the grandest of our multilayered light and prop displays? How impressed would He who listens to angel choirs be with our finest pageants? How impressed would He who created the Grand Canyon, Niagara Falls, and the splendor of fall mountain foliage be with our multimillion-dollar facilities and grand architectures. How impressed would He who listens continually to the heavenly hosts shouting "worthy is the Lamb" and "Hallelujah! For the Lord God, the Almighty, reigns. Let us rejoice and be glad and give the glory to Him" (Revelation 19:6–7) be with a worship service that is fast paced, light on prophetic preaching, and very heavy on music and drama, seemingly preoccupied with being "trendier-than-thou?" In how many of the cited cases would the Son of God feel again what He felt when He first came to the earth? When, according to John 1:11, "He came to His own, and those who were His own did not receive Him." In which of the cases would Jesus leave the church feeling that He had been the object of worship, the subject, center, and sole purpose of worship, and not merely an icon providing justification for the performance?

The argument often goes, we know so much more about the need for societal and cultural engagement than in days past. We are so much better equipped to shape, fashion, and package the church so as to reflect the Head without appearing noticeably different from popular culture. This argument is akin to a sculptor chiseling a block of stone into a shape of his or her own design, then bringing in the model to see how nearly the stone matches that person's image. Sadly, it appears that in many cases our "much learning" may very well be a contributor to such backward attempts at doing church.

Further, in some quarters church is in danger of becoming primarily an academic pursuit, complete with "informed" debate, immovable allegiances, and, in its most extreme result, intense pride, believing as we tend that no mystery is beyond the power of collective human reason. Admittedly, there is a necessary place for studies of the church within the academy. Further admitted is the fact that involvement with the academy will always include debate. This is fine as long as the debate is largely a conversation between inquiring disciples, not competing entities who are more intent on their positions than they are committed to the leadership of the church's one Head. Perhaps it is at this point that we should pause, and instead of yielding to pride and personal demands, humbly recall that Jesus did not come to take sides—He came to take control. Remember, Jesus *is* the Head.

Allowing Jesus His rightful place as head in all our deliberations about church—whether in the academy, individual conversations, or board/committee meetings—would likely yield some enlightening results. For example, we might discover that including sermons and ministries that address human needs as perceived by human beings (felt needs) can be valid and useful, serving as contemporary parables to illustrate the careful exegesis of God's Word. We might find that building the ministry of a particular church within the context of a specific target, instead of dishonoring God, can liberate a congregation and enhance its overall ministry effectiveness. We might even discover that utilizing the spiritual gifts of believers by expressing the highest levels of creativity in worship has the potential to encourage those individuals to give back to God the best of what He has given them, as well as glorifying God in beautiful and unique ways. Most surprising might be the discovery that time-honored, traditional forms of worship still have their place, providing for many a reassuring sense of spiritual well-being in a world otherwise fraught with insecurity.

Each of these observations involves subjects of ongoing debate, yet none of them in and of themselves are inherently right or wrong. Still, when any method, tradition, philosophy, or practice is so routinized as to become in itself the *definition* of true church, the entire enterprise is at worst threatened with irrelevance or, at best, merely running in place instead of running the race (Hebrews 12:1b). Both of the potential outcomes serve only to perpetuate a very real and growing crisis.

Coming to Terms with a Crisis

The church of North America is in crisis. Do not misunderstand. I do not mean to insinuate that the North American church will not survive. Jesus made specific promises regarding the survival and victory of the true church that includes every continent on the face of the earth. Not even hell can destroy it (Matthew 16:18). But there is a crisis, nonetheless. It is not necessarily a crisis of method, style, ecclesiastical form, or cultural relevance (though those issues are debated *ad nauseam*). Instead, it is largely a crisis of identification and biblical understanding.

It is interesting that this conclusion seems to be verified by liberal and conservative observers of the church alike. For instance, while I disagree with many of Bill J. Leonard's theological positions and his criticism of conservative evangelicalism, the founding dean of the Wake Forest University School of Divinity, does offer some interesting insights into the nature of this crisis. In an analysis originally published in *The Baptist Times* of the Baptist Union of Great Britain, Leonard locates the crisis in what he calls "a state of permanent transition"[1] involving all of American Protestantism. He wrote,

---

[1] Bill J. Leonard, "Analysis: Southern Baptists Face the Future—and an Identity Crisis," *Associated Baptist Press* Web Site, abpnews.com/content/view/5341/53/, accessed 14 July 2010. Republished from *The Baptist Times*, the Baptist Union of Great Britain, nd.

These days it is clear that fewer religious Americans think of their primary identity in terms of a denomination. Once the primary way of organizing Protestant communions in the United States, denominations now are only one of *multiple options* along with independent churches, mega-churches, emergent churches and a variety of non-denominational, interchurch coalitions (italics added).[2]

Not surprisingly, given his predilection for arguments against the Southern Baptist Convention, Leonard uses the SBC as a case study to make his point, listing several characteristics of the "permanent transition," which he contends are observable within the Convention. Consider the following summary of his observations (italics added):

- Statistical *declines or plateaus* in the number of annual baptisms reported by SBC member churches
- *Declining* contributions to denominational programs and agencies
- A continuing increase in the age of the average SBC church member (now calculated to be in the mid-to-late 50s)
- Studies indicating that the majority of SBC churches are *declining or stagnant* in membership and baptisms. One recent study suggests that only 11 percent of SBC churches are growing through evangelization of unchurched persons rather than simply transfer of members from other churches.
- A *steady decline* in the number of churches that utilize traditional methods of evangelism—revivals, professional evangelists, direct evangelistic techniques—as means of reaching the unchurched

---

[2]Ibid.

- When transferring membership, they are apt to look for a particular type of congregation before they consider its denominational label.

- An expanding localism by which members strongly identify with their specific congregation but are less identified with more extended . . . alliances

- As churches move away from revivals as the means for annual evangelistic campaigns, many are unclear as how to extend their evangelistic outreach in other ways.

- . . . an increasing number of churches . . . keeping more of their money at home . . .

- The rise of the mega-church has had significant effects on . . . identity and practice. Such massive congregations are usually guided by a central pastoral figure/CEO and offer specialized ministry to target groups . . . organized around intentional marketing techniques. . . .

- . . . a new generation of Internet-fueled and reform-minded . . . activists, who resist denominational attitudes and practices they view as too doctrinally or denominationally conformist.[3]

Several disturbing things stand out in Leonard's analysis, not the least of which is the repeated usage of such words as "plateau," "stagnant," and variants of the word "decline" when applied to the present state of North American churches. The crisis nature of these words is clear when they are understood as qualifiers of such troubling church trends and conditions as reduced growth by evangelism, fewer contributions to larger cooperative efforts, the overall greying of numerous congregations, and the reluctance of numerous congregations to be "typed" by labels they view as potentially harmful to their public persona or that threaten to "hem them in" with certain ecclesiastical traditions or doctrines.

---

[3]Leonard, "Analysis: Southern Baptists Face the Future"

On the more conservative side, in its own self-assessments, the Southern Baptist Convention—the world's largest evangelical denomination—seems to reinforce Leonard's conclusions. As far back as 2002, the North American Mission Board (SBC) estimated that "219.5 million people in the United States and Canada [were] totally unchurched. . . . The gulf between churched and unchurched has grown by over 28 million in the last decade alone."[4] In round numbers, the Southern Baptist Convention has approximately 50,000 congregations. Currently, "this [number of congregations] represents a church for every 5,700 people in the United States and one church for every 227,000 people in Canada. If the North American population stopped growing today, at [the SBC's] current baptismal rate it would take close to 500 years for Southern Baptists to reach everyone."[5] Add to these data the troubling report that "seventy-two churches close their doors each week in the U.S. and Canada,"[6] and the resulting conclusion is undeniable. Stated simply, the increasing divergence between churched and unchurched peoples indicates that too many existing North American churches—whether healthy, plateaued, or declining—are simply not bridging the gap between churched and unchurched peoples.

Sadly, current studies are no more encouraging than those of previous years, indicating that the gap between churched and unchurched peoples is still a gaping one. For example, findings released in 2009 from the American Religious Identification Survey (ARIS) found that "[t]he percentage of Americans claiming 'no religion' almost doubled in two decades, climbing

---

[4] North American Mission Board, Nehemiah Project site menu 1.1, http://www.namb.net/nehemiah/whatis.html.menu.html (accessed June 17, 2002).

[5] Richard H. Harris, "A 20/20 Vision for the Twenty-First Century," 1.1, http://www.namb.net/cp.NAMB.html (accessed June 6, 2002).

[6] North American Mission Board, Nehemiah Project "Introduction," 1.1, http://www.namb.net/root/nehemiah/intro.html.NAMB.html (accessed June 24, 2002).

from 8.1 percent in 1990 to 15 percent in 2008."[7] Further, the study noted that the trend toward "no religion" in response to questions pertaining to religious affiliation was not confined to only one region of the United States. "Those marking 'no religion' [in the survey] . . . made up the only group to have grown in every state, from the secular Northeast to the conservative Bible Belt."[8]

Just as alarming, though not altogether surprising, is the continued—and increased—hemorrhaging of young people from the ranks of the American church. In May 2009, political scientists Robert Putnam and David Campbell presented research from their book *American Grace* to the Pew Forum on Religion and Public Life. In their presentation they reported that "young Americans are dropping out of religion at an alarming rate of five to six times the historic rate (30 to 40 percent have no religion today, versus 5 to 10 percent a year ago)."[9] While Putnam's and Campbell's research addressed religious participation on a general scale, Rainer Research Group and The Barna Group offer more specific application of the data to the local church. Rainer found that "approximately 70 percent of American youth drop out of church between ages 18 and 22. Barna . . . estimates that 80 percent of those reared in the church will be 'disengaged' by the time they are 29."[10] Taken together, these data leave us with the sad conclusion that "[t]he vast majority of outsiders [to the Christian faith] in this country, particularly among young generations, are actually *de*churched individuals."[11]

Still, despite such bad news there are analysts who seek to be more optimistic about the current condition of the North American church. However, even these few more upbeat reports usually present conclusions accompanied by studied qualifications, indicating the tenuous nature of their findings. Clearly, the church

---

[7]Drew Dyck, "The Leavers," *Christianity Today*, November 2010, 40.
[8]40.
[9]Drew Dyck, "The Leavers," 40.
[10]42.
[11]42.

must admit to a crisis and reinvestigate the data for the purpose of not only identifying the trends, but more importantly discovering their root causes as well—even if that discovery lays much of the responsibility for the crisis at our own feet.

Take a moment and reread the material above. If that information is read with an eye for the causes undergirding the trends enumerated, several things stand out. Consider the following personal observations regarding causation.

Much of What Is Regarded as Needed Change Appears Artificial in Nature

Each of the characteristics above have emerged in the wake of the current demand for various changes within the church, including affiliations, worship styles, targets, preaching style and content, etc. But the practical evidence suggests that when changes to these things are initiated, they simply result in repeated calls for and the installation of more change. Additionally, in far too many instances what is offered as real change appears to be little more than the mere exchange of stylishly repackaged, recycled methods and programs, produced in a rushed effort to do something that gives the appearance of doing something—anything—that demonstrates connectedness with the surrounding culture. Leaders, troubled by the much-dreaded perception of being out of step with society's definitions of church, human need, and proper ministry are pressed into (often quite innocently and with the best of motives) redressing tried and failed answers to look like innovation and then implementing them as bold, God honoring, genuine change. However, rushing into human *activity* in response to secular trends—even when doing so appears proactive, progressive, and socially sensitive—as opposed to careful *action* led and fueled by the Holy Spirit, will always yield results that are transitory in nature and so doomed to failure that the call for replacement changes in the future is unavoidable.

It is important to remember that real change in the church, when and where needed, is good if (and this is a big "if") it truly corrects unbiblical trends and provides godly results that are both biblical and permanent. Change that results in greater frustration due to hasty actions, unchecked motives—or even good motives that do not take time to hear out God for directions—is wrong, pure and simple. Actions that maintain the continuing cycle of transitory *exchange* that is not genuine biblical *change* only exacerbates the perception (both inside and outside the church) that the church, like any other earthly organization, must flounder in uncertainty while doing the best it can to solve its own issues. Consequently, the vitality and confidence that accompanies the knowledge that there *is* a permanent answer transcending all human variables in its application are lost. When this occurs, the church of triumph becomes the church of trepidation, with its membership living as stymied residents on earth's shifting sands instead of being confident occupants firmly planted on God's solid rock. The tendency to rush to change motivated by any concern—being out of step with the cadence set by the public's preferences, the desire to achieve relevance through fully identifying with and accommodating the whims of culture, or simply desiring to prove a point by "doing it differently"—are wrong-headed at best and blatantly unbiblical at worst.

The Belief in Absolute Solutions Applicable to the Universal Church Regardless of Time and Culture Seems to Be Lost

The old adage that the only thing that does not change is change itself appears to have moved from the world of ideas into the realm of absolute law. According to professor and author, Robert Don Hughes, Baby Boomers (individuals born between 1945 and 1964) accept change as a necessary evil to be managed and applied when needed. Their children and grandchildren (Busters, Bridgers, Millennials, etc.), on the other hand, consider change an unavoidable inevitability. Further, for those generations subsequent to the Boomers, largely postmodern in their world views, the sense that change is inevitable is understood as a logical consequence of the perceived lack of absolutes and consequent dominance of relativity. In other words, if nothing is ever fully settled by the existence of absolute truth, all solutions are subject to change and replacement as they flow within the stream of relative answers. Consider, for example, the young man, distinctly postmodern in his thinking, who chose to yield to his misgivings and abandon his previous faith. "When his father learned of his decision . . ., he rushed his son a copy of *Mere Christianity*, hoping the book would bring him back. But C. S. Lewis's logical style left him cold. 'All that rationality comes from the Western philosophical tradition,' [he said]. 'I don't think that's the only way to find truth.'"[12] For this young man and multitudes like him, there is no such thing as a single solution that can possibly result in enduring, permanent change. Therefore, for applied changes to fail and require more change in the future is both normative and is to be expected.

When this attitude moves into the church, it rarely does so admitting to a basis of relativity. The argument usually runs something like this: the church is filled with imperfect human beings who cannot be expected to determine and apply permanent change. Admittedly, the first part of the statement is true: the church—the Body—*is* populated by imperfect people. Equally true, however, is the fact that the Body has a perfect head! And answers do not (at least they are not supposed to) flow from the body to the head; they flow from the Head to the Body.

---

[12]Drew Dyck, "The Leavers," 42.

Perhaps this is a good place to reflect on a very basic biblical, theological question. In all the Bible's presentation of the church—doctrinally, historically, propositionally—is any of the information offered in a pick-and-choose, options-oriented fashion? Absolutely not! Everything the Bible teaches about the origin, nature, characteristics, and functions of the church are treated as singular, absolute, and final. The reason is simple: while the earthly church may be a body of yet to be perfected human beings, the head of the body is none other than omnipotent, omnipresent, omniscient God, in the perfect person of the Lord Jesus Christ. He is the same God who declares, "For I, the LORD, do not change . . ." (Malachi 3:6a).

Given God's self-declared immutability, coupled with His sovereign power (omnipotence), His full knowledge of all things from beginning to end (omniscience), His abiding presence and activity among all peoples and cultures in all places throughout history (omnipresence), is it too much to assume that what God has revealed in His Word about the church are both single and unchanging answers? No, it is not. And because God's single and unchanging answers flow from His own character and power, it further stands to reason that what He sets down as answers are permanent in their durability. This understanding of the nature of God is nothing more than basic, primary Sunday school fare; it should never be jettisoned in favor of accommodating any expression of relativity regarding the character and practice of the church.

Private Fear Masquerading as Cultural Sensitivity among Church Leadership

Notice how the point is framed: "private fear *masquerading* as cultural sensitivity." As a young boy, I recall hearing an evangelist preaching on personal evangelism. At one point, he pointed to the men in the congregation and shouted, "I used to wonder why so many men won't be seen carrying a full-sized Bible, but they will put a small Testament in their shirt pockets. I think the reason is, the big Bible is seen for what it is. The little Testament can easily be mistaken for a pack of Winston's!" He continued, "But you say 'No, I'm just being humble.' Don't give me that," the preacher thundered. "You're not being humble; you're just plain scared to death!"

Obviously, that was a long time ago and in a much different era of preaching. As an illustration, however, the story clarifies my point. Sometimes the things we do, or don't do, may appear to be acts or omissions of noble motivation (for example, acting in humility), when in actuality they really serve to cover a particular personal fear. Do not misunderstand; there is no intent here to downplay the importance of being humbly sensitive to how others—lost or saved—view their needs or life circumstances, or how one should go about expressing concern. The church is called to ministry that is bathed in compassion and human identification. What is being stressed is giving the *appearance* of sensitivity, when in reality the argument to sensitivity is actually a convenient way to avoid admitting the personal fear of facing contemporary culture prophetically.

Perhaps some are thinking, *I agree; God's answers for His church are absolute and permanent. I want to know and implement those answers in my church, but I also truly want to provide those answers in ways that are sensitive to cultural trends and nonoffensive in their application.* Fine. Now consider that response a bit further. To accept the absoluteness of any truth is also to accept the nature of its permanence. This being accepted, the logical and correct next step is to implement that truth in its proper, permanent relation to the question at hand. However, adding to this implementation the conjunction "but" interjects an exception that negates the essence of the entire relationship between question and truth. Remember, anything that is truly absolute stands without exception or qualification.

Consider this. How effective would it be to say, "premeditated, cold-blooded murder is absolutely wrong; but if your emotions get the better of you, you cannot be blamed for your actions"? In this case, you void your overall position by making the absolute statement, "cold-blooded murder is wrong," relative by including the conjunctive phrase, "*but* if you can't help yourself, it's okay." This would be true even if you were motivated to make the exception based on sensitivity to the offender. Whenever you add "but" to a statement of absolute truth, that statement can no longer be regarded as absolute and universal. At least in terms of your argument, the absolute is rendered relative.

The same logic is true regarding the Bible's teachings concerning the church. Because God's Word is absolutely true, there is a divine "either/or" in the responses of God related to His church. We either believe and do exactly what God requires—regardless of cultural responses or our personal fears regarding those responses—or we do not. No mitigating conjunction is allowed. There is no middle ground precisely because there is no true distinction between absolute theological truth and true godly practice. One cannot ascribe to the concepts of an orthodox theology and then follow practices that are inconsistent with the precepts of that theology and maintain any sense of credibility or hope of God's blessing. While God's truth remains absolute, when our practices reflect relativity there is always a killing effect, not to the truth as presented in Scripture, but to the effect and longevity of that truth as practiced.

Quite often, it is argued that the practices of the church, especially with regard to its presentation methodologies, should be crafted so as to make the message more culturally relevant and applicable to those *outside* the Body who do not understand Christ or His gospel. While it can be argued that it is not the responsibility of the world to overcome obstacles in order to get to Jesus, rather it is the responsibility of the church to remove those barriers, crafting church for public understanding must be regarded only as a communication principle, not as the definitive, deciding argument for what the church does.

Paul's words to the Ephesian Church are helpful in understanding this point. He wrote,

> As a result, we are no longer to be children, tossed here and there by waves and carried about by every wind of doctrine, by the trickery of men, by craftiness in deceitful scheming; but *speaking the truth in love*, we are to grow up in all aspects into Him who is the head, even Christ, from whom the whole body, being fitted and held together by what every joint supplies, according to the proper working of each individual part, causes the growth of the body for the building up of itself in love (Ephesians 4:14–16, italics added).

When speaking of the church's engagement of the world, the words most often quoted in these verses are, "speaking the truth in love." Notice, however, that these four words taken from verse 15 are lifted from a much larger—and very important—context. Verse 14 makes it clear that believers are not to be swept away by the external forces surrounding them. Verse 16 demands that we be grounded in the stable truth and person of Jesus Christ. These are two vital bookends supporting a central volume of truth. That truth insists that God's people—the church—*voice the truth* grounded in attitudes of Christ's own love (v. 15), but always within the context of refusal to be swayed by external demands and opinions (v. 14), while maintaining absolute fidelity to our Head, the Lord Jesus Christ (v. 16).

As might be expected, the "love" Paul speaks of is *agapē*, the Greek word most often understood as God's own love. This love, among other things, has two broad implications. First, it is expressive of all the goodwill and graces of God Himself. It is winsome, kind, and unconditional. Second, it is courageous in that it gives what is needed, even if what it gives is not necessarily what is wanted. As used by the apostle, the first application speaks to the spirit and attitude in which truth is spoken: be sweet, winsome, and graceful. The second application refers to the content of what is shared: while one's tone may be guarded, content is not to be sacrificed. Never let it be forgotten that both applications are required if we truly obey Scripture and "speak the truth in love."

Without doubt, it is correct to assert that the world does not understand the church, its message, or its Lord. How could they? Better yet, why would they? The church is an alien body sojourning on the planet. It is called to follow a crucified but living Savior, adhere to a counter-cultural book, and live separated lives. If the church is faithful to its purpose, it proclaims a message that admits to being foolishness to many and an offense for others (1 Corinthians 5:18; Galatians 5:11).

Beyond these factors, the world does not understand the church for a much more basic and universal reason: it is spiritually lost! In other words, the world does not know Christ and is therefore without the spiritual mind to comprehend His church, or its Savior. The apostle Paul underscores this global lack of comprehension by explaining, "because the mind set on the flesh is hostile toward God; for it does not subject itself to the law of God, *for it is not even able to do so*" (Romans 8:7, italics added). To the church at Corinth Paul explained, "But a natural man does not accept the things of the Spirit of God, for they are foolishness to him; and *he cannot understand them*, because they are spiritually appraised" (1 Corinthians 2:14, italics added). Note in both verses how the apostle stresses the fact that people outside of Christ are *completely* without the ability to comprehend spiritual truth. They cannot understand the truth of God, nor do they understand the truth tellers.

Many people do come to a point of understanding truth and responding positively to the gospel. However, when this is genuinely the case, it is because the great reveler of truth, the Holy Spirit, illuminated and made plain the message communicated through the instrumentation of the church. When this happens, new believers tend to rejoice in the truth revealed and care very little about the way in which it was packaged.

Perhaps many reading these words have found nothing new in what has been said. The various media are constantly reporting on the assortment of trends—both positive and negative—affecting the modern church. Speculations, predictions, and analysis swell the literature. Much of the material has excellent informative value. However, it has provided little in the way of stemming the crisis nature confronting the modern church, let alone encouraging leadership who desire to recognize and implement godly change. What is needed is for the church to look at itself (not just the literature) with clear eyes and renewed courage to ask a new set of questions. These questions must probe deeper than mere utilitarian, surface inquiries in an effort to slow the process of particular trends. Surface questions will only produce surface answers, the kind of answers that serve only to perpetuate the deadly cycle of change, exchange, and more change. This cycle must be broken, and it will only be broken when the church takes a fresh approach to self-examination: examination that is focused first on probing biblically the reason for our existence, then using those answers as a basis for *defining* our purpose and *designing* our practices. Until the church comes to a point of reappraisal, repentance, and revival and comprehends anew the bare, simple intent of God for Christ's Body as a salt and light, worshiping, ministering community of broken disciples who deny self and exalt Jesus, we may very well in the midst of our "holy wars" over technology, musical styles, doctrinal versus doctrine lite preaching, or demands for traditionalism in polity and worship, hear the words of the prophet Amos directed to us as they were first spoken to Israel: "I hate, I reject your festivals, nor do I delight in your solemn assemblies. Even though you offer up to Me burnt offerings and your grain offerings, I will not accept them; And I will not even look at the peace offerings of your fatlings. Take away from Me the noise of your songs; I will not even listen to the sound of your harps" (Amos 5:21–23).

That is a graphic vision and a potent warning; it is certainly a condition far outside the revealed will of God for Christ's church. The good news is, Amos' words do not have to be applied to the contemporary church, not if correct responses to the right questions are asked and applied.

A Quick Look at Two of the New Questions: What Is? What to Do?

Not long after the classroom discussion mentioned earlier, I told a colleague about the students' observations regarding my question. After we had discussed the exchange, he asked if I intended to explore the issue further, suggesting that I might find it beneficial to spend some time researching church growth theory as part of the discussion. I responded to his question and suggestion by saying that my answer was both yes and no—and my position has not changed. Allow me to explain my reasons, as I did to my friend.

The answer is "no" because that would most likely entail a discussion centered primarily on *what to do*. I hasten to add that my reluctance to frame a discussion around an appeal to church growth theory is not based in any aversion to that discipline. Rather, I am concerned that appealing too quickly to a *what to do* focus could potentially impede the discovery of significant causation issues that are too important to overlook.

That we global Westerners desire a quick *what to do* strategy in response to most critical situations is undeniable. For example, Google recently returned approximately 969,000 sites when the search term "church growth" was used. It appears there are numerous "what to dos" for every church growth taste and theological persuasion, including at least one site committed to recovery for those ministers addicted to church growth strategies and seminars! The problem with yielding to the Western bent toward an early *what to do* approach to problem solving is that one key point is overlooked: *what to do* is normally expressed as a strategy to achieve a particular goal. But—and here is the problem—in order to be valid, *what is done* must be based upon a foundation that is consistent with both the definition and character undergirding the strategy. Additionally, discovery (perhaps rediscovery) of this foundation requires a previous step. It is in reference to this previous step that I also answered my friend's question, "yes."

Repeating myself, I am not interested in a *what to do* discussion—not just yet anyway. My interest is in a *what is?* conversation, specifically, *what is the true church?* Certainly, where Jesus would go to church would be predicated largely upon a congregation's proximity to being what God intended and the Savior died to create. Further, *what is?* must be the fundamental starting point of the discussion in light of the assertion that the church faces an identity and definition crisis. Simply put, effective strategy always follows correct identity and definition. Before it is possible to know *what to do*, it is essential to know and submit to *what is?* the church. Answering this vital question is the needed previous step before considering *what to do.*

First Things First

Essential to the *what is?* step is agreement on a defining, evidentiary source. For this, we have only to commit ourselves to the single source of God's final revelation regarding the church: the Bible. More will be said about this in the following chapter. Suffice it to say now that with this commitment properly made, our task is to lay aside every human strategy related to *what to do*—whether academic theory, political correctness, scientific data, or cultural expedience—and, as the old saying goes, "when all else fails, *read the directions.*" In other words, it is essential that the church take a fresh look at itself and answer *what is?* through the exclusive lens of the Bible, accepting Scripture alone as the Lord's single, absolute, and final source of church definition and identity. For when—and only when—all issues and questions related to the church are addressed from a biblical perspective and responded to positively will church growth follow as a natural consequence. In other words, God honoring church growth is a result of knowing what constitutes the true church biblically *(what is?)*, and then being faithful to uphold the integrity of that truth *(what to do)*.

At the risk of sounding like I am denying my previously stated position, I will quote the following statement discovered some time ago on the Web while doing research on church planting: "There's no need to 'reinvent the wheel.' The keys to growing a vibrant and successful church are the same as the keys to success in any field: (1) find out what works, (2) find a successful model, and (3) then emulate it!" The heart of this book is a close look at Scripture related to *what is?* using these three points as a master outline. By way of setting the stage for the larger discussion, I wish to reflect briefly on only the first point— "find out what works"—before returning to it in more detail in the following chapter.

Simply put, what works has not, does not, and will not change. This is because what works is not a plan; it is not a strategy; it is not a method. What works is not bound to history, culture, nationality, or ethnicity. All these things do change, for they are in constant flux. What works is a person—the Lord Jesus Christ, the church's single Head—and the relationship of the church to Him. He alone is the one who is unchanging, ". . . the same yesterday and today and forever" (Hebrews 13:8).

For reasons that will become abundantly clear as the *what is?* question is explored, one quickly discovers that biblical terminology always unites the church with Jesus. Consider these facts.

- The Greek word translated church throughout the New Testament—*ekklēsia*—properly defined refers to those "set apart," "called apart," or, in the case of the church, *"ones separated unto and for Jesus."*
- Few word images are more telling of Christ's binding union with His church than what is visualized when the

relationship of Jesus with the church is cast in terms of marriage, bridegroom, and bride (Revelation 19:7).

- Paul understood the connection between Jesus and His church as being so intimate that, inspired by the Holy Spirit, he identified the church as Christ's own *body* in the earth (1 Corinthians 12:27; Ephesians 1:22–23).

- Jesus took full responsibility for the church as owner, defender, and guarantor of its ultimate destiny. He declared, ". . . upon this rock *I will build My church*; and *the gates of Hades will not overpower it*" (Matthew 16:18b, italics added). Christ died to create the church; He promised to preserve the church; and He has pledged to return for the church so that where He is it too may be with Him, forever.

Make careful note of Paul's perspective on Jesus' relationship to the church as seen in Ephesians 1:22–23. The apostle wrote, "And He put all things in subjection under His feet, and gave Him as head over all things to the church, which is His body, the fullness of Him who fills all in all." As previously stated, God appointed Jesus to be the supreme ruler—body head—of the church. However, more than merely setting Jesus over the church as its Head, the Bible says God *gave* Him to the church as a *gift*. And talk about the gift that keeps on giving! Jesus is the very soul of God's glory. In gifting the church with Jesus as its Head, God made the church the receptacle of the abiding gift of His revealed glory in the earth. In other words, God called out and separated the church through Jesus Christ, setting Christ as its Head, in order that He might have an earthly receptacle into which He could continually pour out His glory for the purpose of reveling Himself to humanity, and gaining that glory back through the numerous lives that comprise the earthly Body of Christ. The gifted union of Jesus and His church is unique, binding, and inexorable. This union is fully realized when Christ the Head reigns in supremacy over every detail of the church, the Body, and its life. Remember, all functions of a healthy body are accomplished by its parts, but the functions of the parts are controlled by the head—not the other way around. What is true of the human body is equally true of the spiritual, mystical Body of Christ.

Conclusion

In the truest sense, church is not something *we do*; it is something *we are* because of what He—Jesus—is. This essential truth affects everything and serves to put all things in proper perspective. For example, we serve because *in* Christ we are the church; we do not serve to be the church. We worship because in Christ we are the church; we do not worship to become the church. The list could go on and on. Suffice it to repeat once more, definition and identity begin not with *what to do*, but with *what is?* Certainly, if He were walking the earth in flesh today and seeking a church to attend, Jesus would be most comfortable worshiping with people whose understanding of church is undergirded by a clear knowledge of what and who they are, as the determining basis for all they do. It would be in this environment that Jesus would enjoy the highest likelihood of being the sole object of worship, and not simply a venerated personality whose name and imagery provide some legitimacy for what was previously determined by others as the right thing to do.

Chapter 2

A Successful Model: What Works?

What works? How often has this question been asked by church leaders? Whether in seeking practical answers to failed programs, planning for the future, or as the subject of purely philosophical/theological musings related to the church, this question remains the bare-bones, nuts-and-bolts issue for those who desire to see the church healthy and growing. Despite the fact that "what works?" is both a nagging question and a frustrating conundrum, most assume that there is a satisfactory answer imbedded within that simple two-word inquiry. Whether motivated by the proper conviction to honor God or simply driven by the annoyance of the unanswered, concerned church leaders endure the frustration and continue to ask the question.

The good news is, there is a valid biblical answer to "what works?" As suggested earlier, however, it is an answer that flows naturally out of the correct response to the prior question—*what is?* To ascertain the answer to *what is?*, it is necessary to pair both the biblical teachings regarding the *nature* of the church (what is?) with the historical examples of the *application* of that truth by the early church (what works?).

Let me challenge your thinking along this line by asking yet another question. Why is it, as we strive to develop a *what works?* strategy, that we choose to extol the historical record of the first-century church's expansion, often chiding congregations for not achieving similar results, then abandon that same record

as it relates to their practices? Asked another way, why is it that
we use the example of the early church's growth to illustrate our
current shortcomings, then we largely ignore the very principles
and practices by which they grew as a biblical rubric for
addressing the needs of the contemporary church? How much
sense does that make?

History confirms unequivocally that the church's growth
during the first three centuries of its existence was nothing less
than exceptional. In fact, I suggest it was humanly impossible.
"Nothing about the early Christians is more striking than the
extent to which they managed to get about [in] the world."[13] In
just over three hundred years, a relatively small band of post-
Pentecost Christians increased from a one city contingent to a
world-wide movement. By the time of the Edict of Milan (AD
313), ending ten periods of the persecution of Christians, there
was hardly a place in the Greco-Roman world without a Christian
presence of some size. One small but important verification of
this point comes from Pliny the Younger (AD 62-c. 115), a
Roman senator and governor of Bithynia-Pontus. In AD 112,
Pliny despatched a commissioned report to Emperor Trajan
concerning Christians and the expansion of their movement. In it
he intimates that the growth of the Church was so rapid that he
had cause to fear that the shrines of the pagan gods "[would]
come to be wholly destroyed."[14] Writing about fifty-four years
later, in AD 166, another official noted that ". . . the number of
Christians has already surpassed that of the Jews."[15] Arguably, the
first three centuries of the church presents a record of the first
mass movement in Christian history.

This growth was incredible enough as a stand-alone fact.
But realizing that the early exponential expansion of Christianity
was accomplished during a period with few assets contemporary

---

[13]Stephen Neill, *A History of Christian Missions*, 2nd ed. (New York,
NY: Penguin Books, 1990), 24.

[14]Quoted in Neill, *A History*, 28, from J. Stevenson, *Pliny, Epistles X,
96, 97*, (np: 1957), 13–16.

[15]30.

missionaries might consider essential, including modern travel and mass communication technologies, the accomplishment is nothing less than jaw-dropping. Admittedly, there did exist advantages unique to the period, which greatly facilitated the rapid spread of the gospel and the expansion of the church. Such things as the *Pax Romana*, the empire-wide system of Roman roads, and the universal Greek language all contributed to an era characterized as "the fullness of time" (Galatians 4:4). Had the church been born just a century earlier, when few of these things existed as part of the era's social and political reality, the obstacles to church growth would have been enormous. However, contrasted with modern advantages such as jet air travel, satellite-enabled communications, and the increased cross-cultural awareness and understanding fostered by globalization, first-century advantages pale in comparison.

The primary marvel, however, is not in either the unique advantages the church enjoyed at that special moment in time, or in the lack of modern assets. Rather it is in the informed, practical usage the church made of what *was* available to them. Driven by a passionate commitment to Jesus Christ and His gospel, our ancient counterparts utilized what was available and continued to move along the multidirectional missionary trails first blazed by the apostle Paul and his mission teams. As Bishop Stephen Neill summarizes so well:

> What is clear is that every Christian was a witness. Where there were Christians, [in that place] there would be a living, burning faith, and before long an expanding Christian community. . . . that was the greatest glory of the church of those days. . . . The church was the body of Christ, indwelt by his Spirit; and what Christ had begun to do, that the church would continue to do, through all the days and unto the uttermost parts of the earth until his unpredictable but certain coming again.[16]

---

[16]Neill, *A History*, 22–23.

Interestingly, Neill's assessment does not take into account the multitude of believers who witnessed to their newfound faith while remaining in their occupations, living at home, and going about their normal routines. These lifestyle witnesses became an unnumbered, unnamed expansionary force that can only be fully known and applauded in heaven.

Equally amazing is the fact that there is scant biblical evidence that the early church spent much time at all deliberating church growth strategy and methodology. As a point in fact, the most famous meeting of early church leadership—recorded in Acts 15—was not over strategy and methodology per say, but rather it took up questions concerning collateral issues surrounding the doctrines of salvation and Gentile inclusion in the church. What the Bible does record in abundance is the fact that the large majority of early believers postured themselves as lifestyle evangelist missionaries and ultimately engaged the "Jerusalem to the ends of the earth" witnessing program prescribed by Jesus (Acts 1:8).

"Lives as Tools" Ministry

To accomplish their witnessing program, these early believers *invested their lives* as their main tools of ministry, employing five primary means to facilitate Christianity's growth: (1) preaching and teaching of evangelists, (2) personal witness of believers, (3) acts of kindness and charity, (4) faith shown in persecution and death, and (5) intellectual reasoning of early apologists.

It is easy enough to verify that these five items are true regarding the outreach practiced by early believers and not merely the conclusions of some sympathetic historian. To do so, consider the evidence related to the following items from the list.

Preaching and Teaching of the Evangelists

Eusebius of Caesarea (c. AD 263–339), bishop and church historian, offers the following testimony in his seminal work, *Ecclesiastical History*.

At that time [about the beginning of the, second century] many Christians felt their souls inspired by the holy word with a passionate desire for perfection. Their first action, in obedience to the instructions of the Savior, was to sell their goods and to distribute them to the poor. Then, leaving their homes, they set out to fulfill the work of an evangelist, making it their ambition to preach the word of the faith to those who as yet had heard nothing of it, and to commit to them the books of the divine Gospels. They were content to lay the foundations of the faith among these foreign peoples: they then appointed other pastors, and committed to them the responsibility for building up those whom they had merely brought to the faith. They then passed on to other countries and nations with the grace and help of God.[17]

Acts of Kindness and Charity

One of the challenges encountered by early Christians was the determined efforts of Emperor Julian (AD 332–63) to reinstate the ancient Roman religion into a central place of devotion and honor. However, Julian was frequently frustrated by the difficulty he encountered trying to achieve his goal because of the rapid growth of Christianity. Attempting to discover why his program of pagan revival was failing and a religion he regarded as blatant atheism continued to attract followers, Julian ultimately

---

[17]Eusebius, *Ecclesiastical History*, III, 37, 2–3.

concluded that what was drawing many to the Christian faith was their extraordinary exhibition of love in practice.[18] He recorded his thoughts in the following extract from a personal letter:

> Atheism [i.e. Christian faith] has been specially advanced through the loving service rendered to strangers, and through their care for the burial of the dead. It is a scandal that there is not a single Jew who is a beggar, and that the godless Galilaeans [sic] (Christians) care not only for their own poor but for ours as well; while those who belong to us look in vain for the help that we should render them.[19]

Faith Shown in Persecution and Death

During the first three hundred years of the church, "Every Christian knew that sooner or later he might have to testify to his faith at the cost of his life . . . ."[20] This knowledge was the constant context in which early believers lived, day in and day out. They were well aware that Rome was a fickle master. The empire could be at the same time both openly inclusive and monstrously jealous. On one hand, there existed peaceful conditions for travel allowing new ideas to spread freely. On the other hand, there was the constant awareness that Rome's jealousy would never stand by patiently when what it regarded as an upstart movement insisted that Jesus Christ only—not Caesar—should be called Lord. Consequently, "Roman persecution, which flared under the emperors Nero (from A.D. 64), Domitian (from 90), and Marcus Aurelius (in 177) before being exerted systematically by the emperors Decius and Valerian (mid-third century) and Diocletian (start of the fourth century),

---

[18]Neill, *A History*, 37.
[19]Neill, *A History*, 37–38.
[20]38.

took deadly aim at the new faith."[21] While it certainly cannot be maintained that all believers remained faithful to Christ when faced with persecution and death (consider the reason for the writing of Hebrews as evidence of this fact), enough verifiable ancient accounts exist to underscore the conclusion that ". . . in the earlier records what we find is calm, dignified, decorous behavior, cool courage in the face of torment, courtesy toward enemies, and a joyful acceptance of suffering as the way appointed by the Lord to lead to his heavenly kingdom."[22]

The point is clear. Despite being ". . . beset by external foes and [frequently] menaced by ideas and practices threatening its internal character, the church moved out into the wider world."[23] With little of humanly devised advantages to aid its expansion, the gospel ultimately traveled the major length and breadth of the world as known to ancient man.

In the fullest sense then, the astounding accomplishments of the early church had little to do with the question, "what to do?" According to their actions, the answer to that question was self-evident to the early church: *do what Jesus commanded.* In the minds of first-century believers, Jesus' commands were simple, clear, and consistent; all that remained was to obey Him energetically.

Engaging the Primary Source

Because the primitive church's extraordinary success obviously demonstrates the approbation of God for their efforts, the example of early believers recorded in Scripture demands not only our undying *respect* within the context of historical reflection, but our studied *replication* within the context of determining and

---

[21]Mark A. Noll, *Turning Points: Decisive Moments in the History of Christianity.* (Grand Rapids: Baker Books, 1997), 30.

[22]Neill, *A History,* 38.

[23]Noll, *Turning Points,* 30.

applying the most definitive historical record. The Bible is that record. As such, it demands its unique place as God's primary source, in both its propositional *and* its historical forms of presentation—and as our only definitive written allegiance.

Before going further, allow me to quickly acknowledge that two thousand years is in fact a long, long time. But when considering this enormous time distance, two important questions must be asked. First, what has changed in the intervening millennia to make the commands of Jesus and the practices of the early church less clear and less worthy of replication? Second, what has transpired requiring that we must now place stacks of secondary "how to" references alongside Scripture to insure that a recently devised program or some bits of cultural or scientific data that the Bible surely could not have anticipated are not missed? The answer should be as obvious to us as it would have been to our ancient Christian brethren—nothing!

Still, for some today, the idea that the twenty-first century church can and should apply first-century principles and practices as a basis for contemporary answers to church growth issues seems simpleminded, naive, or even ludicrous. However, we should be reminded that the authoritative record to which we appeal is the Bible. We are not simply consulting ancient history; we are relying on ancient history as recorded in the Word of God—and that *must* be enough! The Word of God must be understood as absolutely critical to any question regarding the church. After all, the church is solely a biblical concept; apart from the primary source of Scripture, we would not even know of the church. And what is true of the church in general is equally the case with the specific record of early church growth. In point of fact, "If Luke had never written the Acts of the Apostles, . . . we should have known nothing of the development of the early church, except for such stray hints as are available to us in the Epistles."[24] The most any other resource can do related to the church—as good and instructive as many of them may be—is

---

[24]Noll, *Turning Points*, 26.

offer speculative commentary on what the Bible introduces and teaches. Sadly, far too many contemporary "what is?"/"what to do?" church resources base their commentary on interpretations that view biblical truth through the lens of natural and current trends, instead of the other way around. This approach threatens to render the gospel merely good advice instead of good news. While it is important to understand the world and its peoples, the nature of the greater need is such that secondary commentary is simply not sufficient; the primary source, positioned above all else, is demanded.

The fact that in too many cases the biblical record is not enough for the modern church—and perhaps many of its leaders—is clear evidence that, although most would argue to the contrary, we have not yet reached the point of fully accepting the absolute trustworthiness of Scripture as God's first, full, and final words related to all things, including the church. More to the current point, there appears to be enough of an abiding insecurity with the idea of applying the historical practices of the early church as a component of contemporary church growth methods, that the biblical record associated with the early church's advance is often relegated to a separate interpretive category from Scripture's explicitly stated teachings. However, while one may argue that the Bible's historical records, when standing alone, should be interpreted independently, if what occurred in that record—the history—is a direct response to an earlier teaching, the two things should be viewed as a single unit and interpreted as a coherent whole, comprised of lesson and example. Consequently, where the growth-related activity of the first-century church meets the criterion of example matching teaching, those practices should be understood as being biblically definitive and thus replicated as a fundamental act of obedience today.

Responding to What?

So, if the early church was not responding primarily to *what works?* or *what to do?*, to what were they responding? I suggest that their actions were indicative of a greater concern for asking and discovering *what is?* The missionary and ministry activities of the early church seem to verify that their foundational questions surely reached deeper than issues of mere function. If the entire biblical record of the period is taken as a whole, functions that emerged from those deeper, prior questions—what is the *Ekklesía?*; to whom and/or for what have we been separated?; what are the expectations of the Master?—must have been part of their early reasoning.

Among other evidences, two things lend credence to this conclusion. First, the writings of the apostles to the churches provide evidence that the pervading questions were *what is?* in nature. For example, while the apostle Paul did relate his own plans for the geographical expansion of his mission, such notes are painted in large strokes that mainly reflect his personal desires as opposed to mapping out a specific series of strategic steps to be followed by others. Second, the bulk of his writings, instead of telling the church how to do what, instruct believers in such things as how to understand the church, relate to the church, and live out the church before the world, by informing them (and us) of "what is?" In other words, the question of *what to do?* was of secondary importance because it found its answer in *what is?*

How then does the Bible answer the important *what is?* question? An exhaustive answer is well beyond the scope of this work. However, it is possible to consider a small portion of what is taught by looking at three summary points: (1) The true church is a Body of redeemed people called out by and committed to a single Head; (2) the true church is a submissive Body of well-adjusted members; and (3) the true church is a community of worship.

The True Church Is a Body of Redeemed People Called Out by and Committed to a Single Head

In this sense, the church is uniquely personality driven—it is driven by the person of the Lord Jesus Christ. He gathers the church by calling out and assembling its members into His body. Further, the church is called to return the honor of membership in Christ's body by offering exclusive fidelity to its Head and following His leadership. It is here that the biblical marriage metaphor attached to Christ and His church as a binding covenant is clearly applicable: the church is married to Jesus, not just dating Him! With that truth in mind, let's consider "called out" and "a single head" in a bit more detail.

Called Out

The apostle Peter wrote, "But you are a chosen race, A royal priesthood, a holy nation, a people for God's own possession, so that you may proclaim the excellencies of Him who has called you out of darkness into His marvelous light" (1 Peter 2:9). Central to this verse are the words "chosen" and "called." "Chosen" stresses the facts that God exercised His authority to choose His own family from among a formerly alienated people, and then created a unique identity for those chosen. "Called" makes it clear that God authenticated His choices by actively issuing a call that separated His chosen people from an old relationship (with darkness) to a new one (with light). In fact, Peter verifies these truths in the very next verse: "for you once were not a people, but now you are the people of God; you had not received mercy, but now you have received mercy" (v. 10).

While Peter does not use the word *ekklesía* in either of the two verses, it is clear by implication that the full meaning of the word is applicable. As understood in the first century, the *ekklesía* referred in the broadest sense to a group called out or assembled by a herald. As the church grew, the word came to differentiate

Christians from all people and groups, especially in terms of the Jewish synagogue and the heathen, by denoting those throughout the world called by and to Christ in the fellowship of His salvation. Ultimately, the word came to represent those called into another kingdom. This understanding, coupled with the biblical teaching of the kingdom and its growth led to the understanding that the Kingdom of God is to be expressed and realized in society through visible representation in His church. It is easy to see in retrospect how asking *what is?* first, and understanding God's answer to include call, salvation, kingdom, and separation, would significantly affect the church's understanding of *what to do?*

A Single Head

Ephesians 1:22–23 has been cited several times already, but the verses are germane to the point and cannot be over stressed. Paul stated, "And He put all things in subjection under His feet, and gave Him as head over all things to the church, which is His body, the fullness of Him who fills all in all." Even the most cursory reading of these verses leads to a single, logical conclusion. The church—the called-out Body—has a single Head, the Lord Jesus Christ, who has complete authority over the Body.

While that is a powerful truth, to stop there would be to miss something equally important. Look again at the last phrase: ". . . the fullness of Him who fills all in all." Quite literally, the reason that the true church must rely fully on Christ apart from all others; must seek His Word alone as authority for direction, identity, and function; and must abandon all secondary, lesser loyalties is that there is room for nothing else! Christ is so much the owner and master that He consumes and totally fills up the church. In order to add anything beyond His person, will, and purpose requires that we make room for the addition. The only way to do that is by removing what (Who) already fills the church. Any surrender to our own notions and self-directed leadership is an addition that consequently removes Jesus in order to make room.

Note, I did not say "removes *some* of Jesus in order to make room." Jesus as a person is not fragmented; His personality is not multiple choice. There are no optional components allowing for picking and choosing. The church is not a business affair that allows for corporate compromise, such as between a CEO and his or her board. In fact, if it were possible for the true church to be a business, it would certainly not be a board-administered corporation; it would most definitely be a sole proprietorship with Jesus as its sole owner and decision maker. The idea that the true church somehow comprises a board retaining even limited operational control and having voting privileges is entirely a human construct; it is certainly not a biblical teaching. The old adage, "Jesus is either Lord of all or He is not Lord at all," springs immediately to mind.

The True Church Is a Submissive Body of Well-Adjusted Members

What does it mean for the church to be well adjusted? Obviously, more than the standard psychological definition of "well adjusted" is intended. Perhaps the best way to answer the question is by determining what the term does *not* mean, at least in light of this discussion.

It has been said that the definition of insanity is to continue doing the things done in the past expecting different results. As in the case of insanity, for the church to be non-well-adjusted means that it persists in doing the same things it has always done, or is presently doing, while fully expecting different results. Essentially, the non-well-adjusted church may very well be asking the right questions but in the wrong order. These congregations have not yet come to terms with the biblical truths related to what it is and the laws governing its life as the only biblical way of knowing what to do. While such churches may honestly aspire to be all that they ought to be, nevertheless, they continue to put into practice answers that are based on information derived apart from properly engaging the right first question, fully expecting that with greater sincerity and harder work, God will ultimately bless their efforts with different results.

Sadly, for many churches, the effort to create new results by working harder at doing the same things done in the past is often motivated by a desire to return to the conditions of the "good old days." For these folk, the vision and understanding of church is limited to the overall cultural milieu present at the time of what they recall as the days of their church's greatest success. Thus, for them, the true church is defined less by an accurate biblical understanding as it is by a particular time in history and a contemporaneous society. "The community around these churches may have changed five times, but their members [are] still looking for the 'good old days.'"[25] This mentality produces a body of people who are insistent and industrious about doing things "the way we did them in the past," hoping (perhaps even expecting) that the result will be one day opening the doors of the church to discover that their neighborhoods have been reincarnated into images of their yesterdays. As if by persistently doing the things they've always done they can somehow re-create the eras of the 1950s and 1960s.

Here is a thought. If the intent is to move the clock and calendar backwards, why not be really bold. Instead of moving it back only fifty or sixty years, why not seek to move it back two thousand years? After all, there are no social or cultural mechanisms to make half-century adjustments in society. There is a biblical plan for moving the church back to its fundamental roots, but that plan requires a well-adjusted church.

What then does it mean to be a well-adjusted church? Three things come to mind. First, this congregation willingly

---

[25]Jeoff Hammond, "Innovative Church Planting: Re-potting underway in California," http://www.namb.net/Innovative_church_planting_re-potting_under_way_in_California (accessed July 10, 2010).

adjusts to whatever God reveals and directs exclusively through His Word. Second, they accept the realities of their world as it now exists and the sufficiency of Christ, through His church, to encounter that world head-on. Third, they abandon the futile practice of asking the important questions in the wrong order. For this church, what is open to discovery is the thrilling realization that new answers are timeless answers seen again as if for the very first time.

Here is one of the most important of those old answers to which the church must adjust. Jesus said, "I also say to you that you are Peter, and upon this rock I will build *My* church; and the gates of *Hades will not overpower it*" (Matthew 16:18, italics added). In this declaration, Jesus claimed two things. First, Jesus personally verified His ownership of the called-out ones, the church. Second, as owner, Jesus explicitly took exclusive responsibility for the life, health, future, and survival of the church. For the sake of underscoring a fresh point, I will assert again that these claims, coupled with God's divine appointment of Jesus as Head of the Body, give Christ absolute authority over the church. This fact leaves members of His Body with only two acceptable responses (the fresh point): (1) submit to and (2) follow the exclusive leadership of Jesus. Simply put, there are just no other choices available if the church is to be well adjusted.

The True Church Is a Community of Worship

While teaching an Introduction to Missions class a few years ago, I displayed two pictures for my students to review. The first was of a typical Southern-style, red brick church, complete with looming arches, covered portico, and white Corinthian columns. I asked the class to tell me what they saw. Immediately, they responded, "a church." I then displayed a picture of a small, dilapidated stick-and-straw structure surrounded by what was obviously jungle overgrowth. Again, I asked the students to

61

identify the structure. The room was briefly silent, so I waited. After a few moments, there came a smattering of answers. "It's a shack in the jungle." "It's an old house." One student interjected with a laugh, "It's a chicken coop." I brought the laughter to an abrupt end, however, when I said, "You're all wrong; it's a church." You could have heard a pin drop, until one student spoke up for what I later learned was the majority in the room: "A church. How do they worship? I mean, where do they plug in the amps and projector?"

Granted, the student was young and the product of church during the "praise and worship wars" of the last two decades. However, his background and mission naivety revealed a broader (and rather sad) misunderstanding of genuine worship. I do not refer to amps and projectors; those things are peripheral. What I refer to is the apparent presupposition that true worship is somehow connected to a particular worship style. Said another way, it is the notion that apart from a particular style of presentation, worship cannot exist. My fear is that the student's presupposition was based upon a far more widespread and disturbing assumption among numerous modern believers: the erroneous idea that worship and style are synonymous terms. Even more alarming is the specious assumption (held consciously by some and unconsciously by many) that there exists a specific style of worship that not only facilitates the experience but is in itself the embodiment of the genuine article. To think that a single style is in and of itself worship is like saying that a particular literary genre is all there is to literature. Style exists as expression only. While questions of style persist as leading issues in many of today's churches—in some cases rising (degenerating?) to the place of "bones of open contention"—the fact remains that there is simply no universal, intrinsically holy worship *style*. Nor is any style a magic bullet guaranteeing the experience of true worship. While a particular style may function to facilitate worship among a specific people, true worship has a Spirit-animated life of its own apart from any specific style. At minimum—regardless of the stylistic expression—true worship is transcendent, and true worship has a single purpose.

True Worship Is Transcendent

The practice of true worship is clothed in enormous variety transcending all human differences, including culture, language, geography, and ethnicity. If you doubt this, ask those who have engaged in cross-cultural missions (including short-term mission trips) to recount their public worship experiences while abroad. The reports, almost universally, will include stories of being in humble often impoverished surroundings where the language was not understood, the music was strange to the point of being dissonant, and the rituals practiced seemed awkward and confusing. Yet the returning believers will testify to experiencing the undeniable presence of God, and worshiping Him at a depth rarely experienced before. Despite the fact that some of these folk come from churches characterized as highly contemporary in style while others are from fully traditional congregations, each person discovered in vivid fashion that style is not worship— worship is worship! Understanding this truth is essential because ". . . every time we worship together, we are drawn into the community of angels and saints who are always praising God. Even better, we are being reminded that we are included in the circle of fellowship between the Father, Son, and Spirit."[26]

The very core and source of worship emanates from the transcendent. Jesus said as much when He insisted, "But an hour is coming, and now is, when the true worshipers will worship the Father in spirit and truth; for such people the Father seeks to be His worshipers. God is spirit, and those who worship Him must worship in spirit and truth" (John 4:23–24). In these verses, Jesus identifies true worshipers truly worshiping. His words offer both

---

[26]Carolyn Arends, "Hospitality Sweet: One of the Forgotten Keys to the Dynamic Worship of God," *Christianity Today*, October 2010, 56.

definition and qualification of true worship in a single phrase: ". . . the true worshipers will worship the Father in spirit and truth." According to Jesus, the definition of true worship is an act of *engaging* the Father in spirit and in truth. Said another way, the qualification for true worship—that which makes it true and genuine—is the *engagement* of the Father in spirit and truth. The Lord's point is clear; true worship does not exist where the *spirit*-motivated engagement of God is absent. And, I might add, this is true no matter how stirring, emotionally uplifting, or culturally connected the worship style employed may be.

The concept of engaging the Father in worship may appear at first like trying to nail Jell-O to a wall. And it surely would be if the word "spirit" is overlooked. First, note that Jesus said, "God is spirit." Spirit not only speaks to the essence of God, but in a larger sense to His transcendence. It is in spirit that He moves (transcends) between heaven and earth in this present age. It is also as spirit that God inhabits and relates to His earthly children, the church. Jesus taught that to engage God in worship requires that we must relate to Him within our spirits ("God is spirit, and those who worship Him must worship in spirit and truth"). In essence, in order to truly worship, our spirits must be consumed within God's spirit. The reality, however, is that such a transaction is beyond all human capability, despite our most creative efforts to facilitate the experience.

The good news is, what is impossible for humanity is fully possible for our transcendent God. Recall Jesus' words, ". . . for such people (those who worship God in spirit and truth) the Father *seeks* to be His worshipers." In the same way that the Father takes the initiative to call and provide in all other aspects of His people's relationship with Himself, God takes the lead in worship for those open to the engagement. Jesus is clear; God is actively seeking true worshipers. Through the transcending agency of the Holy Spirit, God seeks and calls His people into true worship, and provides the means by which spirit is able to relate to spirit. Recognizing this activity and responding to it, however, requires a fundamental shift in thinking.

Quite often, the methods and styles employed to facilitate worship are driven by the idea that worship originates in earth then rises to heaven. But if God is the seeker who, by His Spirit, initiates and animates worship on behalf of those who are powerless on their own to truly engage Him Spirit to spirit, is it not the case that true worship flows from heaven to earth, then rises back to heaven? Absolutely! In proper order, Jesus is the true worship leader; the Holy Spirit is the divine energizer; and God transcendently overshadows every style and worship method to engage His people. Following this divine order, what God provides from heaven glorifies Him in earth, then rises heavenward to be mixed with the ever-sung praises around His throne. In other words, true worship in the earth is God's call to participate in what is ever occurring in heaven, and His gift of the ability to do so. All of this the Father provides for those who will humbly respond to His seeking, without regard for place, time, accouterments, or style. So, go ahead. Pound the drums vigorously or play the organ gloriously. Dance and sing new songs, or stand quietly and raise melody from the hymnbook. Pace around on an open stage in T-shirt and jeans, or don clerical robes and remain still behind a monumental pulpit. Remember, if true worship occurs, we didn't initiate it, nor did we animate it, and it may very well have taken place in spite of our styles, not because of them.

Remember, when engagement with God so consumes us that we could stand in an open desert devoid of anything but the breath we draw, unconscious of any presence other than our own and that of the Lord God Almighty, we may claim to have worshiped. When the service, event, or private time ends and we cannot fully recall anything but the experience of being in the presence of God, we may claim to have worshiped. When we have no compulsion to contend with others over music, dress, or sermon style because we know that we have heard from God, then we may claim to have worshiped. When we are able to exit such moments with little regard for the meeting of our felt needs but instead have an exalted impression of who God is, then we may claim to have worshiped. For true worship transcends all earthly matters, be they internal or external, and in the energy of God's Spirit such occasions yield to the Father's call to engage Him fully.

True Worship Has a Single Purpose

The universal Body of Christ, scattered as it is to the four corners of the earth, will necessarily manifest itself in day-to-day life in numerous ways. But when assembled locally as groups in individual churches, the display of who and what we are narrows considerably. It should be noted quickly that the forgoing statement is not intended to reflect some ridged, inflexible legalism. Far from it. What is intended is a reminder that what we do is determined by what we are. And because what we are is tightly focused within the Lordship of Jesus Christ as owner and Head of the church, what we do as local assemblies should never expand beyond those boundaries. In all its variety, the gathered church must give primary attention to what must be the singular focus of the worshiping body, as established by its Head, Jesus Christ.

Nowhere does Jesus speak to this singular focus more forcefully than in one of the best-known events in the New Testament. Soon after His entrance into Jerusalem and the beginning of His last precrucifixion week on earth, Jesus encountered merchants in the temple who were abusing both the process of preparing to offer sacrifices and the people making those preparations by transacting business for personal gain, under the guise of facilitating the worship of God. What follows next almost stuns the imagination. According to the Bible, Jesus fashioned a homemade whip and summarily cleaned house, overturning money-changing tables, toppling cages and coops, and sending the merchants running for cover. As entertaining as all this is to recount, the most important element of the story is not what Jesus did; it is what He said. Basing His words on

Isaiah's prophecy—"Even those I will bring to My holy mountain And make them joyful in My house of prayer. Their burnt offerings and their sacrifices will be acceptable on My altar; *For My house will be called a house of prayer for all the peoples*" (Isaiah 56:7, italics added)—Jesus first repeated the prophecy, ". . . 'My house shall be called a house of prayer.'" Then He added His own divine appraisal of the situation, "but you are making it a robber's den" (Matthew 21:13).

Listen closely to Jesus: "My house." This claim is critical. Jesus assumed the right to make and maintain His house exactly as He wanted it. The millennia-long process of making it as He wanted it was within days of its consummation on Calvary. It was only weeks until the earthly placement of what He had made would be implemented at Pentecost. Thus, His reaction to what was going on that day in the temple—actually, what had gone on for years there—was, especially in light of larger events to come, fully justified and completely within His rights. The church is still His house. Nothing has changed; Jesus is still fully justified and completely within His rights to rule what is His.

With extraordinary economy of words, Jesus succinctly added to His "My house" assertion by declaring, ". . . shall be called a house of prayer." In so doing, He preached volumes concerning His singular vision for what His church is. The Greek word *proseuché,* translated "prayer," in addition to speaking of the place where prayer occurs, refers variously to the *act* of communing with God, and the *activity* out of which that communication takes place. It is reasonable to assume that all these meanings were intended by Jesus. His house—wherever, whenever, and however it meets—is to focus primarily on the act of communing (engaging) with God through the activity of offering worship that directs all attention on Him. This singular purpose is to be so tightly focused that the wider world, whether it understands and approves or not (and they will not!), defines us by this characteristic. In this sense, the words of Jesus could very well read: "My church shall be *known* as a house of prayer," or "My house will be *referred* to as a house of prayer."

I ask you, why would our Head make such an assertion if in fact the true church is not exactly what He described? Understanding the definition of the church's singular purpose should drive our quest to determine *what to do?* In other words, what we do should fully and consistently reflect what we are, according to Jesus.

Jesus, however, was not finished with His declarations. Listen to Him: ". . . you are making it a robber's den." These words form no minor addendum to thoughts already expressed. They make clear a real and present danger if the earlier words of Jesus are overlooked: namely, when the church becomes anything less than primarily a house of prayer and biblical worship, it risks the possibility of becoming a place of thievery. Vital life and truth are stolen from the church body, leaving in their places empty superficiality within, an erroneous witness without, and the sadly pointless quest for the solution to a question that has already been fully answered by the church's Head.

Conclusion

Possibly, those reading these thoughts are asking, "But what about ministry? Is the church to be simply an exclusive conclave of gathered believers who give no further thought to touching the lives of others outside themselves?" The biblical answer, obviously, is no.

The full body of kingdom teachings and principles must be applied to all the church is and does. One of these principles dictates that the surest way for a church to die is by turning inward and focusing on its own survival. In the same way that we are instructed to die in order to live, to give in order to receive, to be abased in order to be exalted, in order to thrive the church must forget issues of survival and freely give itself away (more on this later). Thankfully, the Father has made provision for the successful outcomes of *all* kingdom principles.

Note the immediate conclusion to Jesus' cleansing of His house.

> And the blind and the lame came to Him in the temple, and He healed them. But when the chief priests and the scribes saw the wonderful things that He had done, and the children who were shouting in the temple, "Hosanna to the Son of David," they became indignant and said to Him, "Do You hear what these children are saying?" And Jesus said to them, "Yes; have you never read, 'Out of the mouth of infants and nursing babies You have prepared praise for Yourself?'" (Matthew 21:14–16).

Extraordinary! First, in short order after the restoration of God's house to its proper condition, people in various states of need began flocking to Jesus, and they were not disappointed. Jesus, who is always a miracle waiting to happen if His conditions are met, touched and healed those who came to Him. In that cleansed temple, the Holy met the sinful and the needy at the point of their immediate needs—that's ministry!

Second, real and genuine worship broke out spontaneously in the very place that only minutes before had been the site of spiritual abuse and ritual legalism gone to seed. As I visualize the unscripted outburst of "praise and worship" in that renewed temple, it is difficult indeed to imagine that any of our highly choreographed worship events could produce anything akin to the majesty of that moment. If you listen closely, you can almost hear Jesus' promise, "I will build my church," being repeated time and again in the background. When set free within His own house, cleansed and properly conditioned by His own hand, *Jesus simply kept His word.*

Listen well church; nothing whatsoever has changed! Ministry is still the heartbeat of the Savior. A church of submissive, well-adjusted members that is focused on engaging God in Spirit-led worship, and is singular in its purpose to be a biblical "house of prayer," can expect the spontaneous expressions of God's presence evidenced in genuine worship for those within the Body, and meaningful ministry to those without. Not only *can* such results be expected, they *should* be expected— for that is a church Jesus *will* attend.

Chapter 3
A Successful Model: The Model of Function

In the interest of refreshing memory, it is probably a good idea to repeat the quote supplying the basic outline for this discussion: "There's no need to 'reinvent the wheel.' The keys to growing a vibrant and successful church are the same as the keys to success in any field: find out what works, find a successful model, and then emulate it." Having discussed "find what works," we now move to the second item in the list, "find a successful model."

Have you ever put your face above one of those headless frames often found at fairs and arcades, painted to resemble a muscle man, a clown, a bathing beauty, or some such? Many of us have had our pictures taken this way, and the photos are always good for a laugh, mainly because the head doesn't fit the body. I wonder, if you could superimpose a picture of Christ as the head over your local church, would you in all honesty have to laugh at the misfit? Or would you stand in awe of a body of human beings so closely related to a divine Head? Perhaps the observation of the following pastor answers the question best: "I often visit newcomers in town and find some of them to be church shopping. They want to know what they can get out of my church. For these people, and too many more like them, churches are just one more consumer commodity. Worship services are not a place to serve and honor God but a place where people expect to purchase the best: inspiring worship, good music, moving sermons, quality child care. As if we buy God and not vice-versa."

Regrettably, for many people, the true church is so little understood that even the simplest considerations are too much. For example, a man was answering questions for a national religious survey. When asked for his church preference, he responded, "Red brick." Reminds me of the words of a former college professor of mine who told a class of future pastors, "Some days you will just have to laugh to keep from crying."

It should come as no surprise then that so many church leaders struggle to determine what works when it often seems so difficult to recognize the successful model of the church, even when that model presents itself in the Bible. I suggest that while there is far more in the Bible related to the intended model of the church than can be discussed in a single chapter, there are three fundamental things that are clearly evident: (1) the model of function, (2) the model of order, and (3) the model of structure.

These three things serve as "sub-models," that, when taken together, form the foundational *master* model of the true church as presented in Scripture. Each element provides an essential piece necessary for building the whole. In this chapter, we will look closely at the first of the three items: the model of function.

The Model of Function

Recalling the point made in an earlier chapter—the principles and practices of the early church as presented in the historical account of Acts should be understood as biblically definitive—mentally venture back in time and witness the activities of the newly assembled Body of Christ at Pentecost. Acts 2:41–42 records, "So then, those who had received his [Peter's] word were baptized; and that day there were added about three thousand souls. They were continually devoting themselves to the apostles' teaching and to fellowship, to the breaking of bread and to prayer."

Of course, one of the first things that grabs the reader's attention is the number of additions to the church (I note this for the Baptist readers). Taking the Acts narrative as written, it appears that the apostles began immediately to assimilate this enormous influx of people into an identifiable whole—"So then, those who had received his word were baptized; and that day there were added about three thousand souls." However, if focusing on the number and assimilation of converts is the extent of our understanding of the Pentecost event, important observations related to the *people* themselves, and the nature of the Body they were assimilated into, are lost. Such a loss would be sad, indeed. The reason is simple. If we overlook the people, we cannot properly see the Body; if we cannot properly see the Body, we miss the model. To avoid such an omission, consider the following.

The Conviction of Those Added to the Church

According to the biblical account, those added to the church accepted and acted upon the gospel message as preached by Peter ("Those who *accepted* the *message* . . ."). And what a message it was. Volumes have been written concerning the nature and content of the apostle's obviously dynamic sermon. As a quick overview, consider this brief summary of that message.

- Empowered and controlled by the Holy Spirit, Peter boldly declared truths that were consistently and simultaneously biblical, doctrinal, Christ centered, evangelistic, and prophetic.
- His message did not spend precious time on secondary personal speculations, or indulge the present, personal interests of the audience (note that only a very brief

explanation was offered to refute the charge of drunkenness and set straight the accusation that the apostles were inebriated).

- Peter energetically focused on Scripture and its fulfillment. He located the Pentecost event in salvation history by quoting the prophet Joel. He identified Jesus as the promised Messiah through the words of David. He spoke to the shame and crime of crucifying the Son of God, then pointed scripturally to its purpose and inevitability.

- He called people to account for sin and demanded repentance.

- In terms of the future, Peter offered both a cross to bear and a crown to wear to all those in his audience.

It is hard to imagine that any of Peter's listeners walked away saying "what a sermon" or "what a preacher." The majority—at least three thousand that we know of—were left saying, "What a savior! What must I do?" Without a doubt, this was exactly the response God desired—and required. Those who became part of the church were confronted with truth in its fullest expression regarding themselves, their sin, and Jesus as Messiah Savior. They were made to understand these things from God's perspective and not their own. The message did not attempt to call people to Christ by means of a presentation that omitted the hard points of doctrine (Peter certainly didn't appear to worry that "doctrine might be divisive") or attempt to explain away the prophetic assurance of who Jesus is for the sake of inclusion and political or cultural correctness.

As an interesting aside, it is noteworthy that there is no evidence Peter knew in advance that he was about to be called upon to preach the inaugural message of the church. Because he was given no prior notice of his divine preaching appointment, he was not afforded time to prepare his thoughts in advance. While to the listening crowd his sermon may have sounded either prewritten or delivered as the extemporaneous speech of a gifted orator, such assumptions are not evidenced by the Bible. Peter's words and insights were declared spontaneously under the anointing power and might of the Holy Spirit. In other words, Peter was only an instrument—a voice. The words spoken were God's words, supplied and energized by the Holy Spirit, and made audible through Peter to those who would become part of Christ's Body. Because God was its exclusive author, there can be no doubt that the message Peter preached included exactly what God required be made known and accepted by those who would comprise His church. It also appears that Peter believed this to be the case. For years to come, he would faithfully retain his Pentecost sermon content and preaching style. Listen to him before the Jewish leaders in the temple.

> ". . . let it be known to all of you and to all the people of Israel, that by the name of Jesus Christ the Nazarene, whom you crucified, whom God raised from the dead—by this name this man stands here before you in good health. He is the Stone which was rejected by you, the builders, but which became the chief corner stone. And there is salvation in no one else; for there is no other name under heaven that has been given among men by which we must be saved" (Acts 4:10–12).

Hear Peter again as he addresses many of these same leaders some days later, following his release from jail.

> But Peter and the apostles answered, "We must obey God rather than men. The God of our fathers raised up Jesus, whom you had put to death by hanging Him on a cross. He is the one whom God exalted to His right hand as a Prince and a Savior, to grant repentance to Israel, and forgiveness of sins. And we are witnesses of these things; and so is the Holy Spirit, whom God has given to those who obey Him" (Acts 5:29–32).

In fact, the content of Peter's Pentecost message and his later preaching became in essence a template for apostolic and post-apostolic preaching. As Stephen Neill observes, "From the time of the early apostles onwards, the message by which the church brought conviction to its hearers concerned Jesus, the resurrection, and the forgiveness of sins."[27] It appears that from Peter forward, early evangelists learned well the sermonic lessons of Pentecost. As an older preacher once advised, "State the text, exposit it thoroughly, then apply it to Jesus as quickly as possible!"

Those Added to the Church Publically Identified Themselves with the Truth of Peter's Message

The opening phrase of verse 41 verifies this point: ". . . those who had received his word were *baptized*" (italics added). Those in Peter's audience who believed with their hearts made confession with their mouths, then visibly declared themselves among the disciples of Christ through the very public act of baptism.

For the early church, baptism following conversion was never optional. While the period of time between conversion and baptism increased through the years, due to Christianity's transition from being an initially Jewish church to a primarily Gentile movement, the requirement for baptism was never abandoned. And in all cases, the ceremony was intentionally designed to be an event observed by numerous witnesses. Luke's word construction in Acts 2:41 points to this fact. The word "baptized" as used in the text, is from the Greek word *baptisthēto*. Grammatically, *baptisthēto* ". . . is in the passive [voice] indicating

---

[27]Stephen Neill, *A History of Christian Missions*, 2nd ed. (New York, NY: Penguin Books, 1990), 30.

that one does not baptize himself, but is baptized by another *usually in the presence of others*[28] (italics added).

The reasons for insisting on the public display of one's faith were numerous. Understanding them offers important insights into the expectations the early church held for its members, and the sustained vitality of the Body through years of growth and difficult trials. The following few items will make the point clear.

Baptism and the Impact of Encountering Jesus

In 1936, C. H. Dodd, then professor of New Testament at Cambridge University, published *Apostolic Preaching and Its Development*. In the work, he expressed his belief that all the apostles preached the same gospel message—the *kerygma* (proclamation). He postulated that the gospel, as proclaimed by the early apostles, consistently contained four elements. As set forth by Dodd, these four elements include (1) an account of the life of Jesus including His death, burial, resurrection, and ascension; (2) an explanation of how Jesus fulfilled Old Testament prophecies and eschatological expectations; (3) a theological presentation of Jesus as both Lord and Messiah (the Christ); and (4) a call to repentance and forgiveness from sin. In short, the message as presented was highly informed doctrinally.

Through the years, numerous scholars have challenged Dodd's assumptions as an oversimplification, arguing that the apostles announced Christ's arrival and adapted their evangelistic approach according to the context of their audiences. Those differing with Dodd often cite Paul's Mars Hill sermon (Acts 17:22–34), and his message at the synagogue in Antioch of Pisidia (Acts 13:14–41) as examples of their disagreement. Although debate continues, there is, however, a general consensus among scholars that while Paul and other early preachers may have

---

[28]Spiros Zodhiates, ed, *The Hebrew-Greek Key Study Bible*, (Chattanooga, TN: AMG Publishers, 1984), 1361, text note.

adapted their presentations to particular audiences, certain elements were always included in their gospel presentations. One of those crucial inclusions was the call to respond to Jesus, the central figure of the message. Obviously, the early evangelists believed it impossible for a person to be confronted with Christ and the claims of His gospel then simply walk away unmoved, as if nothing had happened. The early preachers assumed that the gospel demanded a response on the part of their listeners. Therefore, a call and opportunity to commit to Christ was considered essential, was fully expected, and always extended.

It was also considered expedient for those who had accepted Christ and His gospel to establish that commitment by *visibly* demonstrating their obedience to Christ and their identity with His church. The apostle Paul would explain years after Pentecost that accepting Christ meant becoming a fully new creation (2 Corinthians 5:17). As new creations, believers were fully expected to abandon their old identities and assume divinely created new ones, then to declare openly that new identity in public fashion. Water baptism, based upon the Old Testament teaching of ritual cleansing, quickly became that means, by providing *external*, symbolic testimony to the *internal* life-changing relationship between the individual and his or her new Lord. Through baptism, the decisions to repent of sin, be joined to Christ, and participate in His church were announced in no uncertain terms for all the world to see.

Baptism as an Affirmation of Faith Giving Strength for Future Challenges

In the early days of the church, being a Christian meant something. At minimum, it meant aligning oneself with the body of scriptural teachings regarding Jesus as the Messiah and accepting the consequences of that belief, whatever they might be. As can be surmised from previous statements, to the first-century church, the notions of secret Christians and clandestine Christianity were unthinkable. This remained true for generations in spite of the fact that as the Christian movement took hold throughout the Roman Empire, the personal cost for a public declaration of faith became more and more intense—even deadly! For example, in the earliest days of the church, Christians were regarded by official Rome as a sect emerging from within Judaism—a legal religion within the empire, having rights to religious expression. Association with Judaism's status as a *religio licita* protected the Christian Church for more than half a century after Pentecost until Rome's destruction of Jerusalem in AD 70 worked to drive the two religions apart.[29] After AD 70, however, Rome's disruption of Judaism pushed the Christian Church out on its own.[30] As F. F. Bruce observes,

> In the lands outside Palestine, the decade which ended with the year 70 marked the close of the period when Christianity could be regarded simply as a variety of Judaism . . . From A.D. 70 onward the divergence of the paths of Jewish Christianity and orthodox Judaism was decisive. . . . Henceforth the main stream of Christianity must make its independent way in the Gentile world.[31]

The world into which Christians made their "independent way" was one of constant peril and personal jeopardy. Christians ". . . under the Roman Empire [were left with] no legal rights to existence, and . . . liable to the utmost stringency of the law."[32] Without the protection of official status, open persecution by both Orthodox Jews and the Roman government was inevitable. Yet, despite the always-present, ever-increasing persecutions meted out on those who associated themselves with Jesus and the church, the call for the public profession of one's faith, affirmed

---

[29]Noll, *Turning Points*, 29.

[30]27.

[31]F. F. Bruce, *The Spreading Flame: The Rise and Progress of Christianity from its First Beginnings to the Conversion of the English* (Grand Rapids: Eerdmans, 1958), 157–58.

[32]Neill, *A History*, 38.

through baptism, was never lifted. Still, with legendary courage, converts in ever-expanding numbers continued to claim Jesus as Lord and give public witness to this decision through the waters of baptism.

Insisting upon baptism—and that done publically—made a significant *advance* contribution toward maintaining personal faithfulness, possibly unintended in the beginning but nonetheless effective in the inevitable time of crisis. How so? The moment of baptism, witnessed by numerous others, provided a point-in-time experience that individual believers could mentally revisit time and again. Recalling the event and what the various elements of one's baptism symbolized served to remind the believer of pledges made and thus, for many, undoubtedly helped preclude the recantation of those promises.

To demonstrate this point, it is helpful to understand just how the baptismal ceremony was designed and performed in the early days of the church. Every symbolic element was intended to speak volumes about what had occurred in the believer's life, and the future implications of his or her acceptance of Jesus as Savior and Lord. Church historian Justo González provides a brief but insightful account of the entire process. He notes that in the earliest days of the church believers were baptized immediately after conversion—a practice made feasible because most converts came from Judaism and understood the basic meaning of the Christian life and message.

> But, as the church became increasingly Gentile, it was necessary to require a period of preparation, trial, and instruction prior to baptism. This was the "catechumenate," which, by the beginning of the third century, lasted three years. During that time, catechumens received instruction in Christian doctrine, and were to give signs in their daily lives of the depth of their conviction. Finally, shortly before being baptized, they were examined and added to the list of those to be baptized. Early in the third century it was customary for those about to be baptized to fast

on Friday and Saturday, and to be baptized very early Sunday morning. . . . On emerging from the waters, the neophytes were given white robes, as a sign of their new life in Christ (see Col 3:9–12 and Rev 3:4). They were also given water to drink, as a sign that they were thoroughly cleansed, both outside and inside. Then they were anointed, thus making them part of the royal priesthood; and were given milk and honey, as sign of the Promised Land into which they were now entering. [33]

Just as important as the symbolic acts employed in the ceremony was a special declaration added in the second century, and required of every individual being baptized. Around AD 150, probably in Rome, the early text for what would later become the "Apostles' Creed" was formulated. Originally called "symbol of the faith," this basic text became ". . . a means by which Christians could distinguish true believers from those who followed the various heresies circulating at the time . . . Anyone who could affirm this creed [were not heretics]."[34]

Prior to being baptized, as part of the ceremony, candidates were presented with a series of questions, drawn from the "symbol." Each one had to be answered in the affirmative or their baptism was forfeited.

Do you believe in God the Father almighty?

Do you believe in Christ Jesus, the Son of God, who was born of the Holy Ghost and of Mary the virgin, who was crucified under Pontius Pilate, and died, and rose again at the third day, living from among the dead, and ascended unto heaven and sat at the right hand of the Father, and will come to judge the quick and the dead?

---

[33]Justo L. Gonzáles, *The Story of Christianity: The Early Church to the Dawn of the Reformation*, vol. 1, (San Francisco: HarperSanFrancisco, 1984), 96.

[34]Gonzáles, *The Story of Christianity*, 63.

Do you believe in the Holy Ghost, the Holy church,
and the resurrection of the flesh?[35]

In addition to serving as affirmations of the believer's
personal sincerity at the moment of baptism, the public response
to these questions provided a valuable, mentally indelible witness
to each believer of the commitment they had made in the presence
of numerous witnesses. Undoubtedly, recalling the moment of
such a public confession gave many the courage to hold fast in
their declared faith, despite the often deadly consequences.

Baptism as a Foundation for an Enduring Witness

Although the fact has been noted several times already, it
bears repeating that the early church found itself in an
increasingly hostile environment. This hostility faced by
Christians was not due simply to the introduction of a new
religion into Roman society. The empire accepted and assimilated
a plethora of religions and religious expressions. As time would
prove, however, much if not most of the enmity between the
church, state, and larger society grew out of the overt expression
of Christianity's counter-cultural morality and lifestyle ethics.

Owing to its close association with Judaism, for the
greater part of the first century, Christianity went largely
unnoticed in the larger social and cultural world of the Roman
Empire. By the early second century forward, however,
Christianity's extraordinary growth rendered it much more visible
to the surrounding society. Because Christian beliefs and lifestyle
practices invariably ran counter to Greco-Roman values, the
Roman state and surrounding pagan culture grew all too aware of
what Roman historian Tacitus called a "pernicious superstition."
In essence, the second century saw the beginning of numerous
values-based "lines in the sand" being drawn between the empire
and the church—lines that neither side were willing to

---

[35]64.

compromise. Thus, while the Roman world flexed its muscle in an effort to thwart Christianity's burgeoning numbers and increasing moral influence within the empire, Christians matched the fire of unspeakable persecution meted out against the church with its own equally strong resolve and resistance to compromise the moral and ethical teachings of Jesus Christ.

What is remarkable about this historical development is that the counter-cultural lines drawn by the church remained indelible and largely without compromise for generations after first being established. It has been said that when the beliefs and practices of an organization change, it is never due to a shift in the organization; it is the result of *different thinking* among those within the organization. For centuries, the church (the organization) defied the normal trend toward "different thinking over time" and held their ground, because believing converts (the people within) remained true to the fundamental values of the faith as set forth by Jesus through the apostles. "As Peter, Paul, and other apostles gave their witness—both through sermons and public defense—the reason for being apostles, persons sent on a mission, took shape,"[36] not only for them but for generations of believers yet to come.

Nowhere is long-term Christian fidelity to basic truth and ultimate perseverance more eloquently described than in the following extract from "Epistle to Diognetus," written in approximately mid-second century.

> For Christians cannot be distinguished from the rest of the human race by country or language or customs. They do not live in cities of their own; they do not use a peculiar form of speech; they do not follow an eccentric manner of life. This doctrine of theirs has not been discovered by the ingenuity or deep thought of inquisitive men, nor do they put forward a merely

---

[36]Norman F. Thomas, ed., *Classic Texts in Mission and World Christianity: A Reader's Companion to David Bosch's Transforming Mission*, American Society of Missiology Series, No. 20, (Maryknoll, NY: Orbis Books, 1996), 3.

human teaching, as some people do. Yet, although they live in Greek and barbarian cities alike, as each [one's] lot has been cast, and follow the customs of the country in clothing and food and other matters of daily living, at the same time they give proof of the remarkable and extraordinary constitution of their own commonwealth. They live in their own countries, but only as aliens. They have a share in everything as citizens, and endure everything as foreigners. Every foreign land is their fatherland, and yet for them every fatherland is a foreign land. They marry, like everyone else, and they beget children, but they do not cast off their offspring. They share their board with each other, but not their marriage bed. It is true that they are "in the flesh," but they do not live "according to the flesh" (Cf. 2 Cor 10:3; 5:16; Rom 8:4; Jn. 17:13–19; 18:36, 37). They busy themselves on earth, but their citizenship is in heaven (Cf. Phil 3:20; Eph 2:19–22; 1 Pet 2:9–17). They obey the established laws; indeed in their private lives they transcend the laws. They love everyone, and by everyone they are persecuted. They are unknown, yet they are condemned; they are put to death, yet they are brought to life. They are poor, yet they make many rich; they are in need of everything, yet they abound in everything. They are dishonored, yet they are glorified in their dishonor; they are slandered, yet they are vindicated. They are cursed, yet they bless; they are insulted, yet they offer respect. When they do good, they are punished as evil doers; when they are punished, they rejoice as if brought to life. By the Jews they are assaulted as foreigners, and by the Greeks they are persecuted, yet those who hate them are unable to give a reason for their hostility[37] (Scripture citations added).

---

[37]Michael W. Holmes, ed., *The Apostolic Fathers*, 2nd ed., Translated by J. B. Lightfoot and J. R. Harmer, "The Epistle to Diognetus," (Grand Rapids; Baker Book House, 1989), 299.

What does this historical review have to do with baptism as a means of aiding the enduring witness of believers? To answer this question, I will cite a small portion of a recent study conducted among participants in an emerging movement in southern India.

In 1991, Herbert E. Hoefer first published the results of research he undertook over a period of about ten years. As noted, his purpose was to investigate a movement then emerging in the southern states of India—primarily in the rural and urban areas of Tamil Nadu—known as "Non-Baptized Believers in Jesus Christ" (NBBC). The report, entitled *Churchless Christianity*, is both alarming and highly informative.

It is not difficult to identify the nature of the movement that is easily surmised from its name. As practiced, numerous individuals in the Hindu state of Tamil Nadu responded to the gospel by mentally assenting to the message while refusing to follow through with any public confession of faith through baptism or association with the church. While I agree with Hoefer's assessment that, "The refusal of baptism may well be a sign of refusal to repent and thus enter into the new life of the Kingdom to which our Lord calls us (Mk 1:15),"[38] for the sake of this discussion, I am more interested in the author's observations regarding the spiritual characteristics of NBBC participants, especially as they compare to the qualities of converts from the same region who chose to make public their decision by following Christ in baptism and identity with the church. It is in this juxtaposition that the value of baptism as a foundation for an enduring witness can be clearly seen.

Summarizing one set of data, Hoefer reports,

The first thing which is striking in the statistics is that so many (almost one-third) say that *they have learned nothing from Jesus*. . . . He is the object of their devotion, their "ishra deva" who represents the power and love

---

[38]Herbert E. Hoefer, *Churchless Christianity*, (Pasadena, CA: William Carey Library, 1991), 162.

of God to them. *Their contact with Jesus has not yet brought them into a transformation of mind and heart.* . . . At least one-fourth of the NBBC respondents . . . state that *they have never prayed to Jesus*[39] (italics added).

Now compare these data to the testimony of a Tamil Nadu convert to Christianity who chose to declare his faith through baptism and open identity with the church.

Though I didn't see the heavens opened, I knew the Spirit of God had sealed a covenant with me and a deep conviction that I belonged to Christ got implanted in my heart. Although none of my Hindu relatives were around me then to witness my baptism, I knew that after baptism I could boldly declare to them and to others that I had identified with Christ. It meant sanctified separation from my old Hindu ritualistic tradition and superstition. I was prepared to be dead to self and the world. I feel within me an urge to partake of the suffering of Christ by laboring for him and for the blessing of many others. I experience also the resurrection power of the Lord Jesus Christ. . . . The power of the Holy Spirit has been enabling me to refuse to yield to unrighteous gain and deceit. . . . I can say boldly that they (my Hindu relatives) respect me more now than ever before. . . . I am not ashamed of this great name of Jesus.[40]

The contrast could not be more vivid, or telling. While baptism is purely a symbolic act, the power of its visible expression contributes significantly to its value as a means to insure one's endurance as a witness to the life-changing relationship with Jesus Christ. Perhaps, among many others, this is one reason the apostles insisted on baptism as more than just a sign *of* faith but as a first act of obedience *within* the faith.

---

[39]Hoefer, *Churchless Christianity*, 120-121.
[40]162.

Consider the Change
in Those Added to the Church

Luke closes Acts chapter 2 with a brief but stirring account of church life following the initial Pentecost event. Verses 42–47 are enough to make any pastor or other church leader cry out, "Lord, please do it again, in my church!" Whether you choose to explain Luke's account as simply postrevival afterglow or as a genuine, Spirit-led movement (my choice), the fact remains that a God-created change had occurred, change that evidenced itself through dramatically changed lives.

Given the pivotal nature of the church's growth during and immediately following Pentecost, Luke's account of events is remarkably simple and to the point. He says of believers in the new church,

> They were continually devoting themselves to the apostles' teaching and to fellowship, to the breaking of bread and to prayer. Everyone kept feeling a sense of awe; and many wonders and signs were taking place through the apostles. And all those who had believed were together and had all things in common; and they began selling their property and possessions and were sharing them with all, as anyone might have need. Day by day continuing with one mind in the temple, and breaking bread from house to house, they were taking their meals together with gladness and sincerity of heart, praising God and having favor with all the people. And the Lord was adding to their number day by day those who were being saved (Acts 2:42–47).

While all the verses above are wonderful in their description of the young, immediate post-Pentecost church, verse 42 is especially insightful as a foundation for the entire passage. Review the words once more: "They were continually devoting themselves to the apostles' teaching and to fellowship, to the breaking of bread and to prayer."

The verse is informative in two ways. First, it provides a small but vitally important list of underlying *reasons* for the attitudes and actions of believers following the events of Pentecost. Remember, the early church knew absolutely nothing about the church or how to grow one. Yet the church grew and prospered exponentially around them. All they seemed to know for sure was to seek, discern, and obey the leading of the Holy Spirit. Consequently, what might be called their church growth "activity cues" were taken exclusively from the guidance of the Holy Spirit. According to the text, under the Spirit's leading, believers were led to do three things: (1) heed and obey the biblical teaching of the apostles, (2) spend time in shared, intimate fellowship with one another, and (3) give themselves to seeking God in prayer—all of which they did. Said another way, the church studied Scripture, learned to love one another, and communed regularly with God. These steps comprise the reason for the church's actions related in Acts 2:43–47, and became the basic three-point formula for early church growth success.

This is a good time to be reminded of a statement made in the last chapter:

> . . . while one may argue that the Bible's historical records, when standing alone, should be interpreted independently, if what occurred in that record—the history—is a direct response to an earlier teaching, the two things should be viewed as a single unit and interpreted as a coherent whole, comprised of lesson and example. Consequently, *where the growth-related activity of the first-century church meets the criterion of example matching teaching, those practices should be understood as being biblically definitive and thus replicated as a fundamental act of obedience today.*

Related to the three historical activities cited by Luke, the question then becomes, do the named activities correspond to specific biblical teachings? If so, we have an instance of practices matching teachings, requiring that those activities be understood as biblically definitive and worthy of replication by today's church as fundamental acts of obedience. Of course, it is easy to find a wealth of proof texts to sustain the scriptural mandates for Bible study, Body fellowship, and communication with God. What remains is to accept the incumbent nature of those same practices on the modern church and to give them priority over all other foundational church-growth strategies.

Second, the passage provides insight into what happened when the early church initiated those three simple steps and, I believe, what can be expected today when the same actions are taken by the modern church. Look at the text once more, but this time as a list of church-growth outcomes resulting from the three activities listed in verse 42.

- Everyone kept feeling a sense of awe
- Many wonders and signs were taking place
- All those who had believed were together and had all things in common
- They began selling their property and possessions and were sharing them with all
- They continued with one mind in the temple
- They broke bread from house to house
- They took their meals together with gladness and sincerity of heart
- They praised God and had favor with all the people
- The Lord added to their number day by day those who were being saved

Take a moment to reread the list. Digest it completely, then compare the listed outcomes with your church. For that matter, compare them with any church in your area. Keep in mind, early believers had no idea how to be, do, or build the church other than to rely fully on the Holy Spirit and whatever "strategy" He led them to employ. And God, who never disappoints His obedient children, responded by making of them a church *fully reflective of His glory and character*—which, by the way, is the very nature of what it means to be the true church.

Let me ask you, if given the opportunity to have the finest church producible by human skill, methodology, technology, and ingenuity or the church described by Luke, which would you choose? I dare say your answer would be immediate and probably without qualification: you would choose the church of Acts 2:42–47. Now ask yourself, if the three activities of Acts 2:42 were to be prioritized and repeated by the modern church, what has changed that would prohibit the same outcomes from occurring today? I contend, nothing has changed.

While nothing has changed to prohibit Acts 2:42–47 from being repeated in the twenty-first-century church, there is one more thing to consider before we can be assured of similar results. As noted at the beginning of this section, this extraordinary church was comprised of changed people; people changed supernaturally in response to their commitments to the gospel and the saving work of Jesus Christ. This fact is verified by a single phrase in verse 42: "They were *continually devoting themselves* to the apostles' teaching and to fellowship, to the breaking of bread and to prayer" (italics added). In other words, salvation and commitment to Christ produced in these new believers new and changed life devotions.

Not one person among the Pentecost converts, including the apostles themselves, could claim prior devotions to Christ that matched what was experienced after the event. The reason for this is easy enough to discern when you consider what those new devotions included. To help, review the list of outcomes once more, but this time as a summary of four new devotions.

- Devotion to a single line of instruction
- Devotion to unity within the Body

- Devotion to continued identity with the message, the Savior, and the Body
- Devotion to worship of and communion with the Savior

Here is the point: these four items are completely "other(s)" focused. The list does not include one "me" or "self" focused devotion; everything is focused away from self and on Jesus and His church. Not one thing in the list indicates the normal human devotions to "my needs being met" or "my preferences being acknowledged." There is not a hint of "what I think," "what I want," or "what do I get out of it." At the risk of being redundant, allow me to repeat: the entire focus of all the new devotions is on Jesus, the Scriptures, and the church body. This is a vital point because such selfless devotions are fully beyond the capacity of purely human production. They can only be generated and sustained supernaturally, and only lives changed by the power of God are open to this special work of God.

Without doubt, Pentecost was a watershed moment in church history. More of significance occurred that day than can be fully known this side of heaven. There is, however, one thing we can know for sure and should not overlook. Pentecost secured a level of personal commitment to Christ unparalleled in the new devotions it produced among His changed followers. Further, it is evident that these devotions were not taken lightly by those who made them; they were lived out continually in the daily lives of the growing church body as matters of routine faith and practice, ultimately becoming the fundamental foundational means by which the church grew.

Before leaving this section and drawing some conclusions, let me encourage you to do something that may, at first, appear a bit silly. It's a simple little exercise involving some word rearrangement that will help you visualize a very important truth. Read again verses 42–47. This time, though, change the past tense structure of the verses to present tense. What you get will be something that reads like this: They *are* continually devoting themselves to the apostles' teaching and to fellowship, to the breaking of bread and to prayer. Everyone *keeps* feeling a sense of awe; and many wonders and signs *are* taking place through the apostles. And all those who *have* believed *are* together and *have* all things in common; and they *are* selling their property and possessions and *are* sharing them with all, as anyone might have need. Day by day continuing with one mind in the temple, and breaking bread from house to house, they *are* taking their meals together with gladness and sincerity of heart, praising God and having favor with all the people. And the Lord *is* adding to their number day by day those who *are* being saved.

While the exercise may be a simple one, it is nonetheless enlightening. If, as is often insisted, the book of Acts is an open historical record still being compiled today through the ministry of the church, and if the historical data can be understood as being biblically definitive for the operations and outcomes of the contemporary church, then the present tense is quite appropriate. The plans and purposes of God have not changed. Changed people living out new devotions to Christ and His church, energized and led by the Holy Spirit will result in Scripture's historical past tense becoming present tense reality in your church. That's reason to rejoice!

Conclusion

When we survey the evidence thus far presented in this section, it becomes obvious that the first function of the church as depicted in the book of Acts is to call out God's people—people who accepted as true both the person and message of Christ— through the full and faithful exposition of Scripture, and to lead those individuals to public identity with Jesus Christ, His teachings, and His church. I hasten to add that this function applied not only to the ancient church, but it applies equally to the twenty-first-century church as well. There is no need to opine for days that God never intended to end. Planned obsolescence is not part of the true church, either in nature, character, or function.

The second function of the church, as drawn from the material, is to be that place where changed people are led to develop new devotions, namely (1) consistent growth in biblical truth, (2) the perpetuation of unimpaired body unity, (3) maturity in spiritual disciplines, and (4) a worshiping relationship with God that exalts and glorifies Jesus Christ as Lord. This function is vitally important in that the outcomes noted in Acts 2:43–47 are directly connected to the church "continually *devoting* themselves to . . ." the three items listed in verse 42. Thus, the fact that planned obsolescence is not part of the true church—or God's activity within it—not only means that God will divinely repeat Himself in terms of outcomes, it also means that the conditions He prescribes for those outcomes never become obsolete, nor are they superceded by any other methodology.

Undoubtedly, the two functions cited above are not the only responsibilities of the church as taught in Scripture. Even so, they are the primary functions of the early church noted by Luke in the book of Acts. Thus, they stand out as of first importance. Before searching for others, keep in mind that while there are more functions, these two alone were enough to produce the extraordinary church of the first century. They alone yielded the fundamental model and ideal for what God intends His church to be, a church that unquestionably Jesus would attend were He walking the earth in flesh today.

Chapter 4
A Successful Model: The Model of Order and Structure

A Model of Order

Perhaps your mother is like mine, a real stickler for order. I cannot begin to count the number of times while I was growing up that she repeated the well-worn adage, "a place for everything and everything in its place." In raising me, she faced a formidable challenge when it came to maintaining any sort of orderliness. My world was one of many things and a host of places for putting them all. The problem was, I repeatedly lost most of my stuff in the disarray of too many places to put them. This invariably meant having to ask for my mother's help locating misplaced items, while enduring another recitation of her unheeded admonition: "When are you going to learn, Gerald? There is a place for everything and everything goes in its place." The truth of the matter is, I'm still learning. Just ask my wife!

Given this confession, it may seem out of place for me to address the subject of order as it relates to the church. However, I am learning. Because learning is a process, perhaps telling you what I know about order up to this point will aid me in learning new lessons.

A Place to Start: Paul and the Corinthian Church

Among the churches planted by the apostle Paul, none seemed to have struggled more with overt pseudo-spirituality than did the church at Corinth. The church was divided in numerous ways, largely due to misguided loyalties, mismanaged church life, and misdirected personal lives. Add to this, problems ranging from abuse of spiritual gifts and the Lord's Supper, and, most egregiously, gross pride over their supposed broad-mindedness related to the acceptance of sexual perversion within the membership, the Corinthian Church was a poster child for dysfunctional congregations. Obviously, to these people Paul had much to say, and through them much to say to us, as well. Consider, for example, his first letter to these troubled people.

One passage of special note is 1 Corinthians 14:40. In this verse, Paul concisely summarizes several previous chapters of practical theological instruction regarding the proper function of the church. He wrote, "But all things must be done properly and in an orderly manner." While this short sentence contains a mere dozen words, it is loaded with volumes of divine insight regarding the importance of order within the true church and the way in which that order is to be expressed in church life.

So where do we begin to get an understanding of the lessons within this short admonition? I suggest we begin by isolating key words. Thankfully, the key terms are not hard to distinguish. The first is the word pair, "all things." The second and third terms are the words "properly" and "order." Let's look at these in their sequence.

The words "all things" are actually combined in a single Greek word: *pas*. In literal definition, *pas* can be understood to mean "all" or "every," as in everything that exists within a given situation, circumstance, or context—without exclusion. We might say, "as many things as there are." Of course, the context in which all things must be done (included) is the church.

Next are the words "properly" and "order." Looking again at the simplest renderings of the two terms, *properly* translates "honestly, honorably, and decorously." *Order* is defined as "proper sequence." When taken together within the context of the church, these key terms can be understood as saying, in the church there is a place for everything (all things), and everything must be in its proper place (order).

This brief interpretive exercise is well and good, but incomplete. Let's take one more step. Ask yourself the question, is there a most important term among the three? I believe the answer is yes. For clarification, consider the verse without one important word: "But all things must be done _____ in an orderly manner." The statement is still a grammatically correct, complete sentence, but the lack of the significant qualifier "properly" renders it incomplete as to God's full intent. The word "properly" is essential to understanding God's command that all things be suitably ordered within the church.

The reason that "properly" is so important is that in addition to providing the noted definitions—honestly, honorably, and decorously—as a qualifier, "properly" plays another important role within this biblical command. Simply put, the word functions as the *basis* upon which "all things" find their "order." In other words, omitting this key term would leave the church confused about what standard "all things" within the church are to be ordered upon. The church could never fully know if its arrangement of church life and ministry is in fact what God desires. Certainly, this would be an intolerable outcome for the Lord of the church.

Of course, God has no intention of leaving the church to wander in ambiguity, thus the insertion of "properly." As used in the text, the word can be interpreted to mean "in compliance with" or "equal to." In other words, all the things about the church and all the things that the church does must *comply* with something. But what? Denomination? Majority vote of the congregation? Traditions of the local Body? Wishes of current leadership?

This is a good place to remind ourselves of a verse central to this study: "And He put all things in subjection under His feet, and gave Him as head over all things to the church" (Ephesians

1:22). The point is this: the foundation—basis—for church order is its Head. For any of the aforementioned things, or other things like them, to be the basis for church order, they must in fact be the head of the church.

To some, what is being said may sound like a surefire formula for creating more confusion and disorder. How foolish we humans—even redeemed humans—are to persist in the notion that we must somehow manage the administration of Jesus, as if God has appointed some His junior partners for management purposes. In the same way, many argue against a walk of faith with an appeal to "common sense" (i.e. "I know we must exercise faith, but we also have to use common sense." As a quick aside, can you think of anything that makes greater "common sense" than being obedient to God, even if that obedience stretches our faith to its limit?). Too many insist that the leadership of Christ in the church must be balanced with the judgment of other sources. Admit it or not, the basic assumption of such an argument is that while Christ is sufficient to assemble and redeem the church, He lacks in sufficiency to administer its life without outside counsel and assistance. Such an assumption is beyond foolish; it is abominable. It is emphatically so that what is true of an individual life is equally true for the assembled lives comprising the single life of Christ's Body: "The lot is cast into the lap, But its every decision is from the LORD" (Proverbs 16:33). Remember, in the church, "every" means every, precisely because "head" means head.

Some might ask, if full administrative leadership of the church rests in Christ alone, why then does the Holy Spirit give such gifts as leadership (Romans 12) and administration (governments) (1 Corinthians 12)? That question is best answered by asking two others: (1) What is the nature of the two gifts? and (2) What is being led and/or administered? When these questions are answered correctly, it becomes clear that no conflict or inconsistency will emerge when the church submits to the absolute headship of Jesus Christ.

In the first case, the gift of leadership refers to the ascribed authority to lead, while administration refers to the ability to get others to work together. In the second case, what is being led and/or administered are the directives of a superior source—the Head. Taken together, the gifts of leadership and administration exist within the church to insure that the desires of the Head are properly carried out by the Body. And Jesus has insured within the same order that His desires will be made known. Knowing what His desires are is the primary responsibility of the "offices" given to the church, as listed in Ephesians chapter 4.

To those who yet doubt the effectiveness—even perfection—of biblical church order, reread the previous paragraph. Then consider it within the context of what has been said about trusting the sufficiency of the Head to administer the church without confusion and disorder. Here is what you will discover. Jesus is the absolute Head with full and final administrative authority. He has appointed spiritual officers to seek, hear, know, and communicate His will. Through the Holy Spirit, He has gifted individual members to lead and administer other gifted members in carrying out His revealed directives. If confusion and conflict arise out of this order, it will not be because of a weakness in the biblical program. It will be because, at some point, those who doubted the effectiveness of faith-based reliance on Christ's control, expanded their roles—sometimes with the best of intentions—to include that "junior partner" mentality referred to earlier, complete with their counsel and assistance. As a point of warning, let's not blame God for outcomes that are the result of us acting as our own worst enemies.

Sadly, in far too many cases, it appears that many other things do effectively constitute the headship of many local bodies. But as Scripture undeniably asserts, Christ alone is the church's one Head, and this headship extends to every local expression of that Body. Furthermore, to be properly ordered, all things within the church must comply exclusively with that Head. This means that proper order of the church must have as its only basis Christ's lordship, Christ's leadership, Christ's character, and most important, Christ's holiness. These qualities are the absolute standard upon which the church bases all that it is and does. For the true church, order is achieved through faithful compliance with its Head as the only basis for its existence, security, and ministry.

One writer illustrates this point well in the following account.

> Growing up on the Atlantic Coast, I spent long hours working on intricate sand castles; whole cities would appear beneath my hands. One year, for several days in a row, I was accosted by bullies who smashed my creations. Finally I tried an experiment: I placed cinder blocks, rocks, and chunks of concrete in the base of my castles. Then I built the sand kingdoms on top of the rocks. When the local toughs appeared (and I disappeared), their bare feet suddenly met their match. Many people see the church in grave peril from a variety of dangers: secularism, politics, heresies, or plain old sin. They forget that the church is built upon a Rock (Matthew 16:16), over which the gates of hell itself shall not prevail.[41]

You see, it matters not at all how the church is critiqued by society or cultural shifts, what the current trends in style and methodology may insist upon, or what the latest popular tweaking of ecclesiology may dictate; the Head alone is the basis of proper order. In practical terms, this means that for the church to be properly the church it is to do nothing merely for the sake of keeping itself or others happy. Every function, every ministry, every expenditure, every decision, and every member must focus on pleasing the Head. This is accomplished only when "all things" comply "properly" with the person and character of Jesus Christ.

---

[41]George P. Elder, *Sermon Illustrations*, http://www.sermon illustrations.com/a-z/c/church.htm, (accessed December 14, 2010).

A Model of Structure

I have no idea who first wrote the following brief summary of corporate life. It is obvious, however, that he or she knew their way around the intricacies of trying to organize individual human beings into some form of productive whole. Insightfully, the anonymous writer observes, "There are four main bones in every organization. The wish-bones: wishing somebody would do something about the problem. The jaw-bones: doing all the talking but very little else. The knuckle-bones: those who knock everything. The back-bones: those who carry the brunt of the load and do most of the work." Sadly, the unknown author could be describing the church.

In a museum at Greenfield Village in Detroit, Michigan, there is a huge steam locomotive. Beside this complicated piece of machinery is a sign showing boiler pressure, size and number of wheels, horsepower, length, weight, and more. The bottom line indicates that 96 percent of the power generated was used to move the locomotive and only 4 percent was left to pull the load. Again, the similarity to many churches is all too obvious.

Knowing that human beings are the same in all generations, past and present, it is reasonable to assume that even in the glory days of the first-century church each of these classes of folk were present. Perhaps this is one reason why the emerging New Testament church recognized early on the need to secure proper structure within the Body.

Surely, as the apostles spent time praying over the church, it must have become apparent to them that God had accomplished some very unique things in the composition of His earthly body. Three come readily to mind. (1) He had created something uniquely interconnected; (2) He had created something of special design that reflected His own unique desires; and (3) He had created something that required a unique structure through qualified leadership and gifted membership.

Something Uniquely Interconnected:
Body to Head

Don't worry; there is nothing wrong with your eyes. The creative piece you are about to read is exactly as it appeared some time ago in the newsletter of The Medical Service Corp. Replacing the letter "e" with an "x," author Richard H. Looney wrote the following tongue-in-cheek memo. His point is effectively and rather humorously made.

> Xvxn though my typxwritxr is an old modxl, it works wxll xxcxpt for onx of thx kxys. I'vx wishxd many timxs that it workxd pxrfxctly. Trux, thxrx arx 42 kxys that function, but onx kxy not working makxs thx diffxrxncx.

> Somxtimxs, it sxxmx to mx that our organization is somxwhat likx my typxwritxr—not all thx pxoplx arx working propxrly. You might say, "Wxll, I'm only onx pxrson. It won't makx much diffxrxncx."

> But you sxx, an organization, to bx xfficixnt, nxxds thx activx participation of xvxry pxrson. Thx nxxt timx you think your xfforts arxn't nxxdxd, rxmxmbxr my typxwritxr, and say to yoursxlf, "I am a kxy pxrson and thxy nxxd mx vxry much."

One sentence in the piece stands out (I'll correct the spelling): "But you see, an organization, to be efficient, needs the active participation of every person." While the church of Jesus Christ may define "efficient" differently than does a secular organization, efficiency of the sort proper to the church is nonetheless expected. For instance, such items as function, order, structure, and training as used in this work can be included as parts of a complete understanding of church efficiency. Perhaps the most concise yet complete definition of church effectiveness is found in the following brief extract from Jesus' teaching in the Sermon on the Mount:

> You are the salt of the earth; but if the salt has become tasteless, how can it be made salty again? It is no longer good for anything, except to be thrown out and trampled underfoot by men. You are the light of the world. A city set on a hill cannot be hidden; nor does anyone light a lamp and put it under a basket, but on the lampstand, and it gives light to all who are in the house. Let your light shine before men in such a way that they may see your good works, and glorify your Father who is in heaven (Matthew 5:13–16).

In this familiar passage, Jesus employs two effective metaphors to describe the church's role in the world: salt and light. While much can be said about the applications of these two word pictures to the ministry of the church, for the sake of this discussion, let it suffice to say that being effectively salt and light in the world is at the core of what it means to be efficient as a church. Further, as with all matters related to the church, this efficiency occurs only when the Body of Christ is rightly connected to its Head. However, while it is imperative for the church to be rightly connected to its Head, this vital relationship provides only the *basis* for the right results. In order for the effect of salt and light to be produced, something else is needed.

The *light* metaphor Jesus used will help explain what is being said. Say, for instance, that you have a need for light in a particular room. In the room there is a properly wired lamp sitting on a centrally located table with a good bulb in it. You know, however, that there will be no light, even with a well-prepared lamp, unless it is properly connected to the power source. So, you plug it in. But the lamp still gives off no light. At this point, the lamp has the right basis—it is rightly related to everything necessary for light. But illumination awaits another step. The switch must be turned on, allowing the power to flow through the lamp's connection, only then will the bulb shine. In the same way, efficiency in the church (e.g. being light in a dark world) requires not only a proper connection to its Head, it is further necessary that the switch be turned on allowing the power and leadership of the Head to flow through the Body. In other words, the right connection is the *basis* for efficiency; turning the switch on *produces* God-glorifying, redemptive efficiency.

What I am saying is simple enough. For the light that resides in the church to be seen through the church, it requires a properly ordered connection to the power source (basis) and the correct setting of the switch (efficiency). The power source is the Lord Jesus Christ; the right connection is the church's proper relationship to the Head; and the correctly set switch is the activity of the Body as it is obedient to Christ. When all these elements are properly ordered, light is the God-honoring consequence. Apart from this ordering of things, however, even the most creative human initiatives will never produce the "light" efficiency necessary for the world to ". . . see your good works, and glorify your Father who is in heaven."

As pointed out, however, it is undeniable that there is an important role for the individual members of the church to play in effecting overall efficiency. Look again at Jesus' words. "You are the light of the world. A city set on a hill cannot be hidden; nor does anyone light a lamp and put it under basket, but on the lampstand, and it gives light to all who are in the house." Note the essential teachings drawn from the light metaphor in these verses. First, Jesus calls believers the "light of the world." And He does so not as a future potential, but as a present reality. Of course, we know that Jesus is the true light of the world. It would be heresy to claim that individual believers have been accorded equality with Christ as light, or to say that Jesus has abrogated any of His deity by extending a portion of that deity to the church. Yet the Lord is clear that we too are lights, not simply that we will become or be made into lights. What we are to understand is that believers are *designated* reflectors of Christ THE light, placed strategically in a dark world to make visible the one and only true light.

Second, Jesus has purposefully "positioned" us to illuminate dark spaces. After all, that is what lamps are intended to do. In the case of the church, positioning can be understood as having an available power source, a proper connection to that source, and dark locations in which to shine. All of these are constantly available to the church.

Finally, Jesus intends that when the church is correctly positioned, it functions as light for the purposes He has established. In other words, as Jesus said, "Let your light shine before men in such a way *that they may see your good works, and glorify your Father who is in heaven*" (italics added). This is the mission of the church; it is a mission impossible apart from the church's interconnectedness with its true Head.

Something Uniquely Connected: Body to Its Parts

Repeating the previous point briefly, for light to shine from a lamp it is necessary that all the elements be properly assembled and connected. However, while this arrangement may provide the needed basis for light, another step is required for the light to be seen. Recall yet another earlier statement: The power source is the Lord Jesus Christ; the right connection is the church's proper relationship to the Head; and *the correctly set switch is the activity of the Body as it is obedient to Christ*. In modern terms, the switch must be turned to the "on" position (Jesus might have said, "the basket removed") in order that all the assembled elements, working together, can perform their particular functions with the result that the light becomes visible. Said another way, *action* must be added to *basis* in order for the right *effect* to be produced. It is here that the interconnectedness of the church—members to one another—is essential. While the eternal significance of the church is larger than the sum of its parts, the outworking of the mission and ministry of the church is divinely connected to the combined activities of every member.

Paul's instruction to the church at Corinth continues to underscore this truth. In 1 Corinthians 12, the apostle sets out to explain the correct use of spiritual gifts in Body ministry. He does not argue the existence of the gifts; rather, he focuses on their value within the context of edifying the church. In doing so, Paul provides essential insight regarding the nature of the church as a unified body working together to be all that God intended. In broad terms, he makes three important points. First, there is variety in oneness (vv. 4–7). Second, the variety of the various parts is expressed through ministry tasks centered around worship (vv. 8–11). Third, the blessing of variety is not a matter of individual significance but of group honor (vv. 14–31).

There Is Variety in Oneness (vv. 4–7)

It may be more correct to say that God has so constructed the church that oneness is actually achieved out of variety. Nonetheless, it is never God's will for the various members to chart their own course and insist upon doing their own thing because of inherent diversity. Rather, the Lord's command is that everyone perform their part in order to produce the unity and unified results of oneness. This is the essence of what it means to be interconnected.

It is interesting to note the way in which the Bible makes this point. Look closely at these verses from 1 Corinthians 12: "Now there are varieties of gifts, but the same Spirit. And there are varieties of ministries, and the same Lord. There are varieties of effects, but the same God who works all things in all persons" (vv. 4–6).

Two repeated words stand out: "varieties" and "same." They are at the heart of each verse. Together they make the single point that ministry gifts are diverse in both their types and distributions, while at the same time there is a single giver of the gifts who chooses both to give them and to whom specific ones are given. Now, pay particular attention to how the single source of the gifts is presented. Paul presents the one source in three distinct persons: Spirit, Lord, and God. Sound familiar? All three members of the unified Godhead are involved in the diverse but interconnected distribution of the ministry gifts. Remarkably, God created something just like Himself in the earth: a body of parts so tightly interconnected as to be inextricably (and mystifyingly!) one. The diverse yet interconnected nature of the Godhead is the very model for the varieties of gifts at work in the church.

This unique, diverse oneness leads to two important conclusions. First, in its earthly operation the church is to live and operate as a replication of the Trinity's unity. Verse 12 states, "For even *as the body is one and yet has many members,* and all the members of the body, though they are many, are one body, *so also is Christ*" (italics added). Simply put, the church, though made up of many members, comprises one body in the very same way that Jesus is one part of a triune whole. Because of this fact, the church is both a testifier and a functionary. The church *testifies* to the full gospel message by *functioning* as a replication of the diverse unity of the triune God who created it.

The second conclusion speaks to the outcome of the church operating as testifier and functionary. Namely, the replication of the Trinity's unity by the church has as its purpose the production of essential benefits for every member. Paul affirms this point in verse 7 when he wrote, "But to each one is given the manifestation of the Spirit for the common good." The benefit Paul spoke of is identified in the words "manifestation" and "common good." Consider the apostle's use of the words and the benefits to which they refer.

"Manifestation" speaks to the exhibition of God at work in the church through the combined, Spirit-empowered efforts of all its members. Obviously, numerous benefits arise from the Holy Spirit's manifestation in the church, but two are noteworthy within the context of the Body and its individual gifting. First, and most apparent, anytime the Holy Spirit exhibits (manifests) Himself, the outcome will always be a greater focus on Jesus and witness to Christ's supremacy within the church. The spiritual eyes of the congregation will be turned away from any me-centered concerns and self-generated agendas. Such things as style and method of worship—or individual preferences—will pale in the overwhelming awareness of God.

The second benefit points directly to the phrase "common good." The manifest presence of the Holy Spirit always leads to unity—pure and simple. The fact that the Holy Spirit is a unifier is clearly established in Scripture. Interestingly, this aspect of the Spirit's ministry is perhaps no more evident than in verse 13 of the chapter we are reviewing. The Bible says, "For *by one Spirit* we were all baptized *into one body,* whether Jews or Greeks, whether slaves or free, and we were all made to drink of one Spirit" (italics added). The point is, the Holy Spirit is the one who has unified the immense variety of redeemed human beings into a single Body. Further, He is pledged to keep up this process, transforming the Body's continuing diversity into a worshiping, ministering unit. And this Spirit-driven unity, which is at the heart of what is labeled "common," will always produce good for all involved.

So, what of the words, "common good?" The phrase is a translation of a single Greek word, *sumpherō,* referring to that which is "good" or "profitable." Interestingly, the word is a verb, a word of action. As used in the text, that which Paul calls "good" or "profitable" should be understood as including both the performance and result of an activity. When *sumpherō* is interpreted in this way, the result is eye-opening. "Good" and "profitable" now assume an action that produces something beneficial, for example "to bear," "to carry," "to collect," or "to contribute." Furthermore, the action prescribed produces mutual benefit through mutual effort. In other words, using the same list of terms, the phrase can mean "to bear *together,*" "to carry *with others,*" "to collect" or "to contribute *in order to help.*" In summary, the phrase "common good" as used in 1 Corinthians 12:7 refers to activity undertaken jointly by many, in order to produce that which is good and profitable (beneficial) for all.

When the two previously noted potential benefits become actual realities within the Body—(1) in its earthly operation the church is to live and operate as a replication of the Trinity's unity; (2) the replication of the Trinity's unity by the church has as its purpose the production of essential benefits for every member—something much grander than what the best of human church-growth innovation can produce will occur. In the first case, God in all His persons *becomes visible* and is glorified through the diverse oneness of His church. In the latter case, when interconnected, Body diversity combines to create unity of purpose; the presence and purposes of God *are evidenced* through the common good enjoyed by His people.

The Variety of the Various Parts Is Expressed through Ministry Tasks Centered around Worship (vv. 8-11)

This truth flows out of a question. Perhaps you have already asked it, or one similar to it. What is the process by which these benefits express themselves? Verses 8–11 of 1 Corinthians 12 provide the answer.

> For to one is given the word of wisdom through the Spirit, and to another the word of knowledge according to the same Spirit; to another faith by the same Spirit, and to another gifts of healing by the one Spirit, and to another the effecting of miracles, and to another prophecy, and to another the distinguishing of spirits, to another various kinds of tongues, and to another the interpretation of tongues. But one and the same Spirit works all these things, distributing to each one individually just as He wills.

While the text contains the answer to the question, the context of the verses provides an essential key for discovering it. That context is, *the body of Christ, in the energy of the Spirit, facilitating worship by the practice of ministry through its spiritual gifts.* Understanding the importance of this context and its relationship to producing the benefits of "common good" is vital to church life. Look at it again in its various parts.

The Body of Christ

Undeniably, the possession of spiritual gifts is an exclusive characteristic of the church. Among the numerous definitions of spiritual gifts, the best ones make this truth clear. One definition I particularly like because of its clarity at this point states, "A spiritual gift is a special attribute given by the Holy Spirit to every member of the Body of Christ according to God's grace for use within the context of the Body."[42] While those outside the church may be naturally invested with amazing talents, only Christ-bought members of His Body are endowed with spiritual gifts. To distinguish between the two things— natural talents and spiritual gifts—one Bible teacher has suggested that a believer might consider the things he or she is able to do for the benefit of others as a Christian that were inabilities before conversion. No matter how one defines or distinguishes spiritual gifts the fact still stands; believers and only believers are the recipients of the gifts of the Spirit. It can be no other way. Jesus said to His disciples, and to those who would become His disciples, "I will ask the Father, and He will give you another Helper, that He may be with you forever; that is the Spirit of truth, *whom the world cannot receive, because it does not see Him or know Him*, but you know Him because He abides with you and will be in you" (John 14:16–17, italics added). Possession belongs only to those who "know" the Spirit through Jesus Christ.

---

[42]C. Peter Wagner, *Your Spiritual Gifts Can Help Your Church Grow* (Ventura, CA: Regal Books, 1979), 42.

In the Energy of the Spirit

Not only are spiritual gifts endowments bestowed by the Holy Spirit, but they are fueled by the Spirit as well. Natural talents are energized by human efforts: training, practice, experience, and performance, to name but a few. While the development of spiritual gifts may benefit from similar efforts, they are wholly dependent on the supplied energy of the Holy Spirit. What Adrian Rogers once said of salvation—"God has put an engine in your salvation; it is the Holy Spirit"—is equally true of spiritual gifts. Believers do not choose them, nor do they empower the exercise of them; these things are the exclusive purview of the Holy Spirit. By maintaining control of both distribution and exercise, He is able to produce the highest good (the "common good") within the church, to the glory of God.

Facilitating Worship

Under the guidance of the Holy Spirit, the Body of Christ is always led into true and meaningful worship. Given the teaching of Scripture, nothing less should be expected. Jesus promised, "But the Helper, the Holy Spirit, whom the Father will send in My name, He will teach you all things, and bring to your remembrance all that I said to you" (John 14:26). On another occasion, rephrasing the same truth, Jesus further explained, "But when He, the Spirit of truth, comes, He will guide you into all the truth; for He will not speak on His own initiative, but whatever He hears, He will speak; and He will disclose to you what is to come. He will glorify Me, for He will take of Mine and will disclose it to you" (John 16:13–14). Ask yourself, what is more central to true worship than the act of engaging God to His glory, by recalling all that He has promised His children through the revelation of His Word?

This might be a good time for every worship leader to pause and ask, what (or which) current worship methodology or typical "order" of worship is the Holy Spirit obligated to bless?

111

Any? Some? Mine? Anyone but theirs? Scripturally, the answer is obvious. The Holy Spirit is the divine master of leading the way into genuine communion with God precisely because His sole obligation is to the Father, and His desires. No pastor or worship leader ever goes before God's people having prayed or prepared hard enough that the Holy Spirit has been placed under any obligation whatsoever to produce genuine worship out of purely human strategy and effort. The Spirit of God will always do what the Father instructs, and, as we have seen, Jesus has made clear what those instructions are. Because the Holy Spirit is the ultimate facilitator of worship, the church will be drawn into true communion with God on His terms—alone. All of which makes the continued warfare and debate over style and method not just something of a moot point, but a rather futile exercise as well. After all, ". . . who among men knows the thoughts of a man except the spirit of the man which is in him? Even so *the thoughts of God no one knows except the Spirit of God"* (1 Corinthians 2:11, italics added).

By the Practice of Ministry through Spiritual Gifts

Allow me to repeat a point previously made: Because the Holy Spirit is the facilitator of worship, the church will be drawn into true communion with God on His terms—alone. And what a difference this fact makes. While many believers may have exited church services empty and disappointed with various worship styles, no child of God has ever spent time in the manifest presence of God and been anything less than satisfied and full! The difference is not the style; it is the work of the facilitator of worship as He is faithful to the exclusive terms of the Father.

One thing that is apparent is that for reasons known only to Him, the Lord has chosen to express Himself in true worship through the spiritual giftedness of His Body's members. It remains the case that, "Not only are the gifts functional, they are congregational."[43] Because the exercise of spiritual gifts is one of God's terms for worship, the Holy Spirit is faithful to empower and utilize the gifts He has given to the Body's various parts (members) for that purpose. As Nazarene scholar W. T. Purkiser said many years ago, "Every true function of the body of Christ has a 'member' to perform it, and every member has a function to perform."[44] Nowhere is this fact more fully evidenced than when the church is engaged in Spirit-facilitated worship.

Just as important as the realization that the Holy Spirit facilitates worship through the exercise of spiritual gifts is the understanding of how that facilitation takes place, and for what purpose. To be sure, there is no intent to exalt a particular gift— what has been called the "syndrome of gift projection"[45]—or a particularly gifted individual. Because "individual Christians disconnected from the Body are not very useful,"[46] the objective of the Holy Spirit is always activity in union, especially in worship.

To discover how the Spirit's facilitation of worship through spiritual gifts is accomplished, read again the words of 1 Corinthians 12:8–11.

> For to one is given the word of wisdom through the Spirit, and to another the word of knowledge according to the same Spirit; to another faith by the same Spirit, and to another gifts of healing by the one Spirit, and to another the effecting of miracles, and to another prophecy, and to another the distinguishing of spirits, to another various kinds of tongues, and to another the interpretation of tongues. But one and the same Spirit works all these

---

[43]Jack W. MacGorman, *The Gifts of the Spirit* (Nashville: Broadman Press, 1974), 31.

[44]W. T. Purkiser, *The Gifts of the Spirit* (Kansas City, MO: Beacon Hill Press, 1975), 21.

[45]Wagner, *Your Spiritual Gifts*, 160.

[46]44.

things, distributing to each one individually just as He wills.

Notice what is happening as the church worships. The members are exercising their gifts in cross-congregational ministry—people are supernaturally ministering out of themselves and into one another! The focus is not individual or self-centered; it is congregational and others focused. Suddenly, Paul's words to the Ephesian Church take on new clarity and meaning.

> . . . until we all attain to the unity of the faith, and of the knowledge of the Son of God, to a mature man, to the measure of the stature which belongs to the fullness of Christ. As a result, we are no longer to be children, tossed here and there by waves and carried about by every wind of doctrine, by the trickery of men, by craftiness in deceitful scheming; but speaking the truth in love, we are to grow up in all aspects into Him who is the head, even Christ, from whom the whole body, being fitted and held together by what every joint supplies, *according to the proper working of each individual part, causes the growth of the body for the building up of itself in love* (Ephesians 4:13–16, italics added).

Here we see a fundamental truth at work: "the things God does in the world are done through Christians who are working together in community, complementing each other with their gifts."[47] In other words, worship occurs as the Holy Spirit empowers and leads individual believers to work in unity through ministry that builds up the whole Body.

Ministry is consistent with the very nature of the gifts themselves. To verify this point, a quick summary of the gifts as listed in Scripture will be helpful. To avoid venturing too far into the deeper waters of "gift theology," only a listing will be

---

[47]Ibid.

provided with just those comments needed to verify the foregoing conclusion.

The Bible provides three major lists of spiritual gifts: Romans 12; 1 Corinthians 12; and Ephesians 4. In each case, some gifts are repeated and others are added. In two cases, lists include items that have come to be referred to as "offices." I include them because spiritual gifts are essential to the proper operation of the offices. Additionally, three other secondary chapters in Scripture fill in important details. These are 1 Corinthians 13–14; 1 Peter 4; 1 Corinthians 7; and Ephesians 3. The composite list below, however, takes into consideration only the three major chapters. They are as follows.

Romans 12

- Prophecy (preaching, inspired utterance)[48]
- Service (ministry)
- Teaching
- Exhortation (stimulating faith, encouraging)
- Giving (contributing, generosity, sharing)
- Leadership (authority, ruling, administration)
- Mercy (sympathy, comfort to the sorrowing, showing kindness)

1 Corinthians 12 adds to the list (without repeating those already listed in Romans 12)

- Wisdom (wise advice, wise speech)
- Knowledge (studying, speaking with knowledge)
- Faith
- Healing
- Miracles (doing great deeds)
- Discerning of spirits (discrimination in spiritual matters)

---

[48]Words in parentheses are variations on the Greek word as translated in Scripture.

- Tongues (speaking in languages never learned . . .)
- Interpretation of tongues
- Apostle
- Helps
- Administration (governments, getting others to work together)

Ephesians 4 adds (without repeating any of the above)

- Evangelist
- Pastor[49]

Review the list closely, setting aside for a moment your own tradition or interpretation of spiritual gifts in general. Just focus on the lists from Scripture and what they all share in common. Each gift in the list is an item suited for ministry. Knowing that spiritual gifts are given only to believers for primary use within the church, one common theme emerges: ministry to the Body. "This does not mean that gifts are always inward-looking, for use just within the church and for the mutual benefit of believers. . . . The point is that [the] gifts, even when moving outward from the Body, are still to be used . . . by Christians *working as a team*"[50] for *the growth of the body for the building up of itself in love* (Ephesians 4:16) (emphasis added). And there is no greater growth point than when the church is engaged in true, mutually fed worship.

Finally, while a particular process may take time to understand and explain, purpose can often be discerned with far less effort. Allow the apostle Peter in short order to answer the question of purpose.

---

[49]Wagner, *Your Spiritual Gifts*, 59–60.
[50]44.

As each one has received a special gift, employ it in serving one another as good stewards of the manifold grace of God. Whoever speaks, is to do so as one who is speaking the utterances of God; whoever serves is to do so as one who is serving by the strength which God supplies; *so that in all things God may be glorified through Jesus Christ,* to whom belongs the glory and dominion forever and ever. Amen (1 Peter 4:10–11, italics added).

There it is, pure, simple, and to the point: *"that in all things God may be glorified through Jesus Christ."* The ultimate glory of God is the purpose, not only for worship, but for the Holy Spirit's facilitation of the experience through the congregation's mutual exercise of its individual spiritual gifts, as well.

So, we are right back where we started. Genuine worship is totally God-focused; the Holy Spirit moves the church to be its best through true worship; the Holy Spirit facilitates true worship by empowering believers to minister to each other as one Body, through their individual gifts; the Body matures in divine unity when it follows the Spirit's lead; and the promised "common good" is achieved when, because of a single view toward heaven, God is glorified through Jesus Christ. Amen!

The Blessing of Variety Is Not a Matter of Individual Significance but of Group Honor (vv. 14–31)

When it comes to spiritual gifts and their diversity within the church there are generally four different responses to the subject made by four groups of people. First, there are the uninformed. These are those folk who either have no knowledge of biblical teaching regarding spiritual gifts, or who have knowledge of them but regard all of them as a first-century phenomenon, only. Second are those people frightened by the idea of giving any attention whatsoever to the subject. Often these are well-meaning individuals who fear the possibility that dealing with spiritual gifts will result in some form of church-damaging disruptiveness. Third are those who fuel the fears of group two. These people believe in spiritual gifts, but in their practice of them live up to every negative stereotype of misuse. Fourth, there are those people who accept and humbly appreciate spiritual gifts and their proper usage as ministry tools within the context of the Body, just as taught in Scripture. Obviously, only one group—the fourth—will experience the fullest expressions of the "common good" produced in congregational life by the Holy Spirit through the proper exercise of His gifts. Group one will miss out because of denial; group two will miss out because of timidity; and group three will miss out because of abuse.

While each of the first three groups needs instructive and corrective attention, the third group—those who believe in spiritual gifts but live up to every negative stereotype of misuse in their practice of them—miss the point most completely. They miss the point because they miss the fundamental principle undergirding the purpose, possession, and practice of spiritual gifts. Here it is: spiritual gifts are largely unsolicited, completely undeserved, acquisitions of grace, the very giving of which is *a blessing of honor, not of entitlement.* When this principle is coupled with the scriptural context of mutual ministry two very important things become apparent. First, the possession and practice of spiritual gifts is a blessing that transcends individual significance; it is a matter of group honor. Second, when fidelity to Scripture is maintained, the gifts of the Spirit produce humility not self-exaltation.

The first conclusion does not mean that there is no individual significance whatsoever in the receipt of spiritual gifts. The Bible is clear that every part is necessary and important for the role it plays, to the degree that the Body would be incomplete without it. Paul wrote,

> For the body is not one member, but many. If the foot says, "Because I am not a hand, I am not a part of the body," it is not for this reason any the less a part of the body. And if the ear says, "Because I am not an eye, I am not a part of the body," it is not for this reason any the less a part of the body. *If the*

whole body were an eye, where would the hearing be? If the
whole were hearing, where would the sense of smell be?
(1 Corinthians 12:14–17, italics added).

Without doubt, every believer is important for his or her function as a member of the Body. And there is nothing wrong with recognizing the contributions made by faithful, hardworking members of the congregation. Often, this is exactly what the church should do to remind itself not only of the presence and contributions of those who might otherwise never be seen, but also to underscore the fact that the greater and more complex the attempted achievement, the more important the unseen parts. For example, did you know that a microscopic broken wire in a backup computer forced NASA to scrub the maiden voyage of the space shuttle *Discovery?* Joe Militano, spokesman for International Business Machines (IBM) said the broken wire was an integrated circuit within one of the *Discovery's* five identical computers, which controlled all the ship's functions, including communications, navigation, and guidance. Engineers isolated the problem to an opening in an integrated circuit in a memory core unit in the computer's input-output processor. So it is in the church. The smallest parts often have the power to make or break ministry. When these small parts function as they should, their contributions must not be overlooked.

However, it must be remembered that no member is inherently more important than any other, or should he or she be considered individually more significant for the role played. God, through the Holy Spirit, has created a whole out of many, not a host of lone rangers. It is impossible to be unified as one in the Spirit and at the same time individually parceled into separate parts and pieces. The beauty of God's glory would be totally absent in such an arrangement. Keep in mind, dismembered body parts are rarely put on display for their individual beauty. Such an exhibition would be considered in bad taste, or just plain sickening. Beauty is comprised of the whole. In the same way, honor and significance for each member is found in the fact that the Holy Spirit chose to gift that person in connection with every other member to accomplish the single purpose of the whole Body.

We may applaud gifted ones for the effectiveness of their individual contributions, but honor goes to the source of the gifts as He works within the whole. Any recognition that may come to an individual should not be accepted as a matter of personal significance, but as an honor shared by the entire Body. Any personal honor is found in the mystifying truth that God chooses to join any human being at all to Himself as a spiritually gifted member of the Body of Christ.

Understood in this way, the existence and proper exercise of spiritual gifts within the Body becomes exactly what God intended: a very humbling experience. When such humility exists, several things will result. There will be no room for gift exaltation or personal elevation. Attitudes of arrogance and self-importance will be strictly prohibited. The Body will have a greater awareness of its interconnectedness and the essential need to function as one. There will be a general sense of honor among the member parts, not for the gifts possessed but for the privilege of being a connected, gifted part of the Body. Most importantly, the church will experience the glory of God, the exaltation of Jesus, the release of the Spirit, and the experience of the "common good." You might say, Jesus will show up for church.

Something of Unique Design that Reflects God's Own Desires

To say that the church is unique from all other groups residing on the planet would, indeed, be an understatement. The unique nature of the church is so complex and richly nuanced as to be beyond human understanding or explanation. Even the divinely inspired apostle Paul, in discussing marriage, was left to conclude his comments by saying, "This mystery is great; but *I am speaking with reference to Christ and the church*" (Ephesians 5:32, italics added). On this side of heaven, all that uniquely distinguishes the true church from other groups on earth will remain a mystery, precisely because the nature of its characteristics defy the limits of human comprehension. One thing we can know, however, is that the unique nature and character of the church is intended to reflect the desires of its Creator. Said another way, God purposefully created a Body just as He desired, and He created it to be and *do all that He desires.*

A full discussion of the desires of God would require a separate book, perhaps one of multiple volumes. But there is one central desire that warrants noting before leaving this discussion. Granted, looking at just one thing in a list of many is very basic. However, even a rudimentary review of a single desire of God will prove enlightening. It might even serve to demonstrate something essential the church needs to rediscover its primary ministry—it will at least provide a more biblical basis for evaluating current condition and practices. What then is that one key desire? Simply this, *God desires to be made known throughout the earth.* This single desire is the one thing most tightly connected to the purposes of God, as seen in the previous historical review and the brief historical summary that follows:

A Look Back

The entire panorama of salvation history unfolds around the universality of God's plan for human redemption and His desire to be made known among all peoples. Beginning in the pages of the Old Testament and continuing through the New Testament, Scripture reveals the will and intention of God that all the world (nations) know and experience Him through the manifestation of His glory (Genesis 17:4, 18:18, 26:4; 1 Chronicles 16:24, 31; Psalm 67:2, 4, 96:10, 72:17–19, 86:9; Isaiah 2:2, 49:6, 61:11, 66:18–19; Jeremiah 4:2, 33:9; Micah 4:1–5; Romans 11:36, 16:27; Ephesians 3:21; Philippians 2:11). History was set in motion for this purpose; masterfully, God continues to guide history toward the inexorable satisfaction of His desire.

Amazingly, with the full array of divine powers at His disposal by which to fulfill His desire, God gracefully chose to use human beings to make Himself known to other human beings. To this end, He first created a special people whose call it was to ". . . witness to the saving purposes of God by experiencing them and living accordingly."[51] Then much later, after the full work of Jesus had been completed on earth, God called out another people, a universally diverse Body commissioned to continue the "making known" process. This special Body is the church. While the compositions and mandates of the two groups—Israel and the church—differ in certain respects, the fundamental mission of both is the same: to fulfill the desire of God by making Him known throughout the earth. A quick review of the biblical historical process involved in God's purposed choices will underscore this point.

The historical process started with an irrevocable covenant made by God with Abram (Abraham), Israel's progenitor and first patriarch. Genesis 12:1–3 provides the initial record of this groundwork set of promises. The Bible says, "Now the Lord said to Abram, 'Go forth from your country, And from your relatives And from your father's house, To the land which I will show you; and I will make you a great nation, and I will bless you, and make your name great; and so you shall be a blessing; and I will bless those who bless you, and the one who curses you I will curse. And in you all the families of the earth will be blessed.'"

However, as important as the promises within the covenant were and are—a promised land (v. 1); a great nation (v. 2); a great name (v. 3); being and providing a great blessing (v. 3)—the construction of the verses makes it clear that something other than these are of greater importance to God.

---

[51]G. Goldsworthy, "The Great Indicative: An Aspect of a Biblical Theology of Mission," RTR 55 [1996], 2–13, quoted in Andreas J. Köstenberger and Peter T. O'Brien, *Salvation to the Ends of the Earth: A Biblical Theology of Mission* (Downers Grove, IL: InterVarsity Press, 2001), 35.

The focus is on what God will do through Abram.[52] In the call of Abram, we have the divine response to the fall of mankind in Eden and its resulting human tragedy as recorded in Genesis 3–11, and God's response is the very soul of grace. Five times in Genesis 12:1–3 God uses the words "bless" and "blessing" to underscore the fact that the Lord has a blessing to provide and Abram will become the means of that blessing for all humankind. Centuries later, writing the church at Rome, the apostle Paul would provide additional commentary on the significance and reason for God's promise to Abram.

> For the promise to Abraham or to his descendants that he would be heir of the world was not through the Law, but through the righteousness of faith. For if those who are of the Law are heirs, faith is made void and the promise is nullified; for the Law brings about wrath, but where there is no law, there also is no violation. *For this reason it is by faith, in order that it may be in accordance with grace, so that the promise will be guaranteed to all the descendants, not only to those who are of the Law, but also to those who are of the faith of Abraham, who is the father of us all, (as it is written, "a father of many nations have I made you")* in the presence of Him whom he believed, even God, who gives life to the dead and calls into being that which does not exist (Romans 4:13–17, italics added).

Combining Paul's commentary with what has already been noted, the following conclusions can be drawn. Through the call of Abraham—and through him, Israel—combined with the covenant established, God asserts His intentions for humanity and establishes a new paradigm, as it were, for accomplishing them. This new paradigm is based upon a key truth, made clear to Abram and explained to us: God and His

---

[52]Andreas J. Köstenberger and Peter T. O'Brien, *Salvation to the Ends of the Earth: A Biblical Theology of Mission* (Downers Grove, IL: InterVarsity Press, 2001), 28–30.

salvation are to be made known to all on earth, precisely because the anticipated blessing arising out of the covenant is for all the families of the earth. Set at the core of accomplishing this new paradigm are a people of promise, a people created and chosen by God to effect His desire and purposes.

Now, make a historical leap across time to view another step in God's ongoing process. The place is Mount Sinai. The key figure is Moses. This venerable leader has been called by God to Sinai after leading the Hebrew nation out of Egypt and away from over four hundred years of excruciating slavery. We join Moses, sequestered on the mountainside, as he receives the following instructions from God: "Thus you shall say to the house of Jacob and tell the sons of Israel: You yourselves have seen what I did to the Egyptians, and how I bore you on eagles' wings, and brought you to Myself. Now then, if you will indeed obey My voice and keep My covenant, then you shall be My own possession among all the peoples, for all the earth is Mine; and you shall be to Me a kingdom of priests and a holy nation. These are the words that you shall speak to the sons of Israel" (Exodus 19:3b-6).

Pay close attention to the way in which God informs the significance of this encounter. First, he tells Moses to tell the Israelites in figurative language that, "I [God] bore you on eagles' wings." Then, in words to be understood as literal, God reveals that He "brought you [Israel] to Myself." Being borne on eagles' wings can be understood as a reference to the Hebrews' miraculous delivery from Egyptian slavery. In saying, "I brought you to Myself" God stresses that He has safely delivered the Hebrews from Egypt for the purpose of an audience with Himself, in order to make or renew a covenant, both of which take place at Sinai. Taken together, these phrases clarify the immediate reason the Jews found themselves free from bondage and assembled in the presence of God at the foot of Mount Sinai. Namely, a new covenant, one that does not eradicate the old but presupposes the existing promises made to Abraham, is being initiated (v. 4). Further, this covenant will provide the working framework around which Israel is to accomplish God's desire to be made known among all the peoples of every nation.

Drawing directly from the text, this framework is easily discerned. First, Israel is to be God's *se gullâ*—literally, "private property held by royalty." As such, they are His "peculiar" (KJV) or "treasured possession" (v. 5). Second, Israel has a role in all the earth precisely because "the whole earth is Mine"—not just a portion of it or its peoples, but all are God's (v. 5). Third, the obedience now required of the Hebrews at Sinai is a call to live out effectively a previously made covenant and commitment (the Abrahamic Covenant), a covenant of grace and faith, not works (v. 5). Finally, Israel's responsibility is to be a kingdom of priests and a holy nation serving God in the world by being separate unto God (v. 6).[53]

To this end, the crowning moment at Sinai occurs: the Ten Commandments are given to God's *se gullâ*. These commands provided the defining basis of holiness necessary for Israel's call by establishing the guidelines to govern the function of the relationship between Yahweh and His redeemed. This was a vital step to say the least. Vital because the desired revelation of God to which Israel was called was to be realized in the display of God's holiness—a display God intended to achieve through the holy, separate, and distinct lives of His people as they complied with the Ten Commandments.

As the ensuing years unfolded, Israel repeatedly failed to live up to her call; yet God did not cancel His covenants or His plan. Two things remained in place, which made any such cancellation impossible: (1) the immutability of God's holy character, and (2) His unchanged desire to be made known among the nations. Simply put, God could not go back on His promises, and He would not abandon His desire. Both of which means that God's promises and desire remain today. To realize both, God still has a people of promise—the church—whose call it is to be the Body through which He is made known.

---

[53]Köstenberger, *Salvation to the Ends of the Earth*, 32–33.

Reading further into the Bible's historical record, it is difficult to reach any other reasonable conclusion than that the church is the intended channel to make God known to the world. One special New Testament verse of note drives this point home. Scripture says, "Unto him be *glory in the church by Christ Jesus* throughout all ages, world without end. Amen" (Ephesians 3:21, KJV, italics added). Regarding this passage, Marvin R. Vincent correctly observed, "As the Church is the *outward domain* in which God is to be praised, so Christ is the *spiritual sphere* of this praise" (emphasis in original).[54] Simply put, the church is the earthly home of praise to God (outward domain); while Jesus, as the Lord of that home, provides the context and character (spiritual sphere) informing the church's call to display the glory of God before a global audience.

Reflecting on Vincent's words, it is easy to understand "outward domain" as meaning the place and the people among whom praise to God is offered. But what does it mean that Jesus is the context—"spiritual sphere"—*informing* the function of praise? Essentially this means that who Jesus is—all the qualities and attributes comprising His character and ministry—informs, motivates, and provides the framework for glorifying God in praise. More to the point, consider the following characteristics of Christ's ministry on earth as parts of that context. In so doing, see if you can discern a common theme that helps define an essential part of Jesus as the "spiritual sphere" of the church.

Jesus had a global purpose while on earth.
- Testimony of Simeon (Luke 2:30–32)
- Testimony of John the Baptist (Luke 3:4–6)
- Samaritan woman at the well (John 4:7–34)
- Roman Centurion (Matthew 8:10–11)

---

[54]Marvin R. Vincent, *Word Studies in the New Testament*, (Charles Scribner's Sons, January 1, 1914), public domain, *e-Sword* freeware site, http://www.sword.net (accessed January 14, 2011).

Jesus' teachings had global implications.

- "Son of man" mentioned over eighty times
- Hometown synagogue sermon (Luke 4:16–30)
- "Good Samaritan" parable (Luke 10:29–37)
- "Great Feast" parable (Luke 14:10–24)
- "Wheat and Tares" parable (Matthew:36–43)

Jesus' last week of physical life included global applications.

- The Good Shepherd (John 10:16)
- "We would see Jesus" (John 12:20–26)
- "The Vineyard" parable (Matthew 21:33–46)
- "To all the nations" (Matthew 24:14)
- The Sheep and the Goats (Matthew 25:31–46)

Jesus shared the Great Commission.

- "So send I you" (John 20:21)
- "To all creation" (Mark 16:15)
- "Go ye therefore" (Matthew 28:19)
- "To all the nations" (Luke 24:47)
- "To the uttermost parts" (Acts 1:8)

The common thread tying all the listed activities and teachings together is Jesus' emphasis on making God and His salvation known among all peoples. To overlook this truth ignores the biblical fact that the mission of Jesus always matched the global desire of the Father. Scripture is abundantly clear at this point. However, as significant as Christ's earthly dedication to God's desire was, the continuing implications of His commitment are of equal importance to the church. For instance, the mandate to advance God's desire for global worship only intensified after Jesus returned to heaven when in perfect, unbroken succession, He passed His own mission and purpose to the church, God's New Testament people of promise. Consider the evidence. In His position as the Head of the Body (Ephesians 1:22), Jesus baptized the church in the Holy Spirit (Luke 3:16), filled the Body proper with His own consuming presence (Ephesians 1:22–23), and became the abiding context—"spiritual sphere"—within which the Body lives, breathes, and finds its every definition (Colossians 2:9–10). The result of Christ's work in this regard produces a practical outcome through the church that looks something like this. Jesus—who still loves what the Father loves (John 4:31)—expresses His holy character in the church through passion for God's praise and glory (John 17:4). He constantly duplicates His own passion within the church (1 Peter 2:5), and leads it to honor the desire of God through ministries that make the Father and His salvation known to the world (John 20:21; Acts 1:8).

Far from being the exception to the rule, this described relationship between Christ and His collective people of promise is meant to constitute the operational norm for the church in the world. When it does, the church will be at its true best and God's desire to be made known to the ends of the earth will be realized.

Something That Required a Unique Structure Involving Qualified Leadership and Gifted Membership

There are numerous ways to explore this topic. For instance, we could discuss "how to" by addressing various methods and styles of Christian leadership. However, strategies of leadership are not the focus of this study. What is on point are the qualifications necessary for being a Christian leader. This section will focus on that point only.

Generally, when seeking to know the biblical qualifications for Christian leaders, Paul's instructions to the church found in 1 Timothy 3:1–13 and Titus 1:6–9 provide the best places to start.

In these passages, Paul lists the qualifications for church leaders, namely overseers and deacons. In both cases, though each passage is worded a bit differently, the qualifications listed are consistent with one another in terms of the specific items named. Just as important, both lists are grounded by a larger, overarching principle. Keep that in mind; both passages contain a *list* of qualifications and a single *principle* serving as the foundation for the lists. In practical application, the principle usually gets far less notice than the items in the lists. Because this is so, let's reverse the normal emphasis and focus attention on the principle.

It is interesting that for every list God provides in Scripture—whether of laws, regulations, promises, or qualifications—there is always an essential first principle undergirding the items in the list. This feature of construction points to the fact that, while the lists may be diverse in content, there is always a common feature uniting that diversity into a unified whole. And that single feature (principle) is of first importance to God. For instance, recall God's response to King Saul, made through Samuel, when the king disobeyed God by keeping part of the livestock of a recently conquered people despite the fact that God had commanded that none of the booty be kept. Listen closely to Samuel as he rebukes Saul for his disobedience: "And Samuel said, 'Hath the LORD as great delight in burnt offerings and sacrifices, as in obeying the voice of the LORD? Behold, *to obey is better than sacrifice*, and to hearken than the fat of rams'" (1 Samuel 15:22, KJV, italics added).

So what was Samuel's message to King Saul? Perhaps it was something to this effect: "Sacrifice is a good and proper thing, in its proper time and place. It is, after all, a command in God's list of spiritual directives. However, in cases where God, for reasons of His own choosing, calls for an action that seems to deviate from the list, the principle (to obey) is better than insisting on the strictures of the list (sacrifice)." In other words, as important as it is to know and faithfully adhere to the items in God's various lists in the normal course of our lives, it is just as important to understand and defer to the foundational principle upon which they are based anytime God requires. This is nothing less than the exercise of grace over legalism or acknowledging relationship over ritual. Remember, in God's economy, principle guides application; thus, it is of primary importance.

Not yet convinced? Recall how often Jesus, when called upon for specific rules (lists) answered with principles only. For instance, in Matthew 19, Jesus was confronted by the Pharisees who demanded an answer regarding the religious legality of divorce for any reason. Jesus refused to play into this ploy to corner Him with specifics—with a list of rules. Instead, He answered by citing the principle, namely God's ideal for marriage as established at creation—He even grounded the principle by locating it in Scripture (Genesis 2:24). While there does exist a small list of permissible allowances for divorce, the stated principle is intended as a first appeal to inform those specific allowances.

Again, consider Peter's question to Jesus regarding forgiving an offending brother. "Then Peter came and said to Him, 'Lord, how often shall my brother sin against me and I forgive him? Up to seven times?' Jesus said to him, 'I do not say to you, up to seven times, but up to seventy times seven'" (Matthew 18:21–22). The bottom line to Peter's request for information can be paraphrased this way, "Lord, give me a forgiveness rule, or rules." The answer Jesus provides sounds almost like a response in kind, until His words are understood in full. The phrase "seventy times seven" is tantamount to saying, "without limit," "infinitely." In plain English, Jesus actually said, "forgive as often as necessary." Instead of a rule, the Lord answered with a principle—true forgiveness stands without limit.

That said, return to 1 Timothy 3:2–7 and consider the list of qualifications for an overseer with an eye for the principle undergirding the list.

> An overseer, then, must be above reproach, the husband of one wife, temperate, prudent, respectable, hospitable, able to teach, not addicted to wine or pugnacious, but gentle, peaceable, free

from the love of money. He must be one who manages his own household well, keeping his children under control with all dignity (but if a man does not know how to manage his own household, how will he take care of the church of God?), and not a new convert, so that he will not become conceited and fall into the condemnation incurred by the devil. And he must have a good reputation with those outside the church, so that he will not fall into reproach and the snare of the devil.

Most every evangelical who has ever served on a pastor search team at his or her church is familiar with this passage. He or she also knows that most other members of the church are acquainted with the verses and believe they know exactly what is taught in them. I repeat, they think they know.

While serving as the director of missions for a Southern Baptist Association of churches, I was often called upon to assist pastor search teams as they endeavored to clarify issues such as the biblical qualifications for church leadership. I clearly recall one such occasion when I was asked to counsel a team struggling with this issue. As might be expected, I began by asking the team members to join me in opening their Bibles to 1 Timothy 3. As pages were flipped to locate the text, one of the team members said, "We already know what those verses are about; they're the ones that say a divorced man can't be a pastor." After everyone located the passage, I looked at the speaker and asked, "And what else?" My question was met with a blank stare—and loads of silence.

It came as something of a surprise to those good people when I read the verses and pointed out that Paul didn't just speak to marriage and/or divorce; he in fact provided an extensive list of important qualifications. Here is how I explained the verses and the qualifications listed.

If the opening phrase of verse 2—"An overseer, then, must be above reproach . . ."—is taken as a general introductory statement and not one of the specific qualifications, the following list emerges:

Husband of one wife	Able to teach	Free from the love of money
Temperate	Not addicted to wine	Manages his own household well
Prudent	Not pugnacious	Keeps children in line with dignity
Respectable	Gentle	Not a new convert
Hospitable	Peaceable	Have a good reputation with those outside the church

Unless my math is seriously flawed, that is a list of fifteen items, covering far more than the single issue of marriage and/or divorce.

Beneath this diverse list is a single, guiding principle: the pastor is to be a mature, capable man of unassailable moral character. The items that follow this principle are there to provide a standard by which to judge the candidate's moral character—but the principle undergirding the list is of primary importance. In other words, all of the specific items taken as the list of qualifications for service are in fact qualifiers for the actual single qualification: exemplary moral character. To miss this point is to miss the point of the passage altogether. Instead of seeking God's holy ideal, we too often busy ourselves in a legalistic score-keeping exercise set on determining who is best based on a scale of more or less, e.g. who among the candidates complies with the greater number of items in the list?

Do not misunderstand. The list is essential and must be obeyed. Yet as important as the list is, its primary function is to define in concrete terms the essential attitudes and/or actions consistent with the underlying principle. We must not get so caught up with the items on the list that we completely lose sight of the foundational, core principle permeating it.

Thinking back to the brother on the pastor search committee, after pointing out to the search team the same things I have written here, I inquired, "After you have asked a candidate about his marriage history (which certainly you must), will you then investigate his relationship with his children, his credit rating, his practices with alcohol, his attitude toward material possessions and personal financial prosperity, and his reputation within the community he is to leave? Will you take time to discern his overall temperament and qualities of personality to see if they reflect biblical expectations? Are you prepared to determine that a man is disqualified if *any* of these qualifications are absent, and to do so with the same force that you would if you discovered he had a previous marriage? After all, the list begins with this all-important first principle: 'an overseer *must be* above reproach.' There is no *should* or *ought* in that principle."

Why stress this matter so forcefully? The reason is simple. Leadership within the church is no place simply to "settle." God's principled ideals are always nonnegotiable. This is especially the case for those who would lead His church. The church—the Body of Christ where Christ the Head provides the spiritual context for life and operation—is too important for anyone to lead other than one whose life matches not only the individual qualifications in the list, but God's undergirding principled ideal as well. This is true when an individual enters upon leadership; it remains true for as long as that person serves.

Some reading these words might say, "If we insisted on such a person, we would never find a pastor or any other leader." To which I would answer, "Perhaps we need fewer who claim leadership." When did the mandate become many leaders instead of biblically qualified leaders? After all, the apostle James said, "Let not many of you become teachers, my brethren, knowing that as such we will incur a stricter judgment" (James 3:1). Evidently, James understood the need for a qualified few over a partially qualified multitude. It is as if the church assumes that if the standard for leaders is set too high (i.e., as high as Scripture), there cannot possibly be anyone qualified to assume a position of leadership. In the wake of such a notion, the tendency is to surrender to the idea that God's ideal is ultimately untenable. Therefore, as the argument goes, the church must *settle* for some more "reasonable" option. The fact of the matter is, the church has not been given the option to negotiate with God for anything less than the leadership standards prescribed in His Word. But rest easy. What God requires, He supplies. Remember, Jesus said, "I will build My church." When He made this promise He was not just referring to membership and infrastructure, He was also speaking of leadership. God refuses to settle. We must not either.

It is utter foolishness to believe that a man called by God to lead the church will find it impossible to uphold faithfully God's moral ideal and standards. Claims to the contrary are completely fallacious. They originate with the devil who would compromise the church at any cost, and as you should expect, Satan's strategy is covert and effective. He simply produces in believers conclusions that are more informed by contemporary society than they are by the timeless Word of God. Doubt this? Then observe closely the media's intellectual talking heads as they discuss the array of moral lapses evident at every level of society. Listen to the sad resignation in their appraisal and analysis: "Because no one is perfect, it is a waste of time to strive for moral purity, or expect such efforts in others." "Because humans fail, it is necessary to accept failure—including gross moral failure—not just as normal, but as unavoidable." Now, pay attention to many of the voices within the church; see if they do not often reflect, even to the point of direct repetition, the very same sentiments.

Normally, in its assessments, the church will add the oft-used qualifier, "No one will ever be perfect this side of heaven." True enough. Yet, at what point did moral purity—especially as defined in Paul's list to Timothy—become God's definition of complete perfection? The sort of biblical perfection that is humanly unattainable on earth includes far more than simply complying with biblically moral character. However, even though complete perfection is fully unattainable here, we are still commanded to strive for holiness reflective of God's own. The Bible says, "As obedient children, do not be conformed to the former lusts which were yours in your ignorance, *but like the Holy One who called you, be holy yourselves also in all your behavior; because it is written, 'You shall be holy, for I am Holy'*" (1 Peter 1:14–16, italics added). It is difficult to imagine that Scripture could be any clearer.

Still, to be sure, even redeemed humans occasionally fail. Mercifully, God has made a provision for those occurrences, and most believers know it well: "If we confess our sins, He is faithful and righteous to forgive us our sins and to cleanse us from all unrighteousness" (1 John 1:9). Probably, we know the verse so well as a result of the number of times we have retreated to it. It could be that we know it *too* well. Possibly, our emphasis on this single verse has blinded us to other verses meant to keep us from having to run to 1 John 1:9 so often. For example, do we know as well Paul's assertions in Romans 6 concerning the believer and continued sin and failure? Review these verses from that chapter, giving special attention to the italicized portions.

> . . . knowing this, that our old self was crucified with Him, in order that our body of sin might be done away with, so that *we would no longer be slaves to sin; for he who has died is freed from sin.* Now if we have died with Christ, we believe that we shall also live with Him, knowing that Christ, having been raised from the dead, is never to die again; death no longer is master over Him. For the death that He died, He died to sin once for all; but the life that He lives, He lives to God. Even so *consider yourselves to be dead to sin,* but alive to God in Christ Jesus. Therefore *do not let sin reign in your mortal body* so that you obey its lusts, and *do not go on presenting the members of your body to sin* as instruments of unrighteousness; but *present yourselves to God as those alive* from the dead, and your members as instruments of righteousness to God.

For sin shall not be master over you, for you are not
under law but under grace (vv. 6–14).

Using the italicized portions as a guide, Paul's message
can be summarized this way: believers are dead to the old self;
thus, they are freed from enslavement to sin. In their freed
condition, believers are to *consider* themselves dead to sin's power,
refuse to allow sin the power position in their lives, and *stop offering*
themselves for sin's expressions. Instead, believers must *present*
themselves to God as those alive through God's salvation and
assume the posture of those who are no longer mastered by sin.

The Scriptures cited above yield four points along with a
single, implied summary message. As I see them, here are the
points. First, the person alive in Christ is a newly created life
having been moved from death and the deadly state of being fully
overpowered by sin. Second, in the truest spiritual sense, sin has
lost its death grip on those in Christ. Third, in practical
application, the mastery of sin has been replaced by Christ, the
master of true life; now it is up to the believer to accept, assume,
and live this new condition. Fourth, experiencing the full
expression of this new life is accomplished as the believer agrees
with God about the replaced mastery of sin over his or her life,
actively assumes the attitude of a victor, and steadfastly refuses to
live any longer as a victim of sin. Now comes the single implied
message: experiencing the reality of the victorious life currently
resident within us requires the work of Christ in salvation
coupled with a choice made by those He has redeemed. Christ
has finished His work—even to the extent of providing the
indwelling power of the Holy Spirit. The believer must choose to
"reckon" themselves dead to sin (KJV) and work from that
perspective to live as victors, not as victims. Simply put, we must
live as those who can overcome sin, because we belong to Him
who has defeated sin.

Church, it must never be the case that the commands of
God are treated so as to become romanticized ideals instead of
the holy objectives God intended for His Body. Keep in mind

that even if some failure is inevitable, that is no adequate reason for making provision for failure beforehand. Further, the failure of others can never justify our own.[55] To assume the impossibility of finding leaders who fully meet the biblical standard creates an atmosphere of surrender and settlement within the Body that is extremely damaging because, while it may reflect the best thinking of a resigned society, it is in direct violation of the Word of God.

So, where does that leave us? Happily, we are left with at least one very encouraging truth: God does raise up and provide for the church leaders who meet His qualifications, despite times and circumstances that often tempt even the best of leaders to failure. In light of this truth, the church must never settle; it must trust God—and wait upon Him—to provide leaders whose character and lifestyle demonstrate the best of what God requires in His principled ideal. Only after the scriptural qualifications based in God's larger undergirding principle are met should a resumé reflecting training and experience be considered as suitable evidence that a candidate is qualified to lead Christ's church.

While locating such biblically qualified leaders may appear a daunting task, take heart. Recognizing biblically qualified leaders is not as difficult as it may sound when one considers how different their lives will appear when contrasted with the often laissez-faire spiritual lifestyles of others, even in the church. Individuals who meet the biblical standards of leadership are immediately recognizable by a number of distinct traits. For instance, they possess a consistent, sacrificial, servant's heart focused on God's glory instead of their own. They are dedicated kingdom builders, not self-focused empire builders. There is no pretense or superficiality in them; they are genuinely committed disciples of Jesus Christ, His Word, and His mission. In a word, these qualified leaders are identifiable because they are truly "radical." (Far from using radical as a buzzword, as is often the

---

[55]Watchman Nee, private letter, quoted in, Bob Finley, *Reformation in Foreign Missions* (Charlottesville, VA: Christian Aid Mission, 2007), 50–51.

case in much church literature and teaching, the word is here intended to identify a very real characteristic in these leaders.) These individuals realize that what is often called radical—radical discipleship, radical commitment, radical service—is so labeled because it differs so from the actual practice of so many believers. Truly qualified leaders know that when it comes to discipleship, lifestyle, or ministry, there is in reality no such thing as radical; there is only normal—biblically normal. However, because in too many cases the church has strayed from the biblical norms of conduct and service, uncompromising adherence to actual biblical teaching has become abnormal. Thus, when a leader (or any other member of the Body) strives to teach and live out truth just as it is revealed in Scripture, that person appears radical. Despite trends to the contrary, however, qualified leaders do adhere to biblical instruction—even the most difficult parts—striving for the ideal of holiness, and they lead others to do so as well.

Admittedly, what has been written regarding church leaders is hard. The very idea of striving for and insisting upon *ideal* behavior in a fallen world makes any effort to attain it seem childish at best and irrationally foolish at worse. However, apart from some hermeneutical calisthenics combining Scripture with various appeals to society and contemporary culture, it is hard to deny that what has been written is, in fact, what Scripture says. So, for a moment, lay aside the inherent difficulty involved and consider a very common-sense observation.

Remembering that the church is God's creation, that it is the Body of Christ, that Jesus is both its Head and the "spiritual sphere" in which it operates, ask yourself these questions: Why would this organism require anything less than leaders qualified according to God's principled ideal and qualifications? Is it possible that leaders who do not take seriously the mandate of holiness measurable by Scripture's listed qualifications can properly lead the true church into a proper relationship with its holy Head? Why would we expect that God will abide anything less stringent, or settle for anyone less compliant? The answer is simple; it is logically inconsistent to acknowledge the God of the church as being completely holy then expect Him to act in any way other than fully holy, or expect Him to require less in the character of those who lead His people. Again, settling is not an option.

Conclusion

It will come as a surprise to many that one of the most famous landmarks in the world today was, when it was built for an international exposition in the nineteenth century, called monstrous by the citizens of the city where it was erected. In fact, the citizens of the city demanded it be torn down as soon as the exposition was over. Yet from the moment its architect first conceived it, he took pride in it and loyally defended it from those who wished to destroy it. He knew it was destined for greatness. Today it is one of the architectural wonders of the modern world and stands as the primary landmark of Paris, France. The architect, of course, was Alexandre Gustave Eiffel. His famous tower was built in 1889. In the same way, we are struck by Jesus' loyalty to another structure—the church—which he entrusted to an unlikely band of disciples, whom he organized, prayed for, and prepared to spread the gospel. To outsiders, they (and we) must seem like incapable blunderers, people who have made the mistake of our lives by becoming serving parts of the church. But Jesus, the architect of the church, knows this structure is destined for greatness now and when he returns.[56]

The greatness of the church rests in the sacrifice and person of Jesus Christ and the investment He continues to make in its life. However, for reasons that will only be fully revealed in heaven, the Lord has chosen to call redeemed humans to share in His program of demonstrating the church's greatness here on earth. He has, thus, positioned the church as being essential to believers' lives and, in turn, made believers

---

[56]John Berstecher, *Sermon Illustrations,* http://www.sermon illustrations.com/a-z/c/church.htm (accessed January 30, 2010.)

central to the life of the church. The result is a true union of necessity: believers need the church and the church needs believers. Chuck Colson rightly observed,

> . . . membership in a confessing body is fundamental to the faithful Christian life. Failure to do so defies the explicit warning not to forsake "our assembling together." His understanding of this prompted Martin Luther to say, "Apart from the church, salvation is impossible." Not that the church provides salvation; God does. But because the "saved" one can't fulfill what it means to be a Christian apart from the church, membership becomes the indispensable mark of salvation. . . . "So highly does the Lord esteem the communion of His church," Calvin wrote, "that He considers everyone a traitor and apostate from religion who perversely withdraws himself from any Christian society which preserves the true ministry of the word . . ."[57]

This chapter has been an effort to show a few essential ways in which the *union of necessity* between Christ and His church are constructed and operative. To this end, we have explored the church as a model of order and structure. It has been pointed out that *order* within the church is founded on the proposition that Jesus Christ, as the single Head of the church, is the only legitimate basis upon which order within the church is to be structured. This being the case, the *structure* of the church is fully dependent upon the order established by the church's true Head.

The church then is structured by Christ to facilitate ministry that accomplishes the will and desires of God. This is seen in at least three ways: (1) the Body is interconnected—Body to Head and each member to every other member—and in this interconnectedness it matures as individual members, empowered by the Holy Spirit, provide ministry to one another through their

---

[57]Charles W. Colson, *The Body*, (Nashville: Word Publishing, 1992) 70.

spiritual gifts; (2) the Body is called and fashioned to accomplish the great desire of God to be made known to the entire world; and (3) the Body is to be led by individuals whose lives exemplify the highest ideals of holiness as set forth in Scripture.

The great truth overarching all of this is—Jesus is supreme as Lord of His church. He is the "Lord-basis" for order; He is the "Lord-designer" of structure. Because He is a sovereign Lord and fully deserving of the honors of royalty, Jesus feels most at home among people who realize His supremacy, not only by celebrating His deity but by submitting to His full control over every detail of the church's life and function. Such a church would certainly be a place Jesus would attend.

Chapter 5

Law-Abiding Citizens

Several years ago, a Christian pastor in Egypt was asked why, after years of prominence and growth, Christianity had ceased to flourish in his country. According to the story, the pastor answered by saying that over time, with shifts in dominant religious groups and various geo-political changes within the country, the church in Egypt, particularly its evangelical branch, began to fear for its future. This fear came to weigh so heavily on the mind of the church that questions of survival instead of ministry began to dominate congregational thinking. As a result, the Egyptian Church chose to turn inward, believing that as they protectively took care of themselves, their survival would be assured. Instead, the pastor insisted, by turning to an inward focus the church doomed itself. This, he explained, is because an important kingdom principle was violated: to survive you must give yourself away.[58]

It is interesting that the Egyptian pastor framed his response to Christianity in Egypt in terms of the church and kingdom law—interesting but not overstated. Consider these facts:

---

[58] I first heard this story as part of a pastor's sermon, back in the seventies. It was told without citing its source. It is not possible for me to vouch for its accuracy. However, even if it's fiction, the lessons are unimpaired.

- The church is centrally located in the Kingdom of God, insuring that all its born-again members are citizens of God's Kingdom.
- Like any other kingdom on earth, the Kingdom of God has a reigning, sovereign monarch, established boundaries, and absolute laws.
- The sovereign ruler is Yahweh.
- The territorial boundaries of His rule reach to the full extent of His creation.
- The laws governing the kingdom are established by the King and stand as immutable in every culture and circumstance, and are incumbent upon all its citizens as their primary obligations of obedience.
- Given the broad expanse of God's Kingdom, its citizens—the people of God—can be found in every corner of the globe and among every ethnic group.
- Additionally, all who are citizens of the kingdom are subject to its King and therefore have a first-order obligation to obey the laws of His Kingdom, by ordering their lives in accordance with them.

Nowhere is this last point better illustrated than in two simple yet telling verses of Scripture. The first comes from the lips of Jesus Himself in His famous Sermon on the Mount. In one crucial statement, Jesus reinforced the primacy of obedience to kingdom rule by saying, "But seek first His kingdom and His righteousness, and all these things will be added to you" (Matthew 6:33).

Do not rush too quickly to the last phrase in the verse (it's an appealing phrase and very true, but as a promise it's predicated on the command of the first phrase). Jesus seems to be answering those who see in His teachings only ethical comments. In this verse, He makes it clear that the ethics prescribed for God's people are elevated far above simple right behavior. What Jesus taught in the Sermon on the Mount are laws of God's Kingdom

("His kingdom") and they are based upon that kingdom's unique claim to righteousness (His righteousness). Further, these laws are to be sought—desired, pursued, aimed at—by kingdom citizens as first-order priorities. They are never to be mitigated by any counsel or teaching to the contrary.

The word translated "first" in Jesus' command is the Greek contraction *prōtos*. The word means "first in time and place, first in rank," and "at the first." As a part of speech, *prōtos* is a "contracted superlative" adjective. In formal terms, this type of adjective describes something above which nothing is superior—a superlative. In more down-to-earth language it means, this is something *so* important that nothing else should be considered *more* important and placed before it. Listen to Jesus: the Kingdom of God is so vitally important that nothing else should be considered more important than finding it and becoming part of it. In other words, once the kingdom is found and you become part of it, nothing is more important than obeying its laws in keeping with the righteousness of its King. Could Jesus be any clearer?

The second verse of proof is equally familiar to most believers. In Acts 5, the apostle Peter was commanded to cease speaking to Jerusalem's residents in the name of Jesus. To those of the Jewish ruling ecclesiastical court who issued the demand, Peter replied, ". . . We *must* obey God rather than men" (v. 29, italics added). Simply put, Peter and the other apostles understood that in this particular circumstance they were left with no choice other than to obey God above any other authority. The larger lesson is unmistakable: when the statutes of God's Kingdom are in conflict with the laws of any other kingdom, the laws governing the believer's primary citizenship—the Kingdom of God—trump every other command.

Be advised, none of this is meant to incite some form of fringe-style response to governmental or civic authorities. Far from it. Without contradicting itself, the Bible also insists that believers live as exemplary citizens of their respective countries, always respecting the authority of governmental leadership

(Romans 13; 1 Peter 2:13–17). In fact, only the most egregious departures from God's moral laws by political entities should result in acts of civil disobedience on the parts of believers. Even then, actions must be taken with an eye to obeying all other laws of God related to respect and graceful forbearance, even to the point of gracefully accepting the punitive actions that may follow in consequence of one's choices.

What is being pointed out has to do with a life of submission to kingdom laws as they govern lifestyle behavior related to *everyday* issues, those things that so often tend to conflict with the so-called common sense answers (laws) of the earthly kingdom. For instance, reconsider what the Egyptian pastor said regarding the decline of the Christian Church in his country. Think carefully about his words: *by turning to an inward focus the church doomed itself. This is because an important kingdom principle was violated: to survive you must give yourself away.* Face it, the common sense of the world scoffs at the idea of achieving survival by making yourself vulnerable through exposure and self-sacrifice. Yet such is the obvious demand of the kingdom as witnessed in statements regarding the believer's lifestyle: If you want to live, you must die; if you want to receive, you must give; if you wish to be served, you must serve; if you wish to be exalted, you must humble yourself. These and numerous other similar commands stand in stark contrast to the counsel of the world. Yet in far too many cases, believers are willing to believe everything the world says with little argument, but challenge everything God says.

Further, to live in violation of God's principles constitutes disobedience, and as any child in Sunday school knows, continued disobedience robs the believer of the blessings of God, the results of which can be devastating. This is precisely because kingdom laws are firmly established by the King and must be adhered to by all His citizens, individually in lifestyle as well as corporately in the church. Further, these laws are immutable and must be obeyed despite the world's counsel to the contrary. To do otherwise is to flirt with danger, even to invite disaster.

The church then—centered as it is squarely within the kingdom, both in terms of location and obligation—is left with an important question to answer: *are we guilty of trying to live as citizens of God's Kingdom while appealing to the laws of another?* If the honest answer to that question is yes—to any degree—we must admit to an operational pattern that makes about as much sense as insisting that an American citizen should not be tried for committing a certain crime in the United States because that particular act is not against the law in Australia. That argument may make for a novel defense, but it just won't stand up in court. Further, knowing that there are serious consequences for disobeying God's laws, is it just possible that many of the front-burner issues that trouble the modern church most—i.e., numerical decline, apathy, discontent, seeming irrelevance—are less the result of a fallen, deteriorating society and the church's supposed inability to relate to it, and more the result of God's withdrawn blessings, stemming from churches trying to maintain an identity with God's Kingdom while at the same time ordering its ministry life according to the laws of another?

Because that is a lengthy and complex sentence, read it again to make sure nothing is missed. Now, recall the words of Jesus, "No one can serve two masters; for either he will hate the one and love the other, or he will be devoted to one and despise the other. . . ." (Matthew 6:24; Luke 16:13). The importance of what Jesus said in this verse is no trivial matter. The Lord did not mince His words—serving two masters simultaneously is impossible; no one can do it. Human beings are incapable of giving equal devotion to multiple masters. Further, even if it were possible for an individual or group of individuals to provide equal devotion to two masters at the same time, surely the demands for full allegiance by each master would render those efforts insufficient.

Given these truths, a simple and straightforward choice emerges: individual believers and the church as a whole must decide which kingdom—which master—will receive their singular and unadulterated allegiance. If the choice is God and His Kingdom, then the laws He has established to govern His

Kingdom's operation become the single standard upon which the lives of kingdom citizens are to be oriented and the entire church must operate. Granted, any reference to laws within the spiritual realm sounds rather arbitrary, especially given the world's antinomian preferences. However, laws are integral to the definition of a kingdom; a kingdom without them lacks order and essential identity. In the absence of laws there exists only a polyglot of free-floating, generally unattached ideas, concepts that are by their nature negotiable, alterable, replaceable, and fully disposable. But such is not the case in the Kingdom of God; its laws are fixed and final. They are nonnegotiable, nondisposable, and never interchangeable with the statues of any other kingdom.

So, let's summarize. First, the Bible clearly establishes the church's central place within God's Kingdom and God's exclusive rule over the life of His corporate Body. Second, the church's place in the kingdom plus God's sovereignty over the kingdom make any divergence from the laws administering His rule acts of overt disobedience. Third, disobedience always results in the displeasure of the Lord of the kingdom and the disruption of His blessings within the Body. Recall that earlier long, complex sentence? Read it again, this time as a statement of fact rather than a question, with the above three conclusions in mind. . . . *the church just might discover that many of the troubling issues it faces—i.e., numerical decline, apathy, discontent, seeming irrelevance—are less the result of a fallen, deteriorating society and the church's supposed inability to relate to it, and more the result of God's withdrawn blessings stemming from believers trying to maintain an identity with God's kingdom while at the same time ordering their lives according to the laws of another.* If the words failed to ring true before, they should by now.

In light of these things, it makes sense to consider the health of the church within the context of its status as a "law-abiding" citizen within the Kingdom of God. However, in doing so do not focus solely on the more pronounced, overt forms of easily discernable deviations from God's laws. In most churches, the larger, potentially deathblow issues are usually accounted for and dealt with in good order. What are of greater danger are the more impalpable deviations from obedience, which tend toward subtle duplicity—the things that are easily missed because in and of themselves they are not sinful. These are usually good things that have become so bloated and overburdened by added elements counseled by the world as to turn the godly into the ungodly. Given these thoughts, we would do well to remember the preacher's words from Ecclesiastes: "Dead flies make a perfumer's oil stink" (Ecclesiastes 10:1). Allow me to suggest a few "dead flies" capable of turning the sweet perfume of the church into something far less desirable.

The Danger of Missed Lessons

It will surprise no one to say that the church has a fundamental responsibility to teach truth. This instruction in truth includes exposition (theoretical instruction) coupled with demonstration (practical application). In other words, the church is responsible before God to offer verbal instruction in the Word of God then provide real-time, lifestyle illustrations of that truth in practice. It's a simple formula, but very effective.

Nowhere is this formula better observed than in Jesus' call to the original twelve disciples and the process by which He trained them. Jesus, according to the custom of a Jewish master teacher, selected teachable men for personal instruction. As part of this instructional process, the disciples lived in very close community with Jesus, the teacher. In this arrangement, the disciples were required to do three things: hear the instructions of the teacher, observe as the teacher lived His teachings in everyday life, then implement and practice the master's teachings in their own lives. This was the scheme by which essential learning took place.

After Jesus returned to heaven, both Jewish and Gentile leaders of the new church continued this instructional method by replicating it in their own ministries. For instance, the apostle Paul incorporated the mentor method of training as part of his missionary activities, at least on a one-to-one basis. The classic evidence of this point is found in Paul's directive to his young protégée, Timothy. To the young pastor, Paul wrote, "The things which you have heard from me in the presence of many witnesses, entrust these to faithful men who will be able to teach others also" (2 Timothy 2:2). Clearly, it was the apostle's intention that Timothy teach and live out truth as a mentor to others and then instruct those others to follow the same scheme in the future.

Nothing since the first century has altered the biblical imperative of dual instruction; making mature disciples is still Christ's mandate for the church. In a very real sense, while the church has leadership who minister as teachers, the Body itself has a master teacher responsibility as it undergirds the instruction of its teachers by living out their biblical lessons, thus exemplifying the gospel. In essence, the training responsibility of the church is twofold. First, it must provide sound biblical instruction; second, it must model and illustrate the application of that truth.

The church has done pretty well with the first responsibility. Today, numerous programs ranging from traditional Sunday school classes to newer, innovative delivery systems such as small groups and technology-based applications, dispense an ever-growing array of Bible study materials. In terms of those materials, the world of biblical literature is replete with an abundance of items designed to appeal to every age group, presentation preference, time frame, and perceived need. Undoubtedly, the twenty-first century is the age of convenient, accessible Bible study such as never before. The church can look with pleasure at how it has maximized available resources for teaching the Word of God.

The second item—the church must model and illustrate the application of truth—is another matter, however. It is here that a notable weakness is evident, a weakness traceable to the incompatibility of two kingdoms with very different laws. Perhaps the best example of this conflict as it affects the responsibility of the church to exemplify the lessons of the gospel is with regard to a key kingdom principle: sacrifice and the living of sacrificial lives. Allow me to illustrate what I mean by speaking of these two items within the context of worship. The benefits of worship reach far beyond the big three: preaching, prayer, and praise. Worship provides a full range of sensory experiences connected to sight, sound, and emotion. Beyond these, however, true worship furnishes an excellent classroom experience, because true Spirit-filled worship promotes very teachable moments. Given the responsibility of the church to undergird its verbal exposition of God's Word with visible applications of truth, there is no better medium for displaying those visible applications than when the church is assembled in corporate worship. Church leadership must maximize, not miss, these divine moments of opportunity.

So, how does this truth relate to sacrifice? Perhaps better asked, how can worship be used to teach sacrifice and selflessness? Further, why is this lesson necessary? Allow me to explain by way of a very special memory from my own family history.

Throughout much of my childhood, and until shortly before my father's death in 2002, the week of Thanksgiving was regularly set aside for the annual gathering of both sides of my family. Because the promotion and organization of this holiday event was mostly my mother's doing, each year all the relatives gathered at the Roe house. My favorite recollections of those three- to four-day Roe/Pope reunions took place during the years Mom and Dad lived in the tiny, rural East Texas community of Mont Alba. About nineteen miles outside Palestine, Texas, Mont Alba consists of a single blinking traffic light, a Post Office, a gas station, and a lone mercantile store, all of which are situated on either side of a typical, ribbonlike Texas two-lane black top. What there is most of in Mont Alba is land, acres and acres of rich pasture land providing an undulating home to countless livestock. It was a perfect setting for the invasion of kinfolk from all around Texas, Alabama, Georgia, Arkansas, and Tennessee.

The good times experienced at those annual gatherings are legendary in Roe/Pope family lore. No one on either side of the family had much in the way of worldly goods, so the fun was rather simple and always self-made. Touch football, horseshoes, various card games, dominos, and storytelling were regular fare. Nothing, however, could top the inevitable, impromptu family singing. Most years at day's end, when everyone was reasonably worn out, Aunt Coralee, who played every song she knew with a bossa nova beat, took over the piano and the music started. The littlest ones sung and danced jigs to "Jesus Loves Me" and "Jesus Loves the Little Children," followed by the teens' renditions of contemporary Christian songs of that time. The adults, old and young, raised the roof with older standards such as "I'll Fly Away" and "Amazing Grace." On a few occasions, Dad would retrieve his guitar and songs from the Stamps Baxter era filled the room.

Recalling those musical evenings brings back delightful memories of not only the singing but the moans and groans as well. You see, not everyone appreciated the others' taste in music, and they were not shy about making their feelings known. The young folk made light of what the older people sang, and the older family members often grimaced when the teens broke into melody. However, it was all in fun and no one ever seriously thought about stopping anyone else from sharing what they had to share. Truth be told, the experience would have been less enjoyable if any of the music had been excluded.

What was experienced during those special evenings extended far beyond good times and freshly made memories. There were important lessons learned as well. You see, left to our individual devices each of us at the family singing might have ruled out some of the presentations by insisting on our own musical preferences, or separating into smaller affinity niches to do our own thing without the bother of music we didn't care for. However, the standing rule was when the family assembled for the singing, everyone had to remain together for the entire program. I must admit, at the time, this rule seemed rather unfair and arbitrary. In retrospect, however, it is now apparent that a few almost magical things took place. First, the family learned to sacrifice individual or smaller group desires for the pleasure of other family members. Second, we discovered the joy of sacrificing our own desires and preferences for the benefit of those we loved—we learned to find joy in the joy of others. Most importantly, the family learned to sacrifice as a unit. In other words, sacrifice was unilateral—everyone submitted to everyone else—and we benefitted from the experience together, as a family unit.

Through the years and involvement in my own ministry, I have come to recognize some telling parallels between those family singing events and the church. For instance, the most basic descriptive term for the church is family. As a family, the church exists in two fundamental forms: the church scattered and the church gathered. In its local arrangement, for most of the week the membership is scattered throughout the community, or town. In most cases, while smaller groups of the Body may come together at certain other intervals during the week, Sunday is the special day when the entire church "family" joins together in what might be likened to a reunion. These Sunday meetings are designed for whole Body teaching, worship, and fellowship. At minimum, they are intended to foster love and unity. Sunday's full-family reunions, particularly when gathered in worship, provide excellent teachable moments to accomplish these ends.

As an illustration to make a point of all this, consider what happens each week across North America in numerous Sunday family gatherings. Note the growing number of churches large and small that subdivide the Body into separate groups for worship. Listen to the rationale guiding these separations. In many cases, the reasoning has nothing whatsoever to do with any utilitarian justification such as inadequate space to house all the congregation in one service, or genuine needs created by unique communities. (For example, I have in mind a Midwestern industrial town where most of the community was employed as shift workers at a large mill. Many of the workers got off work at 2:00 a.m. on Sunday morning. For obvious reasons, they found it very difficult to make the 10:00 a.m. worship at their local Baptist church. The church responded by creating a 2:30 a.m. worship service for these folk. It was a wonderful success.) Whether we choose to admit it or not, the reasons for separate services are usually far less noble. In fact, they are selfish on one hand and fear-based on the other. Segments of the family are unwilling to accommodate the preferences of others or to attend a service that conflicts in time with their other plans. Church leaders respond in fear that people will be lost to the church if the demands for separate worship are not met. In the process, while the motivation of leadership may be pure, the unavoidable truth is selfishness on one hand and fear on the other has created a family of segregated units living under the same roof, demanding their own way without knowledge of or consideration for the needs of others within the household. In the world of family dynamics, this is called *dysfunctional.*

In 1963, Dr. Martin Luther King, speaking of racially segregated congregations, offered the following sad observation: "At 11:00 on Sunday morning when we stand and sing and Christ has no east or west, *we stand at the most segregated hour in this nation.* This is tragic"[59] (italics added). While the current trend to congregational segregation may not rightfully be called tragic, it is at the very least troubling. Whether these separate services are called contemporary worship, traditional worship, modern worship, or something much more trendy, the church—the *family unit* of God—has acquiesced to the world's counsel, which says in order to gain people and keep them coming, the church must offer a variety of taste-specific worship experiences, each of which should be timed and designed to provide only what specific groups prefer without the interference of accommodating any worship expression not to that group's particular taste or inconvenience with their other plans. You might say, it is the

---

[59]Martin Luther King, "1963 WMU Speech," Western Michigan University Libraries, Archives and Regional History Collections, http://www.wmich.edu/library/archives/mlk/q-a.html (accessed March 1, 2011).

"homogeneous unit" principle[60] gone to seed—a principle meant to foster movements of the lost to Christ, not to accommodate the comfort levels of individual groups of believers. Understood from this perspective, the segregation of the Body into various affinity groupings purely for the sake of cultural pragmatics is visible for what it is: the accommodation of the world's counsel leading to me-centered selfishness within a Body originally brought into existence by the ultimate sacrifice of God Himself.

This sort of self-centered attitude is obviously never espoused in the laws of God's Kingdom. Quite the contrary. Kingdom law demands such things as, "Be devoted to one another in brotherly love; give preference to one another in honor" (Romans 12:10); "Do nothing from selfishness or empty conceit, but with humility of mind regard one another as more important than yourselves; do not merely look out for your own personal interests, but also for the interests of others" (Philippians 2:3–4); "You younger men, likewise, be subject to your elders; and all of you, clothe yourselves with humility toward one another, for God is opposed to the proud, but gives grace to the humble" (1 Peter 5:5). Messages contrary to these passages and many others like them arise solely from the counsel of laws governing the kingdom of the world, the very counsel the psalmist praised people for avoiding when he declared, "How blessed is the man who does not walk in the counsel of the wicked, nor stand in the path of sinners, nor sit in the seat of scoffers!" (Psalm 1:1).

The point is this: the counsel of the world's kingdom, which is opposed to the laws of God's Kingdom, is

---

[60]The homogenous unit principle was first articulated by Donald McGavran in his 1954 book, *The Bridges of God*. McGavran contended that people prefer to come to Christ having to cross the fewest racial, social, economic, and linguist barriers. In other words, people are more likely to respond to the gospel within groups most like themselves. To this end, McGavran encouraged missionaries to utilize the "bridges" of family and kinship ties within each people group thereby prompting "people movements" to Christ.

fundamentally selfish and self-serving, motivating the flesh to demand its own satisfaction. As such, that counsel is fully at odds with the laws of God's Kingdom, which requires sacrificial selflessness on the part of its citizenry. It is utterly foolish, therefore, to expect that acquiescence to the laws of self-interest as counseled by the world's cultural kingdom will produce within the church results that are reflective of and pleasing to the sovereign of the kingdom to which it belongs. Further, outside the King's pleasure it is equally foolish to imagine that God will bless the church with the positive outcomes it purports to achieve through abiding by foreign counsel.

In the paradigm of separation, the diversity that God Himself built into the assembled church is as lost as the old are segregated from the young, couples from singles, parents from the childless, the upwardly mobile from the staid and contented, the hipsters from the hymn-sters, the hand-raisers from the hand-sitters, and so on. Ask yourself, are the variety and diversity God created valid only when the church is scattered? Must they be discouraged and discarded when the church is gathered? Sadly, when diversity is excluded for the sake of group separation, the unavoidable result is the absence of what each group can contribute to the other. Consequently, true growth is stymied. Genuine growth does not come from the sharing of exclusively kindred pleasures, pains, and problems, as is the case when everyone is the same and at the same level of life experience. Genuine growth occurs in the combined experience of diverse needs and backgrounds, and the wisdom that flows from the multiple perspectives present when the whole Body comes together. In a very real sense, God purposefully provides learning and growth opportunities in the intentional diversity He has assembled in the church.

The church is called to join Christ in the mission He set forth in such passages as Luke 4:18–19. There, Jesus applied the words of Isaiah to Himself by declaring, "The Spirit of the LORD is upon Me, because He has anointed Me to preach the gospel to the poor. He has sent Me to proclaim release to the captives, and recovery of sight to the blind, to set free those who are oppressed, to proclaim the favorable year of the LORD." While these words are messianic in nature and identify Jesus as the singular Messiah of God, it is also true that those who follow Christ (the church) are undeniably included in the ministry functions set forth in the text. Is it implausible then to think that the church can effectively bind up the wounds and minister mercy to the masses if it is unwilling to identify with and embrace the whole family by subordinating its individual preferences long enough to worship as a unit?

Remember, the church is not just to declare truth; it is to exemplify it, as well. In separation based on self-interest, then, where is the opportunity to *practice* sacrifice? Where is the opportunity to *practice* selflessness? The answer is simple enough. In a me-centered, affinity-based segregation, the opportunities for learning through the observation and practice of these and other kingdom principles are lost; they are lost because the motivation for and application of affinity-based separation tends to mitigate against them. Simply put, it is difficult, if not impossible, to teach and model the very things you seek to avoid. As a correspondent for the *New York Herald* wrote in 1863 of presidential politics, "The art of riding two horses is not confined to the circus."

Please understand; this is by no means intended as a personal diatribe against multiple worship services. As previously noted, there are situations in which offering more than one service is precisely the thing to do, perhaps even a necessity. Further, there is no desire here to set forth another abstract dogma that threatens to obscure essential truth. Truth and its proper application were never intended to be mutually exclusive or antagonistic systems. I am not berating a particular choice in programming; I am appealing for consistency between the kingdom to which the church belongs and the principles upon which it operates.

So what is the truth to which I allude? It is simply this: the church must be constantly vigilant to assess honestly its fidelity to kingdom principles (laws) and judge with equal candor any possible deviations from them, as well as the motivation for those deviations. Three principles should be kept in mind as a basis for this assessment. (1) When the church gathers it does so as a kingdom family; (2) The laws of the kingdom are never to be preempted in our corporate assemblies—including worship—for the sake of personal preferences or on the basis of cultural counsel; (3) God has purposes for worship that reach far beyond singing and preaching, purposes that include the expectation of actually practicing the things we preach. Keeping these things in mind will go a long way to insure that God is fully glorified and the Body benefits from all He intends to do and teach when His people gather together. Certainly, Jesus would be very much at home in a church like this.

Chapter 6

A Missional Mindset

It has been said that a person's actions will be governed by his or her reactions. This makes sense when you consider the impossibility, for example, of producing acts of love when one initially reacts to people or events in anger. Reactions are largely produced by one's mental predisposition to certain people or external stimuli. This mental predisposition can also be referred to as one's mindset. Everyone has one, and it is a powerful thing because it forms the basis for a person's positions relative to individuals, issues, and circumstances, effectively assuring that certain decisions have been made about these things long before the actual deciding is required.

Mindsets are unavoidable; they can be good or bad, moral or immoral, correct or incorrect. For Christians, three things serve to make the distinction between the right or wrong of a particular mindset. First, a correct mindset must reflect the character and nature of God. Second, it must accurately address the situation to which it is applied. Third, it needs be fully and correctly informed, regarding everyone and everything to which it is applied.

Interestingly, groups of individuals, such as the church, also possess mindsets. These corporate mindsets have all the same characteristics and function within the group in the same way as with individuals. They too can be appropriate or inappropriate and are to be judged by the three things noted above. With these things in mind, what, then, should be the undergirding mindset of the church as it goes about its life and ministry on earth?

In his book, *Effective Church Leadership*, author and teacher Kennon Callahan answers this question within the context of what he refers to as the "day of mission."[61] Callahan uses this phrase as a label intended to identify the foundation for the mindset most conducive to the church's engagement of its assignment in the world. Callahan argues that the "day of mission" mentality, or mindset, is critical for the church because the church no longer resides in a churched culture. Instead, he argues, the church functions in a world where "no major cultural value says that the church is important."[62] Consequently, church values are not shared by the culture at large; few people seek out the church on their own initiative and, in the main, most folk live their entire lives as if the church does not exist or matter.

According to Callahan, "A churched culture is not so much defined as a culture in which a certain statistical percentage of the population is actively participating in church work, although the level of participation is likely to be higher than in an unchurched culture. Rather a churched culture is marked by the presence of a persistent, pervasive, major feeling among the people that the church is important."[63] Furthermore, three characteristics generally serve as markers of a churched culture: (1) The church and culture share the same major values; (2) the majority of people who attend church seek it out on their own; and (3) those attending church are active and participatory.[64]

There was a time in American cultural history—perhaps forty to sixty years ago when a churched culture existed—when the church could look to the surrounding, predominant culture as a sympathetic partner in its moral endeavors. That time is no more. And, as disturbing as the truth is, the result is, "America is

---

[61]Kennon L. Callahan, *Effective Church Leadership* (San Francisco: HarperSanFrancisco, 1990), 1.

[62]Callahan, *Effective Church*, 20.

[63]Ibid.

[64]9.

not a Christian nation, it is rather a mission field."[65] It follows then that the church of North America must now view itself in its alien status, as a long-term sojourner with a missionary assignment on the North American mission field. Further, all that the church on this continent sets out to be and do must be informed by this understanding and conviction.

As a result of living in "the day of mission," three things have become true of the church and its relationship with the world: (1) "The day of the professional minister is over. The day of the missionary pastor has come"; (2) "The day of the churched culture is over. The day of the mission field has come"; (3) "The day of the local church is over. The day of the mission outpost has come."[66] As statements of condition, these three propositions are not looming on the horizon; they exist for the church now as present realities.[67] They exist because of—and as products of—the overarching shift away from being a churched culture.[68]

Proposition 1: The Day of the Professional Minister Is Over. The Day of the Missionary Pastor Has Come.

The meaning of these two sentences is found in the juxtaposition between "professional minister" and "missionary pastor." These are two very different individuals, indeed. The professional minister evolved as part of the churched culture that existed between the 1940s and mid-1970s, emerging out of the larger cultural movement of professionalism, and the "interactive

---

[65]Franklin H. Littel, *From State Church to Pluralism* (Garden City, NY: Anchor Books, Doubleday and Company, 1962), 29.

[66]Callahan, *Effective Church*, 3, 13, 22.

[67]11.

[68]8–9.

relationship between the church and culture during the period."[69] "Prior to World War II, the primary focus [for ministers] was on vocation . . . or calling. Following World War II, the primary focus was on profession."[70] After World War II, the professional ministers' movement was fed by a flow of articles and books on the minister as professional. New standards were developed for the professional minister. Denominations focused on the professionalization of the minister. "Seminaries turned their attention to preparing and graduating—in the best sense of the term—'professional ministers.'"[71] There was a perceived need for the church to reflect culturally the broader cultural movement toward professionalism, and the church responded to the need within the context of a churched culture by providing professional ministers.

The leadership perspective of the professional minister was focused inside the church. The assumed appropriateness of this perspective was endorsed by both churchmen and secular scientists of the period. In 1956, Richard Niebuhr wrote that the minister's ". . . first function is that of building or 'edifying' the church. . . . The work that lays the greatest claim to his time and thought is the care of the church, the *administration* of a community"[72] (italics added). Niebuhr further defined the resulting professional leadership style by referring to the minister as a "pastoral director."[73] Ministers of the period were increasingly preoccupied with the inside of the church, and they could focus their energies there because the world was coming to the church.

Within this paradigm there arose the notion that administration was a significant part of the minister's work. Thus, administration and day-to-day care for church programming

---

[69]Callahan, *Effective Church*, 13.

[70]10.

[71]5

[72]Richard Niebuhr, *The Purpose of the Church and Its Ministry* (New York: Harper & Brothers, 1956), 82–83.

[73]Ibid., 79.

consumed an enormous amount of the professional minister's day. But this was not a problem. Far from it. The church of the period assumed that spending a significant amount of time on administrative chores was appropriate ministry for the professional. Additionally, owing to the characteristics of the churched culture of the day, overall church growth did not suffer appreciably. In fact, churches often swelled with consistently increasing numbers of people, in many cases due to another unique phenomenon of the churched-culture period.

The era of the churched culture was marked by the rise of the suburbs. Following World War II, people in mass moved from the rural countryside to the cities hoping to take advantage of opportunities unavailable to them on the family farm. Ultimately, as the American dream was redefined to include secure jobs in new fields, home ownership, and greater social mobility, tens of thousands of those participating in America's new migration moved again, creating suburban communities on the fringes of the adjacent cities. In time, the suburban church was born. These churches were populated mostly by decent, regular, church-going folk who, in numerous cases, transferred "letters" of church membership from existing churches into existing churches. Most of these people had some sort of church background and a variety of "church skills." Soon these suburban churches became centers of busy programs and activities. The congregations were comfortable with an "inside" the church minister. For the pastor of these churches, "The pace was hectic. . . . but life was essentially safe and secure."[74] This pattern was so thoroughly ingrained that only modest efforts of evangelism and outreach by ministers and key leaders were necessary to win enough people to Jesus to swell the church rolls and fill the sanctuaries.[75]

As might be expected within such circumstances, church planting and multiplication was not a highly placed value among

---

[74]Callahan, *Effective Church*, 11.
[75]9.

professional ministers. Reflecting back over the 1960s and 1970s Charles Chaney, writing in 1982, observed,

> For most of the century, and especially over the last two decades, Christian leaders have depreciated the need for new churches in America. In an age that has emphasized social action and ecumenical interests, the romance has been with church mergers, not church planting, and with the application of the gospel to the various issues and systems of society, not the gathering of churches in the various segments of society.[76]

This is not to imply that new churches were not planted during the period. They surely were. In most cases, however, the ". . . comfortable belief [persisted] that only Home Mission Boards [or other institutional agencies] can plant new churches."[77] Simply put, the planting of new congregations was not the ministry priority of the professional minister. He operated in an established church, maintaining and directing a plethora of programs and support systems designed to provide something by way of ministry for everyone.

"The leadership value set that emerged from [the] inside-the-church understanding of the nature of leadership can best be described as: reactive, passive, organizational, institutional."[78] With minor exceptions, professional ministers and the professional ministers' movement overlooked the fact that there is a significant difference between saying, "the world is my parish [and] . . . the church is my parish."[79]

By the mid to late 1970s, things had changed. All the defining characteristics of a churched culture were no longer true of the culture at large. A new era had arrived, and with it came the need for a new kind of minister. While the profession of

---

[76]Charles L. Chaney, *Church Planting at the End of the Twentieth Century* (Wheaton, IL: Tyndale House Publishers, Inc., 1982), 39.

[77]Donald McGavran, in Chaney, *Church Planting*, 9.

[78]Chaney, *Church Planting*, 12.

[79]10.

ministry—the ordained clergy—continued to exist, the day of the professional minister with its attendant leadership style was over. The day of the missionary pastor had come.

The missionary pastor as a practitioner is something of a contemporary reproduction of first-century missionary evangelists. As did his early church counterparts, he practices ministry as a participant in God's mission on earth, viewing his God-assigned place of service as a mission field, and those he encounters as objects of God's mission through him. "He is a realist who knows that [North America] is a mission field and who behaves as a missionary."[80] His leadership style is from the outside in. As compared to the professional minister, his understanding of church leadership is more intentional and less passive, more relational and less organizational, more missional and less institutional.[81] He participates humbly, yet redemptively, among the people outside, in the world. He is not one to stop at training the "laity," who in turn do the ministry; he actively joins the work. His "focus on leadership is in the world, not in the church."[82] The world—that portion of it assigned to him by God—is truly his parish.

The fact is, the professional minister's way of doing things is lost on a mission field. Perhaps the best evidence of this is found in the many plateaued or declining churches whose pastors still operate with a professional minister's mindset. This mindset functions as if a churched culture continues to exist.

> [Professional ministers] primarily [focus] on doing the same things that used to work in the old days. And when it has not worked, [they] have simply tried harder. [They] have assumed that if [they] throw enough hard work at the declining numbers the situation will somehow turn itself around.

---

[80]17.
[81]21.
[82]Callahan, *Effective Church*, 21.

> [They] have assumed that if [they] work longer hours, take more courses in time management, participate in enough continuing education seminars, and focus on more and more work, then somehow things will get better. But all of these valiant, last-ditch efforts will not work because they are based on an understanding of leadership that no longer works.

> [Their] . . . efforts have not worked because they will not work on a mission field.[83]

As previously noted, there is no question that God blessed the period of the professional ministers movement with significant church growth. "New churches were born (and existing churches grew) . . . because the Holy Spirit of God is still at work . . . in [the] world. Indeed, apart from the work of the Holy Spirit there would be no new churches,"[84] or church growth. But the fact that the church understood and responded favorably to the larger culture's movement toward professionalism—training and providing professional ministers—was also a key factor in the church's, and ministers' success. This understanding of doing ministry performed well for nearly forty years.

North America, however, is not the same place in the twenty-first century as it was in 1940 or 1970. The churched culture is no more; the day of mission has arrived, and the missionary pastor is required if not demanded. The call is for churches that are missionary in their intent and church leaders who serve as missionaries at heart.

---

[83]26–27.

[84]Melvin Hodges, *Build My Church* (Chicago: Moody Press, 1957), 97.

Proposition 2: The Day of the Churched Culture Is Over. The Day of the Mission Field Has Come.

To say that the predominant culture of North America is unchurched is not simply to imply that atheism, secularism, and materialism are more present now than in times past. To be sure, these were all present in the often idealized churched culture of the 1940s and 1950s, and beyond as well. It is not even to say that such things are more present in an unchurched culture. To repeat an important point, an unchurched culture is dominated by the fact that *"no major cultural value says that the church is important"*[85] (italics added). People within the culture do not necessarily view the church as harmful or hurtful; they simply do not consider it particularly relevant or helpful in the details of living life.[86] The church is not directly opposed by society; it is simply ignored. Few seek it out as a necessary component in the total framework of a meaningful life.

The ambivalence of the culture toward the church creates an environment for doing ministry that is nothing less than missionary. Global missionaries regularly face cultures where their message is unknown, the need for change is unrecognized, and people simply do not care to listen. Oddly, in a very real sense, it is probably easier today to do ministry in the crime-ridden, dangerously dark streets of the inner-city among the desperate down and out who are open to relief, than in the neatly scrubbed, well-paid, well-educated, "all the needs covered" lanes of modern suburbia. This is odd because it was in the suburbs that professional ministers previously excelled. Suburbia did not change; however, the nature of the culture has changed. The "churched" folk who created the suburbs passed with the times, leaving behind a new suburbanite, fully uncertain about the value of the gospel and its attendant church. The unchurched mission field was born.

---

[85]Callahan, *Effective Church*, 20.
[86]Ibid.

There are arguably two ways in which the new mission field stands in stark contrast with the environment of the earlier church culture. First, the environment of the churched culture was familiar to the ministers who worked within it. It was familiar in that the dominant values between the culture and church were rarely at odds. With few exceptions, the pastor preached to the choir every time the church gathered. He addressed a congregation that, for the most part, had sought out the church. While most evangelical churches did not talk in terms of parishes, it was generally assumed that each church had a territory all its own (though most opted for the more acceptable term, "church field"). Thus, in time, the minister could drive around the "boundaries" of that field and point out each home occupied by a church member. Sadly, he often assumed a comity perception of the area and overlooked the other homes—the other people—in the community.[87]

Second, the churched culture provided peace and security. As Callahan notes, "It is more peaceful and secure to stay in one's office than to venture out into the world. It is more secure in a committee meeting than it is in the world."[88] Because the professional minister functioned primarily inside the church, giving much of his time to administrative chores, he was able to enjoy far more of peace and security than is afforded to the missionary pastor. Clearly, working out in the world with persons who do not readily acquiesce to the gospel message, in the terrain of the unchurched culture, is far less peaceful and secure. But such is the nature of the mission field and the task of the missionary pastor. His leadership must be from outside the church even though life out in the world becomes more ambiguous and complex.[89]

---

[87]Callahan, *Effective Church*, 50.
[88]Callahan, *Effective Church*, 19.
[89]16, 20.

Proposition 3: The Day of the Local Church Is Over. The Day of the Mission Outpost Has Come.

Make no mistake; the local church has not and will not cease to exist. In fact, quite the opposite is true. The local church of the churched culture era is exceptionally resilient. It is quite possible that we "will discover a hundred years hence that there are many, many local churches continuing in existence."[90] "What I am suggesting is that the way in which local churches have done business, conducted leadership, and developed administration is no longer functional in our time. Churches that cling to the old ways that worked so well in the churched culture will survive for a number of years. Their people will grow old together, and many of those churches will eventually die."[91]

Those congregations that persist in functioning as "churched culture" churches despite the fact that the field is now a mission field are preoccupied with maintenance of the institution. The danger with this preoccupation is that "The more concerned we are for maintenance, the less vital in mission we become."[92] The tendency is to forget that, "Local congregations are intended to be mission outposts of the Kingdom, where the doors to the Kingdom are swung wide and where spiritual warfare is carried on."[93]

Instead of maintenance, the mission outpost focuses on the mission of God as He reveals it to the local Body. In the mission outpost, the preoccupation is with outreach and salvation. Believing correctly that it is on a mission field with a missionary assignment, the mission outpost focuses on sharing the good news of Jesus Christ and His Kingdom, and on making mature disciples of Jesus Christ. In essence, the central concern

---

[90]4–5.
[91]Callahan, *Effective Church*, 22.
[92]65.
[93]Hodges, *Build My Church*, 97.

for these Bodies is helping persons claim Jesus as Lord of their lives.[94] The mission outpost recognizes that the preoccupation with maintenance "is a deceptive merry-go-round. The less vital our mission, the more the institution declines. The more the institution declines, the higher the priority for maintenance rises. The more concerned we are with maintenance, the less vital in mission we become. It becomes a never ending cycle of self-suffocation and death."[95]

As opposed to the mission outpost, the "churched culture" local church also has a disturbing preoccupation with money. There is a marked disposition to manage money for the purpose of thrift almost to the point of hoarding. True enough, many of these churches support missions through either direct or cooperative giving. However, these gifts—though gratefully received by those in need of funding—frequently represent an attitude of "missions by proxy." This attitude is often indicative of the church's views relative to their perceived home field and missions in general. In other words, *this church maintains* the notion that a particular territory is the personal geography of a specific church, while mission is something that happens on a distant land, performed by missionary professionals. Still, one must not depreciate the value of such giving—let alone the obedient response to God's command evidenced in mission giving. At issue, however, is the tightly squeezed way in which the local church often guards its resources. The concern is often more with dollars lost to expenses than with ways to spend more effectively into the mission. In these churches, the concept of Christian stewardship is usually understood to mean carefully hoarding the church's financial assets. In this scenario, the church begins to resemble a sort of institutional, holy savings bank where contributions are placed on long-term deposit to insure a healthy bottom-line rather than serving as a conduit to enable ministry. There is little to no regard for the

---

[94]Callahan, *Effective Church*, 24.
[95]Callahan, *Effective Church*, 25.

fact that biblical stewardship is not about preserving God's resources, as if God needs asset managers to maintain His wealth or sustain His church. True stewardship, rather, is about the church's accountability to do what God says with His resources. Often the churched-culture local church will spiritualize their tight-fisted policy regarding money by arguing that they are guarding the ability to fund future ministries by averting possible financial shortfalls. Totally lost in this misunderstanding of stewardship is the fact that while occasionally there may be inadequate resources to do things that *the church wants* to do, the church will never lack the resources to do the things *God tells it to do*. God is under no obligation to fund a church's desire, but He is fully committed to provide for what He commands the church to do.

The mission outpost understands that on a mission field it will be required to live on the edge of its resources. "This is to say, on a mission outpost, there will always be a shortage of personnel, inadequate supplies, and hardly enough of anything. A mission outpost is always investing its leadership, resources, and money to the outermost limits. It is always stretching to the limit of its means."[96] It is most often in need of God-sized miracles. And God never disappoints!

The mission outpost recognizes and accepts that giving itself and its resources away is at the heart of the mission. Indeed, it knows that missions is not missions without this sort of self-sacrifice. The mission outpost knows that pouring its resources into the mission is a necessity, and ending the year at zero financially, is often a luxury. It's concern is to determine ". . . how to be effectively in mission with the vast number of unchurched persons in their community, with the focus on outreach and mission"[97]—whatever the cost may be.

---

[96]Callahan, *Effective Church*, 30.
[97]26.

Important Implications of a Missional Mindset

As part of its commitment to accomplishing its missionary task, the mission outpost will strive to produce several important characteristics. Callahan suggests that there are twelve such "key" characteristics, divided into two "priority" categories. He labels these categories "relational" and "functional." Both mission outposts and churched-culture local churches will attempt to demonstrate as many of the twelve characteristics as possible. The issue, however, is priority. The churched-culture local church will tend to focus on the functional characteristics, whereas the mission outpost will prioritize the relational.[98]

The chart on the next page lists the twelve characteristics within their respective categories.

In terms of priority, "A mission outpost delivers five out of six person-centered, people-centered relational characteristics. . . . A mission outpost may also deliver several (three or four) of the functional characteristics."[99] By contrast, churches functioning as churched-culture local churches tend toward a different focus. They do a reasonably good job of providing most of the six functional, institutional, and organizational characteristics. However, they usually provide only one or two or three of the characteristics from the relational category.[100]

It is difficult to overstate the importance of prioritizing the "relational characteristics" as tools for effective ministry in the current mission environment. This point is emphasized by the results of an extensive research project undertaken in the mid-1990s by Thom Rainer, CEO of LifeWay Christian Resources, Inc., and a team of researchers. The project sought to demonstrate the primary characteristics of the most effective evangelistic churches within the Southern Baptist Convention.

---

[98]Callahan, *Effective Church*, 34.
[99]29.
[100]Callahan, *Effective Church*, 40.

Each of the churches included in the survey was experiencing significant conversion growth.

Relational	Functional
Specific, concrete, missional objectives	Several competent programs and activities
Personal and lay visitation in the community	Open accessibility
Corporate, dynamic worship	High visibility
Groupings of significant relationships of sharing roots, place, and belonging	Adequate parking
Strong leadership resources	Adequate space and facilities
A solid participatory decision-making process in a streamlined organizational structure	Solid financial resources

In a chapter entitled, "Ten Surprises," Rainer explains some of the more unanticipated findings relative to church growth and evangelism. He writes, ". . . surprise is a relative term. . . . When I speak of surprise in this study, I refer to results that are contrary to the conventional wisdom in most recent church growth literature."[101] Summarizing these "surprises," Rainer adds,

---

[101]Thom S. Rainer, *Effective Evangelistic Churches: Successful Churches Reveal What Works and What Doesn't* (Nashville" Broadman & Holeman, 1996), 1.

> Perhaps more than any single theme, we discovered that the churches successfully reaching the lost focus on the *basics:* biblical preaching, prayer, intentional witnessing, missions, and comprehensive biblical training in small groups. . . . That theme recurs throughout [the study]. If methodology or approach to evangelism appears to stray from these *basics,* the churches reject it. If a methodology or approach to evangelism enhanced the *basics,* the church embraced it (italics added).[102]

It is interesting to note the correlation between Rainer's summary of findings among the surveyed churches—what he calls the "basics"—and Callahan's "relational characteristics" of a mission outpost. What Rainer and his associates discovered as effective church growth and ministry techniques were advocated by Callahan as needed to reach North America almost twenty years earlier. Note the following correlations:

Rainer	Callahan
Basics	*Relational characteristics*
Biblical preaching	Corporate, dynamic worship
Intentional witnessing	Pastoral and lay visitation in the community
Missions	Specific, concrete missional objectives
Biblical training in small groups	Groups of significant relationships of sharing roots, place, and belonging

---

[102]48.

It appears that the experience of what Rainer's team called America's most evangelistic churches affirm the propositions Callahan set forth years earlier. In other words, the churches in Rainer's study experiencing the most significant conversion growth (the only genuine form of church growth) gave ministry priority to the mission outpost relational characteristics—the most missionary in Callahan's list of twelve. Functioning as a mission outpost (at least to the degree noted) was a major contributor to their evangelistic effectiveness.

Such churches prove that the most effective way to reach the unreached of North America is with a missionary commitment and methodology guided by a missional mindset. These congregations have further discovered that "local ministry and global missions do not compete with one another;"[103] simply because the two things are in both nature and practice, one and the same. These churches have learned that "God blesses an Acts 1:8 vision. God returns in many ways any 'losses' of funds or people."[104] Label such churches what you will; the truth is they are relational, unchurched culture, mission outposts. Their testimonies provide compelling evidence that the only mindset equal to the church's task on the single global mission field of the twenty-first century is one that is fully missional.

However, because a group mindset is a composite of the individual mindsets within the group, it is essential that all members share the same mind with regard to the mission. Considering this, two questions arise. First, what are the characteristics of a missional mindset as seen in the lives of a believer? Second, how is this mindset achieved? These are the subjects of the next chapter.

---

[103]Rainer, *Evangelistic Churches*, 155.
[104]Ibid.

Chapter 7

"Let This Mind Be in You"

A friend of mine, describing the administrative pattern of a particular institution, commented that instead of following the logic of "ready, aim, fire" the organization was very likely to operate in the reverse order—"fire, aim, ready!" Before you laugh, consider how often the church is guilty of that very thing. How many church leaders, in a well-intended effort to create a more missional mentality within the Body, begin to toss an assortment of "mission opportunities" at the congregation, while simultaneously exhorting the faithful to think and act missionally? Now, contemplate how often those well-intended efforts are met with either indifference or short-lived enthusiasm from the congregation and, not surprisingly, discouragement by the leaders. It's an all-too-common scenario that begs the question, why?

Obviously, numerous reasons can be suggested as to why a particular congregation does not embrace the "missional" challenge with long-term enthusiasm and support. However, the answer may be as simple as overlooking one basic necessity—preparation. It is said that Abraham Lincoln was once asked what he would do if he had just three days to cut an acre of timber and only one ax with which to cut it. According to the story, Lincoln responded, "I would spend the first two days sharpening my ax." If Lincoln actually said those words, he demonstrated a great deal of wisdom. With any significant endeavor, preparation is essential. In the same way, while it is true that missional ministry is indispensable for the church, it is equally true that missional ministry—at least long-term missional ministry—is motivated and sustained by a missional mindset. And that mindset must be developed over time. Until it is, trying to motivate an unprepared people for ministry that is truly missional in nature will be a process of "fire, aim, ready."

Developing a Missional Mindset

A mindset is something of an anomaly. For one thing, no one can point to a particular item and say, "that is a mindset." Yet, the fact that we all display attitudes, convictions, and behaviors makes it obvious that we possess an internal system that drives our choices and the resultant perspective on life. One of the better definitions I have found explains a mindset as being "a set of assumptions, methods or notations held by one or more people or groups of people which is so established that it creates a powerful incentive within these people or groups to continue to adopt or accept prior behaviors, choices, or tools."[105] According to Stanford University psychologist Carol Dweck, "Whether they're aware of it or not, all people keep a running account of what's happening to them, what it means, and what they should do. In other words, our minds are constantly monitoring and interpreting. That's just how we stay on track."[106] Because "staying on track" is essential to most healthy human beings, these mentally compiled "assumption sets" are constantly employed to make sense of ideas and information, thus guiding the daunting process of interpreting the constant deluge of messages competing for lifestyle application.

When understood correctly, it is easy to see just how vital these "assumption sets" (mindsets) are to us all. They are important first because of the numerous sources, which

---

[105]Wikipedia, "Mindset," http://en.wikipedia.org/wiki/Mindset (accessed April 23, 2010).

[106]Carol Dweck, "Mindset," http://mindsetonline.com /changeyourmindset/natureofchange/index.html (accessed April 23, 2010).

undergird them. Recall sociologist Dweck's statement, "people keep a running account of what's happening to them, what it means, and what they should do." In other words, one's mindset is a compiled gathering of experiences and instructions shedding light on what are the appropriate responses to competing ideas. Each of these things—experiences and instructions—have their source in something or someone. Usually, the source is of some significance to the individual—for example, something or someone loved or considered trustworthy. The source can be a parent or grandparent, beloved pastor or teacher, or an institution. When instructions from these sources become components of an individual's set of assumptions, they not only become part of that person's thinking, they also are attached to his or her emotions, as well. When faced with new information and the prospect of a change in thinking, the conflict is often not so much with accepting new ideas but in the struggle to abandon instructions received from others with whom there is an emotional attachment. Often, even when the mind is willing to yield a particular point, the emotions find it untenable to allow permanent change. Said another way, to change one's thinking by releasing parts of a mindset is, for some, the act of admitting that Granny was wrong!

Because groups of people are capable of developing and maintaining a single, uniform mindset, knowing the role of sources helps in understanding why many congregations refuse change when faced with new information, even when new facts are more correct or advantageous than old ones. It is not necessarily so that the people are stubborn and/or hard-hearted. They may even acknowledge and "amen" new information, in the short term. However, they find it unthinkable to violate prior information received from trusted sources—information now emotionally attached to themselves—by making long-term commitments to new information that differs even slightly from these beloved sources.

Second, mindsets are important because they form the basis upon which decisions are made. Be careful not to confuse a mindset with mentality. Mentality guides behavior; a mindset guides mentality. Remember, a mindset comprises the framework—assumption set—upon which decisions are made. If real, productive change in behavior is to be achieved, it is the thinking produced by the mindset that must be addressed. Otherwise, only short-term alleviation of symptoms will result while the cause remains in place, virtually assuring a new outbreak of symptoms in the future.

Taken together, the forgoing information seems less than encouraging as far as change is concerned. Short of manipulative brainwashing, how is it possible to change the all-important mindset in either an individual or a group of individuals? The short answer is, it is not possible. Yet, productive, necessary, long-term behavioral change requires a changed set of mental assumptions. This is quite the conundrum, wouldn't you agree?

Now seems a good time to remind ourselves of two powerful affirmations from Scripture. The first comes from the mouth of Jesus Himself. Speaking to the disciples after His encounter with the rich young ruler, Jesus said, "The things that are impossible with people are possible with God" (Luke 18:27). My single phrase commentary on Christ's words go like this: it is always true that when we stand with God the impossible becomes possible.

The second affirmation of note occurred when the angel Gabriel announced to Mary, God's promise to birth the Messiah through her. Gabriel was explicit with Mary about God's power to do the impossible by declaring that not only are all things possible with God, but *"nothing will be impossible* with God" (Luke 1:37, italics added). That which Gabriel affirmed specifically was the power of God's stated promises—His Word. Literally, Gabriel's statement can be translated, *every word of God shall not be powerless.* God has never uttered one impotent word. Every word He speaks is fortified by His full authority and limitless power; therefore, for God, nothing is impossible.

Keeping all of this in mind, let's breakdown what has been said to this point. The church is most like Christ when it behaves missionally. Missional behavior is motivated and produced by a missional mindset. A missional mindset requires a new set of mental assumptions to guide thinking, and these must be developed correctly. Apart from the threat of manipulation, it is impossible for one human to fully alter the mindset of another human being. Again, these are not very encouraging statements for the pastor who wants to initiate changed thinking among his people. That is, not until Jesus' affirmation is recalled. Namely, "The things that are impossible with people are possible with God."

Here is the point: God can and does change mindsets and mentalities. And when He does, the outcome is long term and positive because God's process is accomplished correctly. After all, the Bible declares, "Whoever is wise, let him understand these things; Whoever is discerning, let him know them. *For the ways of the* LORD *are right,* And the righteous will walk in them, But transgressors will stumble in them" (Hosea 14:9, italics added). Hosea's phrase, "the ways of the LORD," refers not only to the "ways" God *prescribes* but also the "ways" in which He *guides* what He prescribes. God's "ways" lead some to life and others to death, according to the different attitudes that men and women assume toward God and His processes. Consequently, pastors who wish to see the church's mindset truly changed must adopt an attitude of complete reliance on and submission to the ways of God. It is important that in this submissive reliance a couple of things be kept in mind.

First: When Dealing with Believers You Are Dealing with Re-created People

So what can be known of God's "ways" with regard to the changing of mindsets? Without pretending to have special insight into God's ways—which are, after all, beyond knowing— allow me to suggest that God deals with mindsets in need of change in the very same way He handles all else pertaining to His children—He re-creates (Ephesians 2:10, 15, 4:24, Colossians 3:10). God doesn't busy Himself with housekeeping; He builds completely new structures. It is reasonable then to assume that the same holds true of God's work when He acts to change the mindset of a person or group of people. He will dispose of the old and create something brand new. According to 2 Corinthians 5:17—"Therefore if anyone is in Christ, he is a new creature; the old things passed away; behold, new things have come"—the most important change occurs when an individual comes to faith in Jesus Christ. It is at this point that he or she is transformed—supernaturally re-created—into a new creation. All is made new, including the mind.

Still, Scripture indicates that while Christians have a re-created mind, further development of that mind must take place. Note, for example, that in 1 Corinthians 2:16 the apostle Paul wrote, "For who hath known the mind of the LORD, that he may instruct him? *But we have the mind of Christ*" (italics added). On the other hand, to the Philippian Church he admonished, "*Let this mind be in you*, which was also in Christ Jesus" (Philippians 2:5, KJV, italics added). To one church, the apostle affirms that believers possess the mind of Christ; to another he calls upon believers to allow this mind to operate within them, a mind that fully reflects the mind of Christ. Taken together, these verses make clear that all believers are recipients of newly created minds; however, the godly operation of these minds must be developed. It is for this reason that Paul instructed the churches at Rome and Ephesus (and by extension all other churches) to give attention to renewing the mind. Consider these verses. "And do not be conformed to this world, but be *transformed by the renewing of your mind*, so that you may prove what the will of God is, that which is good and acceptable and perfect" (Romans 12:2 italics added). "And that you *be renewed in the spirit of your mind*" (Ephesians 4:23 italics added).

All of this is because a changed mindset requires not just a change *of* mind but a change *within* the mind, in the most radical sense possible. The assumptions of the old mind must be replaced by new ones compatible with the new mind of Christ. This replacement is a growth process, and growth takes time and nurturing. Remember, while grace is instant, gracefulness takes a while. Becoming graceful is the essence of what is meant by growing in grace (2 Peter 3:18). If there were no other reason to submit and rely upon the ways of God for producing change, this would be enough. What is of central importance is to know that when dealing with believers you are dealing with people who have already experienced God's grace in re-creation. These folk may be at different levels of gracefulness, but they are new creations, nonetheless. God has begun the process; He must be at the center of completing it.

Second: Development of a Missional Mindset Requires More Than Focusing on Behavior

In 1988, Kent and Barbara Hughes provided a wonderful service to the Kingdom of God with the publication of their powerfully insightful book, *Liberating Ministry from the Success Syndrome*. Every minister seeking to be "free . . . from the false demands of 'success' and [to] restore the proper measurements of achievements"[107] in his ministry should have a well-read copy of this volume in his library. In the introduction, the authors rightly contend that a "pervasive, sub-biblical emphasis on 'success' . . . has fallen on the church."[108] I couldn't agree more. Further, the success being emphasized is an outcome guided by a definition contrived by the world. Lost in the world's definition is the biblical fact that the true components of true success include such things as faithfulness, serving, loving, believing, prayer,

---

[107]Kent and Barbara Hughes, *Liberating Ministry from the Success Syndrome* (Carol Stream, IL: Tyndale House Publishers, 1988), quote taken from back cover by Ray Steadman.
[108]10.

holiness, and attitude.[109] As ministry is more and more affected by a "sub-biblical emphasis on success" as defined by the world, ministers increasingly find themselves all but held hostage by a "success syndrome" that demands measurable, hard-figure production within the context of definitions created outside the church, but adopted within it.

The problems created by this syndrome are both numerous and critical. When the church seeks to initiate change or bring resolution to problems, the very nature of the syndrome tends to divert the church's attention away from biblical answers and onto remedies that are more compatible with the world's definition of success. In this arrangement, such things as more money, greater numbers, better programs, and larger buildings have become the tangible markers of success. In fact, the demand for tangibility is the core requirement of the world's definition of success. For instance, the world asks if we can we look around us—whether on paper or on the ground—and see "more" and "bigger" than what was previously there? If so, we have succeeded; if not, we have failed. Tragically, in this scheme, the essence of spiritual life, ministry, and church growth becomes little more than the pursuit of world-defined, tangible evidence.

What the church loses in such unbiblical pursuits is nothing less than the heart and purpose of God for the proper spiritual development of His children. This is not to say that God has no desire for visible behavioral change. It was, after all, God who spoke through John the Baptist declaring, "Therefore *bear fruit in keeping* with repentance" (Matthew 3:8, italics added). Paul, in sharing his testimony with King Agrippa, related that he "kept declaring both to those of Damascus first, and also at Jerusalem and then throughout all the region of Judea, and even to the Gentiles, that they should repent and turn to God, *performing deeds appropriate to repentance*" (Acts 26:20, italics added). Then, of course, there is the Bible's most inclusive statement regarding God's intent for the believer's public lifestyle: "For we are His

---

[109]Ibid.

workmanship, *created in Christ Jesus for good works,* which God prepared beforehand *so that we would walk in them"* (Ephesians 2:10, italics added). There can be no doubt; God demands the visible (tangible) evidence of a changed life. In God's economy, however, the process—*how* behavior is changed—is as important as the evidentiary outcome.

This is precisely one of those points where the world's definitions and God's processes are most visibly at cross-purposes. The world focuses on designing and acquiring the end result; God is focused on the process of change, for He has already determined the end result. God knows that external actions are fed and motivated by the internal realities. Therefore, the Lord always pursues the heart of man. Jesus said, "The good man out of the good treasure of his heart brings forth what is good; and the evil man out of the evil treasure brings forth what is evil; for his mouth speaks from that which fills his heart" (Luke 6:45). For this reason, "God sees not as man sees, for man looks at the outward appearance, but the LORD looks at the heart" (1 Samuel 16:7). With God, it is always about the heart, the internal. A change of heart will produce a change of mind and, ultimately, a change in behavior that is genuine and long term.

Joining God in the Process of Change

So, how does the church cooperate with God's processes of change and development? The Bible, of course, is replete with instruction on this question. I will suggest only two things from this volume of information. One is a drawn from a biblical example of conflict resolution; the other is a supporting principle drawn from Scripture.

A Biblical Example

It is a fact of life that conflict happens, even in the best of families. This was evidently the case in the church at Philippi. Among all the churches either planted or in some way influenced directly by Paul, none seemed as nearly perfect as the Philippian Church. A close reading of the apostle's letter to this congregation reveals nothing of the difficulties he encountered with, for example, the churches at Corinth, Colossae, or Thessalonica. The closest Paul comes to a statement of warning or correction is found in chapter 3 verse 15: "Let us therefore, as many as are perfect, have this attitude; and if in anything you have a different attitude, God will reveal that also to you." Even here, Paul seems convinced that this good church would do the right thing if led by God to make any needed corrections.

Still, while the Philippian Church was a very good church, it was not a perfect church. In the closing chapter of his letter, the apostle alludes to a conflict within the Body between two devout women. Paul wrote, "I urge Euodia and I urge Syntyche to live in harmony in the Lord. Indeed, true companion, I ask you also to help these women who have shared my struggle in the cause of the gospel, together with Clement also and the rest of my fellow workers, whose names are in the book of life" (Philippians 4:2–3). One cannot miss the fact that Paul holds these two women in high regard. He recounts their service to him in ministry ("who have shared my struggle in the cause of the gospel") and affirms that he regards them as true believers ("whose names are in the book of life"). Yet, there is conflict between the women that needs to be resolved, and reconciliation that must take place.

There is no biblical evidence as to just what the conflict was. It was probably not of a moral or doctrinal nature or Paul would have no doubt addressed it specifically. Quite possibly the issue was some minor thing that had grown into open conflict. However, because conflict that is minor in its essence can become great in its potential for damage within the church, Paul wanted the matter rectified. His instruction to the church for securing this outcome is remarkable for its pointed simplicity. He wrote, "I urge Euodia and I urge Syntyche to live in harmony in the Lord. Indeed, true companion, I ask you also to help these women, . . ." (4:2–3a). There is a single imperative in the apostle's words: achieve resolution by focusing first on the women, not the conflict. This is vastly different from the definition of and steps toward success posited by the world. The world's scheme runs something like this: focus on the offense; find and assign blame; call out and charge the offender(s); excise the offense (and the offender(s) if deemed necessary); and set penalties for any reoccurrence of the problem. In this formula, the goal (success) is the arbitrary removal of the offense. The lives of the individuals at the center of the conflict are important only to the degree that they aid or hinder reaching the goal, or achieving success.

This was certainly not Paul's approach. Note his complete focus on the reconciliation of the women. It is as if, without saying so explicitly, Paul is asserting that the present conflict will disappear if and when reconciliation between these two sisters in the Lord is achieved. In other words, focus on the internal change that needs to take place within the individuals and the external behavior (conflict) will take care of itself. (By the way, for those who may be thinking, *What about such passages as Matthew 18:15–17?* I urge you to reread Jesus' words. Note that Christ's concluding admonition—"let him (the offending brother) be to you as a Gentile and a tax collector" (basically, to put him out of the fellowship)—is proceeded by two verses of instruction to focus first on recovering the individual.)

Make note of the steps Paul prescribes. First, reconcile without bias. Pay attention to the repetition of "urge" preceding each name—"I urge Euodia and I urge Syntyche." Paul makes the exhortation individual, specific, and equal. He is not seeking to take sides, ferret out a specific offender, or assign individual blame. He calls upon each lady to assume equal responsibility for both the conflict and need for reconciliation. Taking responsibility requires internal spiritual work, which is Paul's focus in the process.

Second, reconcile with intelligence. Doesn't it almost sound a bit naive for one so wise as Paul to request simply, "Live in harmony in the Lord"? Of course, Paul was anything but naive. This becomes obvious when the basis of his simple request is properly understood. Harmony in the Lord requires Christians to make the Lord alone the great object of their affections, and, in their regard for Him, bury all their petty differences and animosities. Now, consider what Paul called upon these believing women to do. Among other things that might be suggested, the apostle urged the ladies to love Jesus more than themselves, their opinions, their positions, their rights, or their pride. In short, they are to assume the truth that the church is larger than its individual parts, including themselves. You see, when all the components of church are added up all that is available is a subtotal. That is until the most important part is added to the equation. That part is the Head—the Lord Jesus Christ. He is the main part; all else is rather petty. Those things that comprise "all else" are certainly unworthy of the church's affection and devotion, not to mention allegiance. These go to Christ alone.

Devotion that results in making the Lord alone the great object of our affections to the exclusion of all our petty differences and animosities hinges on the internal operation of the mind of Christ. His mind alone produces the desire and capacity to obey the Bible's earlier instruction: "maintaining the same love, united in spirit, intent on one purpose. Do nothing from selfishness or empty conceit, but with humility of mind regard one another as more important than yourselves; do not merely look out for your own personal interests, but also for the interests of others" (Philippians 2:2b-4). Intelligent reconciliation seeks to remedy conflict by appealing to the motivating force governing behavior. It calls upon God's children to allow the mind of Christ to operate fully, deepening one's love for Jesus and informing a life that makes all else subservient to the character and will of God.

Third, reconcile with engagement. This is a word to the church: "Help these women." Said another way, "Church, take hold of the need for reconciliation alongside these sisters." To the Body, Paul seems to say, "Their struggle is likewise your struggle. What they must do requires your aid and participation; join them in their recovery."

Admittedly, it is much easier to make arbitrary demands and simply bury the wounded alongside the already dead. While this may be the way of the world, it is never to be the course of the church. The church as a Body cannot escape its interconnectedness. It is always best for the Body to work to heal its sick or broken parts rather than to attempt amputation. In fact, healing and restoration are the limits of the Body as it attends to itself. Removing and pruning are the exclusive purview of the Father (John 15:1). The duty of the church in matters of reconciliation and conflict resolution are to reflect the Holy Spirit's work in the lives of believers. In other words, just as the Holy Spirit is the *paraklētos*—intercessor, consoler, advocate, comforter, and one who is summoned to another's side, especially called to one's aid—who comes to believers in need, the church too is summoned to come alongside struggling brothers and sisters and render help. Believers are never to act in an effort to supplant or usurp the ministry of the Holy Spirit. We function only as instruments of support for what God, through His Spirit, is working to accomplish. Nevertheless, the church has a helping role to play in the resolution of conflict and restoration of believers. It is time consuming, involved, and sometimes messy. Yet, as the Holy Spirit never shirks His responsibility to believers, we should not seek to avoid our duty to our brothers and sisters in Christ. Most importantly, we must always render aid that is biblically focused on the correct goal— internal change in people—even if it does not appear to be the most expedient goal.

The lesson from this example is clear. The biblical way to achieve change in lives (whether conflict or some other need) is to focus on work that moves from the inside out, not the other way around. No one will *act* like a disciple of Christ until he or she begins to *think* like a disciple of Christ, and this requires a change of assumption sets within the inner person.

The Larger Principle

The principle has already been stated in the paragraph above. It is, "no one will act like a disciple of Christ until he or she begins to think like a disciple of Christ." I could state it this way. Thinking determines action and action constitutes behavior. If one is to behave like a disciple, he or she must actively think like one. Because thinking is influenced and controlled by assumptions held mentally—often emotionally—to change thinking and thus behavior, the assumptions guiding one's thoughts must be compatible with the desired behavior. Now, aren't you glad I opted for the simpler statement?—no one will act like a disciple of Christ until he or she begins to think like a disciple of Christ.

Missional thinking and action (the goal) is often contrary to the current mindset of many churches (the conflict). This must be changed if the church is to be most like Christ in its ministry. The biblical way to produce change is to focus on people from the inside out. So, what must be the focus of the pastor's work in order for change to happen? The answer to this question is found in a single phrase within the principle stated above, namely, *disciple of Christ*. Simply put, to change a mindset requires primary focus on making true disciples of Jesus Christ. This is so because at the heart of true discipleship is the recognition that believers are called to be on mission with God in the earth (John 20:21). This recognition assumes the fact that God has established a mission on the planet, one that requires active missional participation by the church. Through new birth, believers possess a mind capable of this conviction. And God, by His Spirit, is committed to build within that mind missional assumptions, which will motivate and drive a missional lifestyle. Said another way, as with the case of Philippians 4:2–3, when the primary focus is on developing people as mature disciples of Jesus Christ, the desired change of mindsets will take care of itself.

Developing Disciples for a Missional Mindset

At the threat of boring you with things previously stated in this book, allow me, as an introduction to this section, to reinforce the importance of true discipleship. First, as time moves forward, there is going to be ever-increasing opposition to the gospel message (2 Timothy 3:1–5; 4:3–5). In consequence, the gospel message will become more and more "historically biblical." This is to say, the response to the gospel and those who faithfully share it will be more and more reflective of the historical record found in Scripture. The gospel will be viewed as radical and revolutionary. It will be seen and treated as a very real threat to the world system and the gods of contemporary culture. And where and when true disciples of Christ take stands in unwavering fidelity to the gospel message, the results will be the same as in the book of Acts. There will be uproar, opposition, persecution, and the mighty movements of God—both in blessings and in judgment.

Second, at the same time that antagonism to the gospel is growing, the church is faced with an increasing number of members whose commitment to Christ will not stand when shaken, and it doesn't take much to shake it before these folk abandon Christ for a growing list of lesser loyalties. Sadly, these lesser loyalties are the very things that many believers today, in their zeal to be safe and culturally nonoffensive, are claiming as genuine values of true discipleship. Whether called cultural contextualization, political correctness, or being open and affirming, in their efforts to be trendier than thou, many believers are buying into little more than shabbily Christianized versions of cultural compromises. In such cases, believer loyalty is attached not to the biblical Jesus who is the Lord and sovereign of a separated, sacrificial, disciplined life, but to a self-created Jesus who is simply the grand source of numerous options to meet the social demand for religious inclusivism. The result is that when the options fail—as surely they will—so does their groundless allegiance to Christ and discipleship.

The church must come to terms with the fact that loyalty to the one true God and identity with His Son, Jesus Christ, leave all other allegiances in the dust. This is only possible when we concentrate everything we believe and practice on the biblical definition of true discipleship, and what it means to be a true disciple of Jesus Christ.

It is necessary then that we ask ourselves two questions: Am I a true disciple of Jesus Christ? If I answer yes, how do I justify my answer? Consider this; true discipleship is normally gauged in two primary ways: position and practice. In terms of *position*, individuals become disciples the moment they come to faith in Jesus as Lord and Savior. Believe me; a person can no more avoid becoming a disciple of Jesus at salvation than he or she can remain alive without breathing. Remember, Jesus said you *are* salt; you *are* light. He didn't say you would become; He said you are. All who are born-again believers are right now positioned as disciples of Jesus Christ.

Beyond position, however, another common gauge of true discipleship is the personal *practice* of certain commonly assumed "disciple-like" practices. These include such things as prayer, Bible reading, sharing of one's faith, and so on. (In some cases—as when comparing the depth of one's level of discipleship to another believer—the amount of time spent in the practice of these disciple disciplines becomes something of a tiebreaker.) Think back for a moment. How did you answer the two questions regarding your discipleship? Did either or both answers include things you do that might evidence your relationship to Jesus? Most likely the answer is yes, because we tend to think in terms of activity when offering proof of our discipleship.

Now comes a more important question. Are position and practice all that define and authenticate true discipleship?

Fortunately, for us, Jesus speaks a clear word on the matter. Look closely at the Bible's record of Jesus' words in Luke 9:23. "And He was saying to them all, 'If anyone wishes to come after Me, he must deny himself, and take up his cross daily and follow Me'" In a handful of carefully chosen words, the Lord provides us with a concise and final answer to the question. True discipleship is comprised of more than merely claiming position and working to practice. According to the Savior, three additional things demand a disciple's attention: self-denial, cross bearing, and following. All of which Jesus insists His disciples must do, daily. These three things do not minimize or overshadow position and practice. Quite the contrary, they are the evidentiary proofs that undergird and verify both our position in Christ and our practice within a kingdom of disciples. Take a look at each of the three commands in the order Jesus listed them.

Three Commands

Once more, view the verse in its entirety. "And He was saying to them all, 'If anyone wishes to come after Me, he must deny himself, and take up his cross daily and follow Me.'" Seeing the whole text is important because, while the verse contains three specific commands, the commands are preceded by contextual information that is valuable in its own right. First, the Bible is clear that what Jesus is about to say is intended for general consumption ("He was saying to them all"). Jesus is not speaking to just one disciple in His audience; His words are directed to every disciple in the group, just as they are to all disciples today.

Second, following Christ as a disciple is an act of the heart ("If anyone wishes to come after Me"). Following Jesus in true discipleship often seems a paradox in that it is at the same time a wonderful and difficult endeavor. In so many ways, being a disciple of Christ resembles the original Peace Corps slogan: "The toughest job you will ever love." There are more sound, intellectual reasons to follow Christ than can be counted. However, faithfulness amid difficulties requires passion that reason alone cannot provide. It is said that the heart has a language that the mind cannot comprehend. This seems true in that the mind convinces by way of reason, while the heart wishes by way of passion. To follow Christ faithfully, the disciple's heart must be even more convinced than his or her mind. The mind will respond to the difficulties; the heart will resonate with the Savior.

Finally, what Jesus is about to say is by way of command ("he must"). The three statements that follow are not suggestions; they are commands. Further, each one appears to be listed in the order of its relative priority and difficulty. Together, they resemble three important materials that must be assembled in a particular order, assuring that the finished structure will be capable of withstanding every destructive force hurled against it. In other words, Jesus calls upon His followers to begin with the "easiest," and most fundamental command then proceed to the next two in the order He prescribes. Keep in mind, everything Jesus builds or brings to maturity is constructed for the long term. Said another way, Jesus builds for eternity. This is certainly true where His disciples and their discipleship are concerned. Disciples built up according to the order set forth by Jesus in Luke 9:23 will become solid structures equipped for present strength and eternal value.

Pastors and church leaders committed to initiating change by building mature disciples of Christ must share His same eternal perspective. Otherwise, their discipleship efforts will be much like trying to reach the rich young ruler by throwing money at him. Put simply, strategies other than the steps set forth by Jesus will always prove ill-suited to the task. They will never produce more than short-lived alterations in thinking and behavior. Keep in mind, true discipleship produces changed lives consistent with the gospel. "The gospel doesn't say, 'You've got most things right, you just need to throw some Jesus in there.' Rather, it says, 'You've got everything wrong, because you're not correctly related to God. Therefore, you've got to be willing to give up everything—mother, father, sister, brother, daughter, whatever—to follow Christ. And if not, you're not worthy of Him.'"[110] As counter-cultural as these words sound, they are nonetheless true. Therefore, the church is left with a single option; make true disciples—in two parts: (1) build disciples *with* Jesus, and (2) build disciples *according to* Jesus. With this in mind, let's take a brief look at the three disciple-building commands.

"He Must Deny Himself"

Several years ago, while serving as pastor of a church in southwest Texas, my day was suddenly interrupted by a highly agitated woman. She was the mother of a gifted son who was soon to graduate with distinction from a prestigious medical school. He had trained for a career in orthopedic surgery. Because of his skills and academic prowess, he was being showered with numerous offers for lucrative future placement. All of this, of course, seemed like a marvelous answer to prayer following years of hard work by the son and financial sacrifice by his parents. But remember, the woman was upset—actually, she was beside herself in anger!

Not knowing what else to do, I asked why, with so much good news, she was so upset. She arose from her chair and stepped directly in front of where I sat. Looking down at me she exclaimed, "He's going to throw it all away. And it's your fault!"

I couldn't imagine. What had I done?

"It's your preaching on missions the last few Sundays!" she exclaimed. "He just announced to his father and me that he is going to become a medical missionary." She spit out those words as if her son had just announced his intention to follow serial killing as a career path.

---

[110]Mark Moring, "Pop Goes the Worship," interview of T. David Gordon, *Christianity Today*, March 2011, 25.

Then, for over a half hour, I listened to a recital of why his decision for missions was a complete waste of his training, life, and future, followed by a demand that I try to talk her son out of his decision. In all candor, I was momentarily tempted to comply with her demand, if for no other reason than to calm her down. However, one statement changed my mind completely.

While recounting the emotional moments just after learning of her son's intentions, the woman explained how she and her husband had tried to convince the boy that he could build a secure medical practice at home and serve periodically on mission trips. She said they told him how, with the money he would make as a surgeon in the United States, he could build and support clinics in needy places around the world. Then, she let it slip; she noted what the young man had said in response to his parents. He said, "That's all true. But God doesn't want my money; He wants my life." With those words ringing in my head, I couldn't help but think—"he gets it!"

Later conversations with this young man revealed that his decision had not come easily. Like any other human being, he had been tempted by the money, the prestige, and the promise of a life filled with stuff. He explained how his personal will had battled long and hard with what he knew to be the will of God. In the end, he had determined that God's will must reign supreme in his life. Again, he got it!

You see, denying self, as commanded by Jesus, has little to do with a decision to do without. True enough, doing God's will may mean giving up certain things. For some, it may very well entail selling property, moving to a distant location, learning another language, living on the edge of resources, or living without certain creature comforts. However, it is just as likely that none of these things will be required. Believers should never assume that God's will is best determined by judging the degree to which the doing of it is painful or requires living in near destitution. It is a sad testament to the overriding self-centered, materialistic view held by many in the church when biblical self-denial is understood as being about lifestyle condition and relative comfort, especially when applied to what it means to be a true disciple of Christ.

Self-denial has to do with the will. Clearly stated, to deny oneself is the act of making and following this commitment—when my will runs contrary to God's will, I will choose God's will over my will, all the time. This statement comprises a commitment so large and all-encompassing that it effectively answers a world of smaller questions even before they are asked. Likewise, it makes numerous commitments before they are required. For instance, when a young man or woman is inducted into a branch of the US military, he or she declares an oath of allegiance to the United States. It is the one and only such oath—commitment—he or she will make. And, it is enough. From the moment of induction forward, there is no question as to whether or not the individual will go where told or do what is commanded, even to the point of facing death. That person has sworn full allegiance to the country and its defense; all other questions and commitments have been settled in one single pledge. In the same way, to accept Christ as Savior and Lord is to make a commitment that forever settles a world of subsequent issues, including the conflict of wills.

Without question, subordinating one's personal will consistently to the will of God is not without difficulty. Even the great apostle Paul confessed,

> For we know that the Law is spiritual, but I am of flesh, sold into bondage to sin. For what I am doing, I do not understand; for I am not practicing what I would like to do, but I am doing the very thing I hate. But if I do the very thing I do not want to do, I agree with the Law, confessing that the Law is good. So now, no longer am I the one doing it, but sin which dwells in me. For I know that nothing good dwells in me, that is, in my flesh; for the willing is present in me, but the doing of the good is not. For the good that I want, I do not do, but I practice the very evil that I do not want. But if I am

doing the very thing I do not want, I am no longer the one doing it, but sin which dwells in me. I find then the principle that evil is present in me, the one who wants to do good. For I joyfully concur with the law of God in the inner man, but I see a different law in the members of my body, waging war against the law of my mind and making me a prisoner of the law of sin which is in my members (Romans 7:14–23).

Every disciple can identify with Paul's struggle. Regrettably, for many believers, this is where identity with Paul stops. For these folk, struggle and failure are interpreted to mean impossibility. And this would be a logical conclusion if the apostle's next statements are ignored. So keep reading. "Wretched man that I am! Who will set me free from the body of this death? Thanks be to God through Jesus Christ our Lord!" (7:24–25a). In the middle of stating his struggle, Paul breaks out in praise. Paul offers no specific formula for just how he will win victory in his personal, spiritual dilemma. All he says is, "God through Jesus Christ." That is answer enough. Even while we must struggle with the remaining power of sin and corruption, God has made a way for victory through the all-sufficiency of Jesus Christ. In simplest terms, what God requires, He empowers through Jesus Christ. Therefore, even in matters of the will, committed disciples are able to declare, "thanks be to God, who gives us the victory through our Lord Jesus Christ" (1 Corinthians 15:57).

"Take Up His Cross Daily"

When interpreting Scripture it is always valuable to put yourself in the place of the original audience, to hear what they heard within the context of their time. Whole teachings, various phrases, and individual words tend to come alive when understood within the framework of the daily experiences of those who first heard the words recorded in Scripture. The phrase "take up his cross" is an excellent case in point.

Two thousand years ago, a cross was yet to become the sacred symbol it has become for today's Christians. Even among many today who do not comprehend or appreciate its spiritual/theological meaning, the cross is a symbol of peace, love, and selfless sacrifice. It is worn as jewelry, lovingly placed on grave markers, and displayed on places of worship. In most cases, those who see it are warmed by its very presence. This imagery, however, is drastically different from what was felt or understood two millennia ago.

The cross in Jesus' day had only one meaning; and that meaning was based upon its single purpose. The cross was an instrument of death by Roman execution. Those who heard Jesus issue this command saw nothing attractive in his chosen imagery. They envisioned (through personal encounters) Rome's deadly authority poured out against its most violent or seditious offenders. They recalled images of suspended, grotesque human figures writhing away in bloody agony, begging for death to end their often days-long torture strapped to rough cross bars. Jesus' audience knew well the stench and terror of human corpses left on crosses until vultures turned bodies into skeletons. In their minds, there was nothing attractive attached to a cross.

In reality, unless you have lived in a brutalized nation under the heartless authority of a maniacal regime, fully grasping what Jesus' original audience pictured as they heard His words is impossible. Perhaps it will help us to put it this way. For Jesus to say to His disciples today, "Take up your cross," is akin to Him saying, "Take up your electric chair"; "Take up your lethal injection"; or "Take up your gallows."

But even these analogies seem a bit weak. Perhaps the best that can be done is to forget imagery and simply accept that what these early Christ followers heard and understood was a call to discipleship that demanded enormous sacrifice and personal cost. It is little wonder then that each of Christ's initial disciples, save Judas Iscariot, followed by an untold number of early believers, willingly died martyrs' deaths. They grasped what it means to take up one's cross, and despite the cultural and historical distance, so can we. Clearly stated, in the words of twentieth-century martyr Dietrich Bonhoeffer: "When Christ calls a man, He bids him come and die."

Recall my earlier assertion that Jesus' three commands are stated in order of their difficulty? One of the reasons I believe this to be true is grounded in the response of those who first heard the words recorded in Luke 9:23. Let me ask you, who would willingly abandon himself or herself to the point of death unless their personal desires were first fully surrendered to the will and desires of another? The answer is simple—no one. The point is, faithfully obeying Christ's call to self-death (taking up one's cross) is wholly dependent on the full surrender of one's personal will (deny self) to that of God. Anyone who would work to develop true disciples of Christ must always keep this truth in mind.

The world may call this kind of surrender "crazy"; the church may call it "radical"; Jesus would simply call it "normal." The fact of the matter is, other than in juxtaposition to what is often passed off as discipleship by the modern church, there is no biblically sound extreme of devotion to Christ that can rightly be called radical, revolutionary, or any other descriptive buzzword used to indicate something extraordinary. What Jesus described in Luke 9:23 is basic; it is the baseline of what constitutes a normal disciple, with every action that flows from such devotion being normal, as well.

"Follow Me"

How often have we heard those words? We have been admonished to "follow Christ" in sermons, Bible studies, small groups, and accountability relationships. They are two rather innocuous, simple-sounding words. In fact, they are so familiar and easy going that it's a wonder Jesus did not begin His three commands by using them.

Once again, context is essential. To understand the specific context to which I refer, allow me to restate the verse in a couple of different ways. Perhaps the exercise will clarify why this simple phrase is the third and most difficult of the list.

Restatement #1—"Follow Me after you understand what it means and have committed to deny yourself and take up your cross."

Restatement #2—"In continued denial of and death to self, follow Me."

Did that help? The point is, following Jesus is not about being good, peaceable, and kind. It's not about imbibing good teachings and seeking to be a nice person. In fact, it's not even about studying Jesus' life and trying to replicate it to the best of our abilities. That is religion, not discipleship. Of course, following Jesus will produce many of these worthy lifestyle features. However, following Jesus as a disciple, according to Christ's intent in Luke 9:23, reaches far beyond mere external work to touch the deepest parts of the inner person. In other words, "following Christ" continues the overarching discipleship characteristic of total abandonment to Jesus Christ.

By now, if you have been reading closely, it should be apparent that a picture is taking shape. Call it the portrait of a true disciple. So far, two elements have come into focus, making clear what a Christ-defined disciple looks like: (1) the abandonment of self will, and (2) death to one's self. But the picture lacks the third and final part; without it the image is incomplete. In keeping with the full context of the verse, the remaining part is self-emptying.

It is tempting at this point to cry out, "That's too much. Surely, God would not expect so much." Let me ask you, what biblically literate believer has not marveled at the grace-filled humility of Jesus when, for the sake of lost humanity, He willing laid aside many of the attributes of deity and took on human flesh and frailty in an act theologians refer to as Jesus' *kenósis* (self-emptying)? Read again the biblical record: "who, although He existed in the form of God, did not regard equality with God a thing to be grasped, but emptied Himself, taking the form of a bond-servant, and being made in the likeness of men. Being found in appearance as a man, He humbled Himself by becoming obedient to the point of death, even death on a cross" (Philippians 2:6–8). What a mind-boggling picture of complete and total surrender.

The image of Jesus' self-emptying is powerful and convicting just as a standalone feature of His life and ministry. It is even more powerful, however, when it is coupled with Philippians 2:5, the verse preceding the scriptural record of His selfless act. The Bible says, "Have this attitude in yourselves which was also in Christ Jesus." This verse forms a bridge connecting two sets of teachings regarding the conduct of the church. The first is a general teaching calling for humility in dealing with others in the Christian family (2:1–4). The second set of verses comprise the *kenósis* record (2:6–7). According to verse 5, both teachings reflect the attitude or mind of Christ, and both are incumbent on believers. Directly to the case in point, believers are not only to marvel at the self-emptying of Jesus, *they are expected to replicate it.*

Think of it this way. Say you own a home that is now much larger than you need or can care for, so you decide to downsize. However, you really love the place. Inside its walls, room by room, are all your fondest memories. Torn between the sensibility of selling and the emotion of past family life, you set a rather high price and determine not to budge from it by even a dollar. Then, within days of placing the house on the market, a well-dressed young man appears at the door asking to view the property. You take him inside and watch as he inspects every square inch of your beloved home. After a thorough inspection, the gentleman tells you he wants to buy the property. Firmly, you tell him that the price is nonnegotiable. Without so much as a flinch, the man tells you he is prepared to pay the full asking price. Further, to speed up the process, he pledges to pay all expenses, including yours, related to the sale—in cash! Stammering in amazement, you agree to sell. It is then agreed that you will fully vacate the premises within thirty days.

Everything in the process goes perfectly according to plan. Thirty days pass and the man along with his family and a loaded moving van pull up to their new house. However, when the new owner tries to unlock the front door, he discovers that his key is useless on the lock. He goes from door to door trying every lock, with the same result. Frustrated, he retries all the locks, peers in windows, and pounds on doors. Then, from the very back of the house, he is able to make out voices and the sound of approaching footsteps. Imagine the man's surprise when the back door swings open and there you stand, spouse by your side, smiling from ear to ear. Imagine his greater surprise when you begin to explain your presence.

"I know this looks strange," you begin, "but let me explain. We know you bought and paid for the house; it's yours. But when we started packing to move out, well, the memories were just too much for us. There's so much here that we still love. We just couldn't give it all up. So, here is what we did. We moved all that we just couldn't part with into one room in the back of the house. Every other room is empty. We will occupy this one small space and you will have everything else. You get 95 percent of the house. Surely you can let us continue to have one room."

If you were the new owner, how would you respond? Would you say, "I fully understand; that sounds reasonable"? Of course you wouldn't, and no one would blame you. Your response would probably go something like this. "I didn't force you to sell this house. I paid the full price for it, for all of it. In every legal sense, this is now my house and these are my rights as owner. I intend to occupy and control every room. You must fully vacate." I doubt anyone would disagree with the demands of the new owner.

Similarly, believers' lives are much like the house in the story. Our lives and destinies were at one time, as it were, on the market. The Bible says, however, "You have been bought with a price" (1 Corinthians 6:20a). What was that price? Scripture says, "Knowing that you were not redeemed [bought] with perishable things like silver or gold from your futile way of life inherited from your forefathers, but with precious blood, as of a lamb unblemished and spotless, the blood of Christ" (1 Peter 1:18–19). God makes the offer to apply the blood price paid by Jesus to those who will willingly receive Him. He does not force. But when accepted, He pays in full. And the full price demands a complete purchase—every room. We must empty out. Do not expect that God will allow His disciples to retain even a few old things in a single room, and never consider Him harsh for making such demands; He is, in fact, the owner.

A Few Closing Thoughts

Setting the Matter Straight

To guard against the notion that Jesus calls believers to become will-less, mindless, zombies without the capacity for original thought, let me hasten to say—all that a Christian is required to surrender, God fully replaces. He requires self-denial. When we seek to obey, He overpowers our rebellious, alien wills and creates within us wills that ever-increasingly desire the very things He chooses for us. He requires death to self. When we seek to obey, He goes to the mind, the motivating source driving us to live in control, and replaces the mind of the flesh with a spiritual mind capable of understanding His Word, drawing accurate conclusions from it, and living out His truths. He requires self-emptying in order to follow Him. When we seek to obey, He fills up every newly emptied space with the indwelling person of the Holy Spirit.

Let it be affirmed, what results from obedience to God's commands is no zombie-like existence. Reflect on the apostle Paul's testimony and rejoice in the fact that it speaks to the life of every true disciple. "For through the Law I died to the Law, so that I might live to God. I have been crucified with Christ; and it is no longer I who live, but Christ lives in me; and the life which I now live in the flesh I live by faith in the Son of God, who loved me and gave Himself up for me." Pay particular attention these truths within the verses:

- We have died to what is past in order to live for the future.
- The death we experience identifies us with the price Jesus paid on Calvary.
- Our new life is made possible by the animating life of Jesus.
- The life we now live is one of gratitude and complete dependence on the life giver.

Here it is in short order: The past is gone. A brighter future is before us complete with a new identity, and a new life source, one that is fully worthy of our trust. This is certainly not the picture of a pitiful, robotic people too weak to chart their own courses. It is the biblical image of vibrant, newly created individuals who were broken enough to follow God's course to Jesus.

Some Distinguishing Characteristics of a True Disciple

Thus far, the discussion has been about what constitutes a true disciple of Jesus Christ. Before concluding and moving on, it would be a good thing to note a few traits that serve to distinguish a true disciple's life and practice from many of the less-than-biblical ideas in vogue today. This is only a brief list with minimum commentary. No doubt, you can add more. The list is limited to only those things ultimately traceable to Scripture. None of the things I consider less than biblical are noted. As has been said in the past, the best way to recognize the counterfeit is to be thoroughly acquainted with the genuine.

A True Disciple Follows in Genuine Repentance

A true disciple of Jesus doesn't just repent of the areas in life where he or she feels *inadequate* without God. The true disciple will daily acknowledge and confess those areas of life where he or she feels *adequate* without God. This individual knows that while it is necessary to repent over things that should have long been overcome (inadequate), it is just as important to admit any sense of being able to function in a particular area or task without God (adequate). This sort of deeper repentance is not designed to make believers constantly berate or belittle themselves, as if they are prodigals who can never get home. Instead, it is motivated by an acute sensitivity to personal sin; for the true disciple is keenly aware that being part of the Bride of Christ requires being divorced from the world. And because repentance is always followed by God's gracious forgiveness, a life of such full surrender to Jesus is nurtured, growing so deep God can ask us to do anything and we will do it.

A True Disciple Follows in an Ongoing Lifestyle

The true disciple knows that there is no finality to the Christian life this side of eternity; as long as we have minds and are breathing, we are engaged. A true disciple understands that he didn't come to Christ for salvation only to secure his eternal destiny, but to live out his human destiny as well, by following Jesus.

A True Disciple Follows by Living the Normality of a Sacrificed Life

One of the most stirring stories found in contemporary missions is that of five young men, missionaries to Ecuador, who were speared to death in 1956 in their attempts to reach the Auca Indians with the gospel. For over sixty years, the story of their martyrdom has been an inspirational staple in the missions community. Readers of the various accounts have marveled at the depth of each young man's commitment to Christ. Many have called it extraordinary. Knowing, for example, that the men made a pact among themselves that the handgun they had was, under no circumstances, to be used against the Auca, is almost unbelievable. They reasoned that the Indians were not prepared for eternity, but the missionaries were. According to one of the Auca, who later came to faith in Christ, when he was about to spear the young missionary holding the pistol—a weapon that could have saved his life—he fired it in the air instead of into his attacker, and allowed himself to be killed.

As extraordinary as these acts seem, it is noteworthy that what these men did on that Ecuadoran beach was to them normal. Jim Elliot, the team leader, wrote many inspiring words in his brief life, but none so telling as these two entries in his journal. "That man is no fool to give what he cannot keep to gain what he cannot lose." "God, light these idle sticks of my life and may I burn up for Thee. Consume my life, Oh God, for it is Thine. I seek not a long life, but a full one like Yours, Lord Jesus." His heart was shared by all those who died on the beach with him. For them, as will be the case for every true disciple, a sacrificial life is a normal life.

Just before being burned at the stake, Joan of Arc is reported to have said: "Every man gives his life for what he believes. And every woman gives her life for what she believes. Sometimes people believe in little or nothing, and yet they give their lives for that little or nothing. One life is all we have; we live it and it is gone. But to live it without belief is more terrible than dying, even more terrible than dying young." The true disciple believes and lives out that belief.

A True Disciple Is Intentional about Sacrifice

True disciples are not haphazard about sacrifice. They are not only willing, they are intentional. They anticipate sacrifice as a normal matter of course. Therefore, much of that sacrifice is made assumably even before it is required practically. Among these assumptive sacrifices, one seems paramount: *They willingly sacrifice all expectations related to pride and esteem.*

There is a fallacy today that authentic Christianity can be lived in this world without giving offense to anyone, and that we can expect that everyone will sooner or later come to appreciate us and our convictions. We have only to consider the history of the One we serve to know better than this. There was no room for Jesus in the inn; the innkeeper turned Him out. When He got a bit older, there was no room in His family; His family turned on Him. He went to the temple and found no room in the temple; the temple turned on Him. And when He died, there was no room to bury Him; He died outside the city. Why then is it that we expect to be accepted everywhere and by everyone? How is it that the world couldn't get along with the holiest Man who ever lived and yet we expect it to get along well with us?

True disciples are undaunted by the world's attitude regarding who they serve. The world will chide and ridicule us for our faith. Let the world do as it will; you need never apologize for Jesus! Remember, He that is from above is above all. Consider this. He came to earth with a single redemptive purpose (Luke 19:10). He sacrificed all to live among humanity (Philippians 2:5–8). He endured all that was necessary to save humanity from sin, death, and ourselves (1 Peter 2:22–24). Furthermore, the Bible declares, "For this reason also, God highly exalted Him, and bestowed on Him the name which is above every name, so that at the name of Jesus every knee will bow, of those who are in heaven and on earth and under the earth, and that every tongue will confess that Jesus Christ is Lord, to the glory of God the Father" (Philippians 2:9–11). In Jesus, there is all to glory in and nothing to apologize for.

A True Disciple Follows Christ by Living a Refocused Life

Refocused Ideas about Happiness

There is an idea circulating in contemporary Christianity asserting that the end of all being is the happiness of man. Though not often stated in these words, the message is, God reigns in heaven for the happiness of man; Jesus Christ was incarnated for the happiness of man; all the angelic hosts exist for the happiness of man. In other words, everything is not only centered around, but exists for, the happiness of man. True disciples know that this message is unbiblical, ungodly, and un-Christian. True Christianity says, "The end of all being is the glory of God." The true disciple lives a life of humility and service focused on this truth.

Refocused Ideas about Prayer

No one is more keenly aware of the primacy of prayer than the true disciples of Jesus Christ. More than any others, these folk are aware of the many intricacies involved in prayer: types of prayer, methods of prayer, frequency of prayer, components of prayer. Additionally, their refocus on prayer will also give attention to what needs to be prayed about and what does not. As was noted earlier in this chapter, numerous smaller issues have been settled as a result of one's overarching commitment to Christ and following Him in discipleship. True disciples know and believe this. Therefore, they spend little time re-asking questions in prayer that have already been answered.

To understand what I mean, think about this. Say you are discussing college and life options with your son or daughter. During the conversation, your child tells you he or she has decided to study law, or medicine, or business, or education. In most cases your response, as well as those of most other concerned family, would be, "That's wonderful." Now, imagine if that same child tells you, "I want to be a foreign missionary."

What is the typical response? Isn't it normal for us to answer, "That's good, but you need to pray about it."

Think about that answer compared to the response to the first question. Now, it is never wrong to call for prayer. However, why is it that we would hasten to call for prayer over missionary service and not any other profession? Here is the point. Jesus has already commanded us to "Go . . . and make disciples of all the nations." Is it really necessary to pray over whether or not to obey an explicit command? Why not a call to pray and ask God for permission to stay? He has, after all, already told us to go. The point is this, true disciples assume the primacy of their larger commitment to obey Christ unquestioningly, and they pray accordingly.

Refocused Ideas about Service

Have you ever wondered why God insists that a person must come to Him by way of the cross? Why does He require that a person embrace death with Christ? I know there are a myriad of theological elements to consider in answer to these questions. But beyond these, could it be because coming to the cross and embracing Christ's death is the only way God can get glory out of a human being? Truthfully speaking, when all that we know of humanity is understood properly, we are left to admit that there is absolutely nothing in the combined best of human beings that can bring a single moment of glory to God, apart from first being joined to Christ at the cross.

This, then, leads to a second question. Why are we called to serve God as obedient disciples of Jesus? The answer remains the same: because it is the only way God can continue to get glory out of us. When convinced of this truth, a true disciple will pray, "Lord Jesus, I'm going to obey You and love You and serve You and do what You want me to do as long as I live even if I lose everything in the process, simply because You are worthy to be loved, obeyed and served."

Nate Saint, one of the five missionaries killed by the Auca Indians in Ecuador, wrote in his diary: "People who do not know the Lord ask why in the world we waste our lives as missionaries. They forget that they too are expending their lives, and when the bubble has burst they will have nothing of eternal significance to show for the years they have wasted." Refocused service cringes at the thought of such waste and determines to bring glory to God by living a life for the gospel that makes sense in the light of eternity.

Conclusion

In God's economy, the church will only achieve results that are fully reflective of the divine character when they are accomplished by true disciples of Christ. Nothing mirrors divine character within the church more than a Body mindset that is missional in nature. Only when a genuinely missional mindset permeates the church will God-exemplifying, missional ministry occur on a consistent basis.

There are two primary ways to go about changing the church's mindset if it is other than missional. The first is by means of appealing to external motivation through programs, promotions, and other schemes designed to stir momentary emotional responses to causes and more programs. These efforts may work for short-term effect, but they will never produce long-term affect. The second way is to focus on the inner person by developing true disciples of Jesus Christ. This process begins with helping people learn to think like disciples, for a person must learn to think like a disciple before he or she will begin to live like one. Until thinking and living line up, descriptive qualifiers such as "radical" or "revolutionary" attached to "disciple"—even when discussing missional objectives and activities—are just buzzwords for people acting on temporary emotions or according to some other person's instructions. They are meaningless adjectives describing what ought to be instead of what actually is.

Some time ago my pastor was discussing the pastoral challenge of developing believers into true disciples. He spoke for ministers everywhere when he, rather tongue in cheek, observed, "Circumstances are easy to change; it's human beings that present the problem." A century and a half before my pastor's observation, evangelist Dwight L. Moody shared his own take on the difficulty of developing disciples. He said, "It is better to train ten people than to do the work of ten people. But it is harder."[111] Yet, despite the difficulty, developing mature disciples of Jesus Christ is absolutely necessary. It is necessary because, as the Bible makes clear, Jesus commanded it. Jesus issued the mandate as part of His parting instructions to the twelve men who first walked with Him (Matthew 28:18–20, et. al.). Further, Jesus demonstrated the importance of making mature disciples by making this vital work part of His ministry while on earth, and as you are no doubt aware, the process was no less difficult for Him. The level of difficulty, however, cannot be the deciding factor for whether or not we follow God's plan. As Martin Luther said, "A religion that gives nothing, costs nothing, and suffers nothing, is worth nothing."

Further, the task is well worth the work involved. When the church has a missional mindset by virtue of a membership functioning as true, maturing disciples of Christ, missional thinking and ministry will flow as a natural consequence, and so too will the benefits. The missionary heart of God will show itself to the world as God's people, without the need for continued prodding, reflect the example of the church's Head—"the Word [who] became flesh, and dwelt among us, and we saw His glory, glory as of the only begotten from the Father, full of grace and truth" (John 1:14). This is far better than as Karl Barth said, "The Word became flesh—and then through theologians it became

---

[111]Dwight L. Moody, *Sermon Illustrations*, http://www.sermon illustrations.com/a-z/d/discipleship.htm, (accessed May 27, 2011).

words again."[112] Most beneficial, this sort of missional church would surely be a church Jesus would attend.

---

[112]Karl Barth, *Sermon Illustrations*, http://www.sermonillustrations. com/a-z/d/discipleship.htm, (accessed May 30, 2011).

Chapter 8

The Power of Passion

It is said that words possess a life of their own, and in a sense, this is true. Words come and go with the years. If you doubt this, take time to peruse an Old English dictionary. Reading many of the entries will feel like visiting a museum of little known, long-discarded artifacts.

It is also true that a host of the entries you will find, while unrecognizable in their early English forms, will prove vaguely familiar. This is because so many of the words used today are rooted in these often strange-looking and sounding structures. Thus, words are also transitory in nature. In other words, they are retained and modified by different generations and cultures as time progresses. This is true of the forms and spellings of words, as well as their assigned definitions.

One such word is "passion." Say the word and dozens of emotions flood the mind, emotions that are actually included in dictionary definitions. For example, according to the *Collins English Dictionary*, passion, among other things, is defined as "*any* powerful or compelling emotion or feeling, as love or hate"[113] (emphasis added). To prove the point of broad meaning, the *Collins* dictionary adds the following denotations related to passion.

---

[113]passion, Dictionary.com, *Collins English Dictionary - Complete & Unabridged 10th Edition*, HarperCollins Publishers, http://dictionary.reference.com/browse/passion (accessed: June 02, 2011).

An instance or experience of strong love or sexual desire; a person toward whom one feels strong love or sexual desire; a strong or extravagant fondness, enthusiasm, or desire for anything: the object of such a fondness or desire: an outburst of strong emotion or feeling: violent anger. [T]he state of being acted upon or affected by something external, especially something alien to one's nature or one's customary behavior (contrasted with action). [T]he sufferings of Christ on the cross or His sufferings subsequent to the Last Supper; the narrative of Christ's sufferings as recorded in the Gospels; the sufferings of a martyr.[114]

Check the definition of passion in most other reputable dictionaries and you will get the same results: meanings so broad that the word can be applied to most any person, place, thing, or experience about which one feels strongly.

What may come as a surprise is that in its earliest form "passion" had a much tighter definition. The Latin noun that is the ancestor of the modern English word passion is *passio*. The word originally meant "suffering," and it is still used today in this sense in the very specialized context of the sufferings of Jesus, e.g., *The Passion of the Christ*, passion play, etc. Over time, however, the word developed not only an "undergoing" sense—"fact or condition of being acted upon"—but also a separate *extended sense*, a generalization from experiencing pain to experiencing any sort of intense feeling or emotion.[115]

In modern parlance, "passion" is used in the broadest sense possible. However, for all the ways the word is defined, there is very limited regard in contemporary usage for its original meaning, other than in the specialized context noted above. This is noticeably true in the modern church where passion has become something of a buzzword to describe deep commitment

---

[114]*Collins English Dictionary.*

[115]Arnold Zwicky, *Language Log,* "No Pain, No Gain?," http://itre.cis.upenn.edu/~myl/languagelog/archives/002454.html (accessed: June 4, 2011).

to Christ. For instance, I was asked recently to fill out a recommendation form submitted to me by a major mission-sending agency on behalf of a former student. One of the more prominent questions on the form asked that I respond to the applicant's "passion" for missions and missionary service. I say prominent because the question was in two rather extensive parts. First, there was a long list of characteristics (perhaps the agency's definitions of missionary passion) from which I was to choose all that applied. Second, I was asked to provide additional detailed information in narrative form giving reasons and examples for each of my choices. More to the immediate point, not one of the "passion" characteristics listed on the reference form was related in any way to the fundamental, original definition of the word. Instead, each one had to do with such things as commitment, fervor, work ethic, initiative, ambition, and attitude. There was nothing at all related to the candidate's willingness to suffer for the name of Christ or the gospel. Yet, "suffer," "to suffer," or "suffering" comprise the original meaning of passion.

As I considered my response to the question, I found myself wondering, *If by overlooking and not including the original meaning in the broad definitions of passion, do modern believers miss an important requirement when we speak of being passionate about Christ and His church?* Asked another way, do we miss the full meaning of passion simply because we fail to grasp fully what early believers understood when they used the word?

Admittedly, it is difficult if not impossible, to know just what was in the minds of the rank and file of our spiritual ancestors when they used certain words to described their own commitments to Christ. In fact, we can't say with certainty that *passio* (suffer) was ever used popularly in either noun or adjective form to identify or describe personal commitments to Christ. What we can know is that the word was available to early believers, and if used by them for descriptive purposes it would certainly have been used within the context of its definition at the time.

Considering these things, while at the same time contemplating the original meaning of *passio*, I am left to wonder how many of us could (would), in good conscience continue to use "passion" or "passionate" as qualifiers to describe our depth of commitment to Christ, the church, and the gospel message if the modern usage of the word maintained its original meaning? Now do not misunderstand me; I am not advocating abandoning the array of meanings that currently define passion. All I am suggesting is that the original definition of *passio* should be reinserted into our personal spiritual lexicons in order that suffering and the willingness to pay that level of price for Christ is included in what the church understands and means when passion is advocated and claimed by contemporary disciples.

Keeping "to suffer" in the definition would certainly align more accurately with Scripture. Take for example Paul's words: "For to you it has been granted for Christ's sake, not only to believe in Him, but also *to suffer* for His sake" (Philippians 1:29, italics added). Or Peter's admonition in 1 Peter 4:19: "Therefore, those also who *suffer* according to the will of God shall entrust their souls to a faithful Creator in doing what is right." In both verses, the word translated "suffer" is from the Greek word *paskho*. Note the root stem, *pas*. Does it look familiar? It should (hint: *pas-sio*). The biblical word is defined, "to experience a sensation or impression (usually painful), feel, *passion*, suffer, vex." If suffering is removed from the root for passion, even the biblical text would be altered. I think you will agree, that would be unwise.

Without doubt, the idea of suffering is vitally linked to both the early semantic and biblical meanings of passion, and it should be for the contemporary church as well. Without accepting the potential for suffering, the church, while it might claim a deeply felt love and adoration for Jesus, even a willingness to expend energy in occasional selfless service to His Kingdom, cannot rightly claim passion. To omit this essential part of the definition will render us like the young soldier who boldly proclaimed his willingness to give his "last drop" of blood for his country. But when asked by his commanding officer if he would be willing to give his "first drop" of blood for his country, the outspoken soldier retreated into silence.

By ignoring the original definition of passion and making it a purely feelings-based description of one's commitment to Christ, the church today finds itself with numerous "last drop" disciples. These folk tend to speak proudly of their devotion then linger at a safe distance in the secure rear. They can be seen week after week comfortably ensconced within the church's sanctuary environment with their arms raised in praise, choruses ringing from their voices, and praise language dripping from their lips. Essentially, they appear to be living pictures of genuine passion for Jesus, and by today's standards, they are. Yet when the Kingdom of God presses them for service that may require personal loss and sacrifice—on any level, physical or emotional—they grow suddenly silent, even invisible. Their priority is to retain every drop of life until retreat is no longer an option. And hopefully, they pray, that day will never come.

On the other hand, there are those willing to turn the feeling of passion into a living expression by sacrificing everything as their fundamental act of devotion to Christ. Theirs is more than a "first drop" commitment; it is a cost-counted, no retreat, fully emptied surrender of their lives from the start of their walk with Jesus. They take seriously the Lord's admonition that there are costs to be counted before committing one's self to a relationship with Christ (Luke 14:28–32). They accept that the Lord meant exactly what He said when He insisted, ". . . none of you can be My disciple who does not give up all his own possessions" (Luke 14:33). For these disciples, surrender begins with the abandonment of that most precious of possessions: their lives.

In fact, "first drop" believers share in a rich spiritual heritage dating back to the early church. For ancient believers, passion—*passio*—was understood to mean "suffering," first and foremost. This understanding of passion, energized by the Holy Spirit, undergirded the fire of the early church. For that fire to blaze once more, the element of suffering must be intentionally and prominently reinserted into the church's definition of passion. In other words, when we who call ourselves disciples of the Lord Jesus use passion to characterize our adoration, commitment and surrender to Christ, suffering must not be omitted from what we mean. To do so robs the church of numerous benefits.

The Benefits of True Passion

When "suffering"—both the willingness to suffer and the actual circumstances of suffering—is understood and accepted as part of the church's definition of "passion," then and only then can our claims to being passionate about Christ be regarded as fully legitimate and become truly powerful. It is not just powerful in the sense of emotional expression, but rather powerful in the numerous practical, God-glorifying ways that fully sacrificial surrender affects the ministry of the church, the lives within the church, and the world around the church.

For instance, true passion will expand the positive response of the church to God's command to "go." For years, church and mission leaders have questioned why it is that with the fields so "white unto harvest," such a relative few in the church are willing to go. Why is it that so many church members who profess a desire to go with God insist on staying where they are? Perhaps the honest answer is as simple as the threat of sacrifice and suffering. The idea of abandoning creature comforts and accepting personal insecurities is too much for many believers to contemplate. True passion changes that. True passion positions itself with the apostle Paul who said, "But whatever things were gain to me, those things I have counted as loss for the sake of Christ" (Philippians 3:7). Those genuinely passionate about Christ and His cause in the fullest, most literal sense possible will, as it were, march on hell with a water pistol, regardless of the outcome. Theirs is the confidence of Shadrach,

Meshach, and Abed-nego who declared to King Nebuchadnezzar, "If it be so, our God whom we serve is able to deliver us from the furnace of blazing fire; and He will deliver us out of your hand, O king. But even if He does not, let it be known to you, O king, that we are not going to serve your gods or worship the golden image that you have set up" (Daniel 3:17–18). If this kind of true passion reigned in the church, the current limited response to engage the world would be reversed, resulting in a dramatic increase in the numbers of those willing to follow God anywhere and at any cost.

Second, if genuine passion ruled the commitment of contemporary believers the voice of the church would be more widely respected around the world. Of course, the world at large will never fully respect the voice of the church, no matter what it says or how it says it. The respect spoken of here is that which is to be gained from believers around the world outside the North American continent, those brothers and sisters who have paid and are paying a suffering price for their faith in Jesus Christ. I speak of those persecuted believers in the two-thirds or majority of the world who are part of the largest "human rights" violation issue on the globe. That multitude of saints who, according to the World Evangelical Alliance, make up the over 200 million Christians in at least sixty countries who are denied fundamental human rights solely because of their faith. In short, those who are part of "[an] injustice so great that by its very nature it defies being statistically analyzed with any degree of certitude."[116]

Glenn Penner of Voice of the Martyrs explains the difficulty in gathering reliable persecution statistics and in so doing illustrates further the suffering endured by the global Christian family. He writes,

> . . . despite our modern technology making today's world a much smaller place, much of today's

---

[116]Glenn Penner, "The Limits of Statistics," *The Voice of the Martyrs Persecuted Church Weblog,* http://persecutedchurch.blogspot.com /2009/04/limits-of-statistics.html (accessed June 26, 2011).

persecution still takes place in remote areas of countries often cut off from or with restricted access to modern communications. *Most martyrs suffer and die anonymously,* unknown, forgotten, their deaths unrecorded except in heaven. Even email, which most of us consider a basic everyday tool is a struggle to use in places like Ethiopia, Burma, and much of central Africa. Even where it is more readily available, it is not secure. Much goes unreported or is reported months, even years later. *For many, persecution is such a part of life that it hardly dawns on the afflicted to tell the world.* Many are nervous about sharing what they know for fear of retribution[117] (emphasis added).

Keep in mind, these suffering believers are thinking people. They made their choices to follow Jesus knowing full well the price they would likely pay. Yet, in the face of grave threats, they gave themselves completely to the Savior, and in most cases, they did so openly, not in secret; otherwise, they would not be suffering persecution. The question for the Western church as we look into the faces of our global brothers and sisters in Christ who daily endure so much for the sake of the gospel: how can the comfortable church of the West earn the respect of the persecuted church around the world?

There is no more effective way to earn respect than through *points of identity* between involved parties. Normally, when seeking points of identity, the first consideration is to look for points of common belief. While agreement on essential doctrines is crucial, points of common experience between groups are equally important, and should not be overlooked. In fact, common experiences are often the best first step toward building enduring and mutually beneficial relationships. The majority-world church experiences persecution and suffering on a daily basis. While believers in the West do not as yet face overt physical persecution for the faith, we are nevertheless

---

[117]Penner, "Statistics."

commanded to remember those who are. Suffering, then, is a point at which the entire global church can and should find identity with all its members.

Certainly, it is not suggested that believers in more secure areas of the world foolishly place themselves in intentional jeopardy for the sake of greater identity with the plight of the persecuted. What is urged is that nonpersecuted believers in the West adopt a sincere *willingness* to identify with those suffering for their faith. Acting on this willingness will draw us into the truth that suffering is a normal cost of true discipleship. It will allow us to become feeling participants in the lives of distant strugglers, all of which will provide a needed point of identity between the West and the rest of the global church.

Scripture is clear that this sort of identity between believers is exactly what God intends for His people. The truth is, the nonpersecuted are not without personal responsibility to and for those who suffer for the faith. We in the West need to ask ourselves honestly, is it possible that we actually believe God gives His disciples the right to choose the extent to which we are willing to share in the experiences of our brothers and sisters, wherever they may be? Do we imagine that the Bible's repeated teachings regarding the church as a body of interconnected parts, feeling each other's joys and pains, applies only to those parts within our own particular region of the world, or, more specifically, those with whom we worship each week? That certainly does not appear to be the message of Hebrews 13:3, which says, "Remember the prisoners, as though in prison with them, and those who are ill-treated, since you yourselves also are in the body." Quite clearly, the church is admonished never to forget those being persecuted for the cause of Christ.

Further, the Body of Christ is commanded to remember these suffering saints as though suffering alongside them. It might be a stretch, but perhaps part of what Paul meant when he told Timothy, "Indeed, all who desire to live godly in Christ Jesus will be persecuted" (2 Timothy 3:12), is captured in the "as though" portion of Hebrews 13:3. In other words, while it is true that many may never undergo severe persecution or intense suffering for their faith, and while it is also true that it would be foolish to place ourselves intentionally in dangerous situations when unnecessary, our identity with those in such circumstances can and should be so real, so deeply felt, as to sense that we too are undergoing the very same persecution, alongside them.

Make no mistake; our persecuted brothers and sisters are not necessarily asking that we physically join them in their circumstances. However, when they look at the church of the privileged West, they cannot help but wonder at the lack of a basic willingness to follow Christ into such conditions, if commanded. They must question a commitment to Christ that does not assume struggle and can claim passion without including suffering. It is important to remember that the relative security and freedom Christians experience as the norm in the West is largely atypical for the church in the rest of the world. Further, we must not mistake our peace for God's approbation; as if the West's lack of persecution is an indication of God's pleasure with our supposedly more mature understanding of the limits of discipleship. It is more likely that our level of discipleship lacks the depth and surrender to bring persecution on the church. We fool ourselves if we believe that the freedom, ease, comfort, and prosperity that marks the life and message of so many churches in the West impresses the global church or provides us with credibility and respect among our global brothers and sisters.

Of course, some may be asking, "Why is it necessary to identify with believers around the globe in the midst their circumstances?" The are several reasons; here are just a few.

Identity Will Increase Sensitivity and Empathy in the Church

The *Oxford English Dictionary* notes that when the word "identify" is followed by the preposition "with" (e.g., to identify with), it can be defined as, "to feel oneself to be, or to become, closely associated with or part of a person or thing."[118] To achieve this level of identity between persons, shared points of reference are needed. Indeed, the command of Hebrews 13:3 and the promise of 2 Timothy 3:12 provide the biblical and, thus, most important connection between all believers. However, because we are human beings operating within a human context, it is also important for there to be a point of reference that binds individuals together on an emotional basis. While it is true that obedience to the Word of God is in no way dependent upon one's feelings, being connected to our brothers and sisters emotionally allows biblical obedience to be undergirded by Christ-honoring motives, motives that are faithful to Scripture's admonitions and more aligned with the heart of God.

A connection on this level calls for sensitivity and empathy for another person that is so deep and personal that it leads to an emotional engagement of that individual's plight as though it were our own. Obviously, this is a difficult proposition when considering the fact that the overwhelming majority of persecuted believers will never personally be known to us. Yet, Hebrews 13:3 and similar passages stand, and the church must obey them. The first step in obedience is to put forth the effort. Let me suggest the following initial steps.

Ask God to Give You a Truly Sensitive and Empathetic Heart

People who are both sensitive and empathetic are more attuned to the conditions and needs of others. Sensitive people are more likely to notice someone else's feelings and to feel something themselves. Empathetic people find ways to identify with another's feelings by putting themselves emotionally in the place of another. Ask God to give you His eyes with which to view the world around you; ask Him to let you see what He sees

---

[118]*Oxford English Dictionary*, http://www.oed.com/view /Entry/90999?redirectedFrom=identify (accessed, July 4, 2011).

when He looks upon His persecuted children. Then ask God for a burden for your suffering brothers and sisters, not just a concern.

Make it a Habit to Obtain the Most Correct Information

When we feel empathy for someone, we are getting emotional information about them and their situation. By collecting information about other people's feelings, you get to know them better. As you get to know others on an emotional level, you are likely to see similarities between your feelings and theirs, between your basic emotional needs and theirs, and between their present condition and your possible future. When you recognize the similarities between their life and yours, you are more able to identify with them, relate to them, and empathize with them. Ask God to help you read beneath the statistics, reports, and stirring stories. Strive to experience the humanity beneath the numbers and narratives.

Seek to Know and Understand Yourself as Part of the Whole

While empathy begins with awareness of another person's feelings, the ability to empathize is directly dependent on your ability to feel your own feelings and identify them. If you have never felt a certain feeling, it will be hard for you to understand how another person is feeling. This holds equally true for pleasure and pain. On the other hand, when we say that someone "can't relate" to other people at all, it is likely because they have not experienced, acknowledged, or accepted many feelings of their own.[119] They cannot relate because they fail to see accurately their own humanity. The great tragedy is that many who claim faith in Christ fall into this category. They fail to realize that "When our feelings are turned off or insulated by layers of protective defense, life loses something precious. We trudge on,

---

[119]S. Hein, *Emotional Intelligence*, "Showing Empathy," http://eqi.org/empathy.htm#Showing Empathy (accessed July 3, 2011).

accomplishing plenty but appreciating little."[120] Chief among what is lost is the acute awareness that each of us are undeserving sinners saved by (and living on) the abiding grace of God.

For others, particularly in the West, there is an underlying assumption that the difficulties and trials experienced by majority-world peoples are to some degree their own fault. There is little to no regard for the all-inclusive nature of Paul's words to the entire Christian family, "Indeed, all who desire to live godly in Christ Jesus will be persecuted" (2 Timothy 3:12). And, sadly, as long as we persist in the fallacious notion that the marks of God's blessing are prosperity, health, personal well-being, and cultural approval, such oversight will continue.

It is time to break with this pattern. Ask God to help you feel and understand your own experiences within the context of His Word and as a connected part of the interconnected, global Body of Christ. You may never know exactly what another brother or sister feels; however, by connecting with your own struggles, you will find identity with these and other saints a very real and enriching possibility.

Identity Will Increase Accountability within the Global Church

Judging reality and personal progress are fundamental purposes of accountability. Engagement with global believers, particularly those undergoing persecution for their faith, will provide needed accountability by which to judge the actual depth and growth of our own commitments to Christ (Proverbs 27:17).

For any accountability relationship to work, certain things are essential. First, the objective and standard for judging one's

---

[120]Michael McGowan, *Christianity Today*, "The Heart Has Reasons: Rational Proofs Alone do Not A Christian Make", review of Clifford Williams, *Existential Reasons for Belief in God: A Defense of Desires and Emotions for Faith*, June 2011, 70.

progress toward the goal must be established. In the case of discipleship, the goal is to attain the deepest level possible, according to the standard set by Jesus in Luke 16:33. Second, there must be a partner in the relationship who is credible because he or she has attained the objective by the established standard. It makes no sense to judge ourselves according to ourselves, or modified versions of the biblical standard. Further, nothing is gained by teaming with an accountability partner who demonstrates little experience and spiritual growth as a disciple of Christ. The relationship is only effective when the standard is biblically accurate and the life of the partner is a witness to personal victory through God's faithfulness in the midst of struggles.

Proper accountability will keep the church honest. The testimonies and examples of saints who are faithful to Christ, despite having to pay a suffering price for their fidelity, provide excellent examples by which the church can judge the validity of its claims and the progress it has yet to make.

Identity Will Increase Awareness Regarding the Condition of the Global Church

Many, if not most, Western believers are unaware that the epicenter of the global church has shifted away from its traditional position in Western Europe and North America to other parts of the globe. There is little awareness that the pendulum has swung from a majority of the world's Christians living in the West to a majority of them living outside it. Clearly, the global West no longer dominates the world Christian movement; to large degree, the West has become a subordinate participant.

Because of this trend, those concerned with the overall health of the church should not draw conclusions based solely on the condition of the church in the West. Ongoing evangelism accompanied by numerical and spiritual growth are centerpieces of the church in many places such as South America, Africa, and large portions of Asia. Significant evidence of this is found in the fact that many former mission fields of previous years are now increasingly becoming enthusiastic mission-sending countries. Despite meager resources, limited training, little to no outside support, and, for many, constant physical and political jeopardy, the fervency of majority-world believers is bringing a vibrancy of faith to areas where the gospel has never been preached, as well as reigniting lost passions for Christ in parts of the world where the fires of faith had long since died away.[121]

If for no other reason, Western believers need to be aware of these things for the sake of comparison and the insights such comparison will bring. Common sense observation is enough to discern that the ardor for Christ and His mission, which was once a hallmark of American Christianity in particular, has, in too many instances, become little more than a quest for individual gratification without too much personal sacrifice. At the same time, in two-thirds of the world, Christianity is ablaze with holy intensity, moving steadily forward, fueled by believers whose commitment to Christ is so truly passionate that no personal cost or sacrifice is considered too great. Comparison will make two things very clear. First, when compared to the growth, vibrancy, and sacrificial surrender of Christians in the majority world, Western Christianity in general and American Christianity specifically are notably deficient. Second, the phenomenal growth of majority-world Christianity bears every mark of a global movement created and blessed by God. Because the blessing of God is reserved for those who are fully obedient to His teachings and leadership, there is every reason to conclude that the extraordinary discipleship of our global brothers and sisters exemplifies what it means to walk is correct obedience to the will of God, and thus to receive and sustain the blessing of the Father. Certainly, there is much for us to see and learn from the

---

[121]Pocock, Michael, Gailyn Van Rheenen, and Douglas McConnell, *The Changing Face of World Missions: Engaging Contemporary Issues and Trends* (Grand Rapids: MI, 2005), 150–151.

willingness of our majority-world brothers and sister to pay a suffering price in their passion for the advancement of the gospel.

The Western church needs to be aware of these things; it must be convicted by them, and it must learn from them. When we humbly identify with our sacrificing, suffering brothers and sisters around the world—willing to join them at their level of surrender and true passion—we will be more apt to engage those closest to us who are in need. Even more importantly, we can join the forward progress of the global church as God moves it toward its final consummation in Christ (Ephesians 1:10). You see, while scholars may debate the reasons why Christianity has established itself so strongly in certain areas of the world without any real answers, what does seem obvious is that Christianity is moving back home, to the Zion of God (Isaiah 49:12–23). It is time for the Western church to abandon its lesser, more comfortable definitions of passion and align itself with ultimate obedience to God's call to true discipleship, and join the movement—at any price.

Identity Will Aid in Preparation for the Future

When considering ways in which the church can be more effective in the world it is rare that the issue of its "status" on earth is raised. It is, however, important to know and accept our position on the earth relative to all other people and ideas. Getting directly to the point, the church is a minority population on the planet. The church is something of a spiritual ethnic minority, and this should come as no surprise. After all, the Bible teaches that believers live as aliens, strangers, and exiles in the earth (Ephesians 2:19; Hebrews 11:13). Furthermore, the church is also a minority in its mindset; for ours is the mind of Christ (Philippians 2:5; Colossians 2:18, 20).

The West, however, where triumphal language and power rhetoric have long dominated both our attitude and discourse, finds it difficult to accept the church's minority status as anything more than a biblical metaphor related mostly to believers living in less developed areas of the world. For this reason, we continue to advocate, as if it were part of the Gospel's content, altering the balance of power here on earth through such things as politics and social engagement. Yet it is a mistake to overlook the twin facts that the church's minority status on this planet is obviously by God's own design, and that this status carries important implications. Most notably, when we teach and live the unadulterated biblical gospel, our message, our ethics, and our values will also be in the minority, and there will be a price to pay.

Obedience to God requires that the church move beyond viewing its minority status as merely an abstract concept that can be altered by compromise, public relations, and political strategy. The church must acknowledge and accept its earthly minority status as being God's will and learn how to live and minister faithfully as unappreciated, unwelcome aliens on planet Earth.

Our brothers and sisters outside the West live this status as a present, physical reality on a daily basis, and they do so with remarkable effectiveness. They understand that being in the minority means less political voice, limited rights, and little respect from those around them. They anticipate these things because they understand them to be the normal cost for having pledged their allegiance to the cross of Jesus Christ. From these people we need to draw fresh lessons to inform our own minority status in the world.

While it is true that believers in the global West are not undergoing persecution and physical suffering because of their faith in Christ, prophetic Scriptures makes it certain that the question is not if, but when? Western Christianity has lived for centuries in relative peace and security, able to function pretty much at will. Biblically, however, this is destined to change—dramatically. Believing this to be true, Western Christians would do well to think through God's response to the prophet Jeremiah's complaint about his own difficulties. Listen to the Lord. "If you have run with footmen and they have tired you out, then how can you compete with horses? If you fall down in a land of peace, how will you do in the thicket of the Jordan?" (Jeremiah 12:5). To paraphrase, God said, "Your experience up to this time, despite the struggles you have encountered, can be compared to living in a peaceful land. But you will come into much greater dangers, where you will never for a moment be sure of your survival. If you do not learn to persevere now, how will you ever survive then?"

God's wisdom is unassailable and, as always, it bears immediate relevance to the present. For those believers who find themselves struggling to bear up faithfully in lands of peace, willing identity with and learning from those who know how to live victoriously in "the thicket of the Jordan" will do much to prepare them for tougher times ahead, times that are sure to come.

The Elements of True Passion

There is one other reason, beyond those stated above, that should be noted for identifying with our persecuted brothers and sisters in their true passion for Jesus Christ. Namely, genuine passion—that which is fully aligned with the whole definition of the word—is *visible* to others. In other words, it can be seen, known, and openly contrasted with lesser commitments, no matter what one may claim to the contrary. The reason is, true passion is composed of certain elements that will show forth in the life of the church. If these elements are absent, true passion does not, and will not, exist.

It is said that many years ago a nun in South America was reported to be performing miracles of healing in a small village. Curious about the reports, a bishop dispatched one of his monks to investigate the claims. The monk traveled for days and upon arriving in the village, he asked that the nun in question be sent to wash his feet. Within minutes, the monk was told that the nun was offended and refused to oblige his request. With no further investigation, the monk immediately returned to his bishop. His report was simple and to the point: "The rumors are false," he said. "For where there is no willingness to wash feet, there are no miracles."

In the same way, true passion has elements that both precede it and sustain it, without which it does not exist. The most important—the essential elements—are extraordinary love, uncompromising allegiance, and godly anguish.

True Passion Is Founded upon Extraordinary Love

As the old song goes, "Love makes the world go round." This is certainly the case with love's relationship to passion. Truly passionate believers have an unbounded, unconditional, self-sacrificing love for Jesus Christ. The love that drives them to passion for Christ is wholly obedient to the accurate interpretation of Jesus' words: "If anyone comes to Me, and does not hate his own father and mother and wife and children and brothers and sisters, yes, and even his own life, he cannot be My disciple" (Luke 14:26). In other words, unless your love for Jesus makes your love for anyone or anything else, including your own life, look like hate by comparison, you cannot be His disciple. The love for Christ possessed by the truly passionate disciple of Christ willingly meets the scriptural standard set by Jesus.

If you feel that the words of Jesus in this case are difficult, you are not alone. In comparison to the lesser definitions of discipleship and passion in vogue among much of the contemporary church, the standard Jesus set for His disciples appears nothing less than exceptional. But it is what it is—making nothing less than an extraordinary love sufficient to match the command with obedience. In fact, truly passionate followers of Christ cannot imagine the standard for discipleship being anything less than what Christ has commanded, and why should they? The Bible tells us that Jesus exemplified extraordinary love (John 15:12–13; 1 John 4:19; Revelation 1:5); Jesus endured the cost of extraordinary love (Hebrews 12:2–3; 1 Peter 2:21–24); and

Jesus enjoyed the gratification that was His because of His extraordinary love (Hebrews 12:2). Further, Jesus insured that His disciples had the capacity for His own extraordinary love: "and I have made Your name known to them, and will make it known, so that the love with which You loved Me *may be in them,* and I in them" (John 17:26, italics added). Yes, the standard is difficult but not impossible. Along with the command comes the example of Jesus and the power of God to obey it. It is only left for the church to accept Christ's standard, without modification.

Of course, it is one thing to discuss extraordinary love as an abstract concept and quite another to determine just how that love should look when applied to a given situation. The best way, I believe, to understand the *affect* of extraordinary love is to witness the *effect,* or behavior, that such love produces in and through the lives of those who possess it. Allow me to draw from my own testimony to illustrate the point.

I come from a long line of woodworkers. This is particularly true of the men on my mother's side of the family. My maternal grandfather and his brother were both master craftsmen who provided for their families by building everything from houses to furniture. As old-school artisans, they were capable of crafting extraordinary pieces without the aid of electrically or battery-powered tools. I still marvel when I think of what they were able to produce with nothing more than arm strength, sharp tools, and skilled patience.

From these men I inherited both a respect for the craft and a love for building things out of wood. Over the years, I have amassed quite a shop of my own. It is a room that is much more than just a space full of tools; it is my retreat. Another woodworker and great friend of mine calls time spent in a wood shop "saw dust therapy." I couldn't agree more. Time spent in my own shop, surrounded by the sounds of various tools and the smell of fresh saw dust, provides for me some of the most enjoyable and relaxing hours of any given day.

Yes, I love woodwork. However, for all the time, energy, and money I invest in building things, I *only* love doing it; I am not passionate about it. There is a difference. True enough, love and passion go hand in hand. It is quite possible to love something or someone, even to love deeply, and keep that love hidden from others, never allowing any external expression of that love to show itself. In other words, an individual can love and, at the same time, restrain that emotion from becoming more than a manageable, internal feeling.

Hiding one's true passion, however, is impossible. Whether the focus of one's passion is a person, cause, project, or idea it is absolutely impossible for a person to be passionate without first loving the object of his or her affection so extraordinarily that a life-defining spillover is inevitable. Simply put, without an undergirding love so strong that it creates a willingness to abandon all else for the object of one's affection, there is no passion.

Let me illustrate what I have just said by making it a bit more personal. I love woodwork enough to continue doing it, but not enough to abandon all else for it. In other words, I love it but not enough to claim honestly that I am passionate about it. However, I am not without an abiding passion. When asked about my passion, I do not have to stop and study the question. For me there is not a vast array of interests through which I must sort in order to answer. My response is exactly the same as Count Nikolaus Ludwig von Zinzendorf, the eighteenth-century Pietist missionary and founder of the Moravian Church who said, "I have but one passion; it is He [Jesus], He only."

Please understand, I say this humbly and with ample fear and trembling. For while my passion is real, so too are my feet of clay. I have failed enough to know that I have no cause or right to claim a life that has always kept track with my passion, no matter how sincerely I may hold to it. The words of Jesus are fully descriptive of my own daily struggles: "the spirit is willing, but the flesh is weak" (Matthew 26:41b). But know as well, I lay claim to this passion sincerely and unashamedly. There are many people and things I love. There are numerous causes I believe in and would gladly affix my name to. But Christ alone is my passion. If there is anyone who deserves my attention, my loyalty, my time, my money, my efforts, my adoration, my devotion, my worship, and praise, it is Jesus Christ. I cannot imagine life without Him. I would most gladly sacrifice all else to please Him. Further, my passion extends to all the specific ways in which Christ has chosen to express Himself through me: my wife, my family, the church, missions, preaching, teaching, and mentoring. Passion for Christ provides me with the complete earthly fulfillment of Jesus' promise that in Him, I "have life, and have it abundantly" (John 10:10b). In short, I gladly join with the apostle Paul in declaring, "For to me, to live is Christ" (Philippians 1:21a).

The point is this: the only love conducive to Jesus' prescribed standard for discipleship is a love so extraordinary that it cannot be contained. As an uncontainable response to the love of Christ, true passion (the very expression of Jesus' standard of discipleship) cannot help but overflow the disciple as abandoned surrender to the Lord that becomes visible in lifestyle, works, and words. Extraordinary love produces an effect so powerful that lesser standards of discipleship are not considered; rather, they are discarded as untenable. While it is possible to live without some loves ever being realized, the extraordinary love that makes Christ the object of its affection renders life apart from full surrender to Him unthinkable. Simply put, there is no true passion that is not first motivated and undergirded by extraordinary love. So, the bottom-line question is, how much do you actually love Jesus? The answer will define your passion.

True Passion Faithfully Adheres to Uncompromising Allegiance

Just as true passion rejects lesser standards for discipleship that attempt to reduce the demands made by Jesus, true passion accepts the cross alone as the foundation of its outflow, for it was Christ's finished work on the cross that made provision for man and woman to have a disciple's relationship with God. The cross of Christ, therefore, informs the response of the truly passionate to and in the world.

However, simply to say the cross of Christ informs the truly passionate may not be enough to accurately make the point. Many in the contemporary church appear to assume that there are multiple crosses—or, at least, versions of the cross—to which disciples may appeal as the basis of their commitments to Jesus. In a rather prophetic article that appeared first in *The Alliance Witness* of 1946, then again in 2000, A. W. Tozer (1897–1963) spoke of two crosses. He labeled these crosses, "the old cross and the new." Because this article so thoroughly addresses the subject of this section, I have decided to include it in full as the primary text of this section. Read it carefully, keeping in mind that the "old cross" is the true cross, the cross of genuine passion.

> All unannounced and mostly undetected there has come in modern times a new cross into popular evangelical circles. It is like the old cross, but different; the likenesses are superficial, the differences fundamental.

> From this new cross has sprung a new philosophy of the Christian life; and from that new philosophy has come a new evangelical technique, a new type of meeting and a new kind of preaching. This new evangelism employs the same language as the old, but its content is not the same and its emphasis not as before.

> The old cross would have no truck with the world. For Adam's proud flesh it meant the end of the journey. It carried into effect the sentence imposed by the law of Sinai. The new cross is not opposed to the human race; rather, it is a friendly pal and, if understood aright, it is the source of oceans of good clean fun and innocent enjoyment. It lets Adam live without interference. His life motivation is unchanged; he still lives for his own pleasure, only now he takes delight in singing choruses and watching religious movies instead

of singing bawdy songs and drinking hard liquor. The accent is still on enjoyment, though the fun is now on a higher plane morally if not intellectually.

The new cross encourages a new and entirely different evangelistic approach. The evangelist does not demand abnegation of the old life before a new life can be received. He preaches not contrasts but similarities. He seeks to key into public interest by showing that Christianity makes no unpleasant demands; rather, it offers the same thing the world does, only on a higher level. Whatever the sin-mad world happens to be clamouring after at the moment is cleverly shown to be the very thing the gospel offers; only the religious product is better.

The new cross does not slay the sinner, it redirects him. It gears him into a cleaner and jollier way of living and saves his self-respect. To the self-assertive it says, "Come and assert yourself for Christ." To the egotist it says, "Come and do your boasting in the Lord." To the thrill seeker it says, "Come and enjoy the thrill of Christian fellowship." The Christian message is slanted in the direction of the current vogue in order to make it acceptable to the public.

The philosophy behind this kind of thing may be sincere, but its sincerity does not save it from being false. It is false because it is blind. It misses completely all the meaning of the cross.

The old cross is a symbol of death. It stands for the abrupt violent end of a human being. The man in Roman times who took up his cross and started down the road had already said goodbye to his friends. He was not coming back. He was going out to have his life redirected; he was going out to have it ended. The cross made no compromise, modified nothing, spared nothing; it slew all of the man, completely and for good. It did not try to keep on good terms with its victim. It struck cruel and hard, and when it had finished its work the man was no more.

The race of Adam is under a death sentence. There is no commutation, and no escape. God cannot approve any of the fruits of sin, however innocent they may appear or beautiful to the eyes of men. God salvages the individual by liquidating him and then raising him again to newness of life.

That evangelism which draws friendly parallels between the ways of God and the ways of men is false to the Bible and cruel to the souls of its hearers. The faith of Christ does not parallel the world; it intersects it. In coming to Christ we do not bring our old life up onto a higher plane; we leave it at the cross. The corn of wheat must fall into the ground and die.

We who preach the gospel must not think of ourselves as public relations agents sent to establish good will between Christ and the world. We must not imagine ourselves commissioned to make Christ acceptable to Big Business, or the Press, the World of Sports, or Modern Education. We are not diplomats but prophets, and our message is not a compromise but an ultimatum.

God offers life, but not an improved old life. The life he offers is life out of death. It stands always on the far side of the cross. Whoever would possess it must pass under the rod. He must repudiate himself and concur in God's just sentence against him.

What does this mean to the individual, the condemned man who would find life in Christ Jesus? How can this theology be translated into life? Simply, he must repent and believe. He must forsake his sins and then go on to forsake himself. Let him cover nothing, defend nothing, excuse nothing. Let him not seek to make terms with God, but let him bow his head before the stroke of God's stern displeasure.

Having done this let him gaze with simple trust upon the risen Saviour, and from Him will come life and rebirth and cleansing and power. The cross that ended the earthly life of Jesus now puts an end to the sinner, and the power that raised Christ from the dead now raises him to a new life along with Christ.

To any who may object to this or count it merely a narrow and private view of truth let me say, God has set His hallmark of approval upon this message from Paul's day to the present. Whether stated in these exact words or not, this has been the content of all preaching that has brought life and power to the world through the centuries. The mystics, the reformers, the revivalists have put their emphasis here, and signs and wonders and mighty operations of the Holy Ghost gave witness to God's approval.

Dare we, the heirs of such a legacy of power, tamper with the truth? Dare we with our stubby pencils erase the lines of the blueprint or alter the pattern shown us in the mount? May God forbid. Let us preach the old cross and we will know the old power.[122]

Nothing of substance can be added to Tozer's words that will make them any clearer or to the point. As he puts it, "The old cross would have *no truck* with the world." And so it is with true passion for Christ. Bound to the old cross, true passion has "no truck" with any version of the cross that minimizes the demand and high privilege of joining in the sufferings of Christ. Genuinely passionate disciples understand well and accept fully the words of Scripture which declare, "For to you it has been

---

[122]Reprinted from *The Alliance Weekly*, Vol. 81 Number 41, October 12, 1946. Used with permission, The Archives of The Christian and Missionary Alliance. The original article can be found online at http://www.cmalliance.org/resources/archives/alifepdf/AW-1946-10-12.

granted for Christ's sake, not only to believe in Him, but also to suffer for His sake" (Philippians 1:29).

True Passion Embodies Godly Anguish

It may be troubling to some that in discussing true passion, so much emphasis has been given to including the important defining element—suffering. Some may be troubled by the insistence that without a willingness to suffer for the name and cause of Christ, a person cannot rightly claim to be a passionate disciple of Jesus Christ. Others may be troubled by the very fact that they have never been called upon to suffer for their faith, that they have much and live comfortably.

In reality, suffering is not just about physical hardship, danger, or deprivation. If you have never been in such overt circumstances, thank God for your blessings. But know also that there are numerous forms of suffering that have little to do with physical hardship, ways of suffering that many in the church seek to avoid with the same energy they would exert if placed under a sentence of death. I speak of experiencing godly anguish because of the sinful state of the world around them.

Once more, I have chosen the words of a well-known preacher to clarify my point. The following is from an audio recording of a sermon preached by David Wilkerson (1931–2011), founding pastor of New York City's Times Square Church and author of the 1963 bestseller *The Cross and the Switchblade*. Read it carefully, asking God to let it truly speak to your heart.

> I look at the whole religious scene today and I all I see are inventions and ministries of man and flesh. . . . I see more of the world coming into the church and impacting the church rather than the church impacting the world. I see the music taking over the house of God. I see entertainment taking over the house of God . . . .

> Whatever happened to anguish in the house of God? Whatever happened to anguish in ministry? . . . Anguish means extreme pain and distress. . . . Acute, deeply felt inner pain because of conditions about you, in you. The agony of God's [own] heart.

> . . . *All true passion is born out of anguish. All true passion for Christ comes out of a baptism of anguish.* You search the Scripture and you'll find that when God determined to recover a ruined situation He would share His own anguish for what [He] saw happening to His church and His people.

> Does it matter to you today . . . that . . . the church, is now married to the world?

> There is going to be no renewal, no revival, no awakening until we are willing to let [God] once again break us [to the point of anguish].[123]

Those truly passionate about Christ are passionate about the things that touch the heart of God. They love what He loves, hate what He Hates, and share His heartbreak over those who continue to reject Him. These folk tend to see with the eyes of God and react with the heart of God. They not only see the sin around them, they feel its consequences and are driven by what they experience, compelled to sacrificial service out of passion for the Savior. The question then is not so much are we willing to suffer for Christ in the most extreme forms? Rather, it is, are we willing to be pained as Christ is pained over the conditions of the lost world and compromising church just outside our doors? If we are unable to answer yes to the second question, we are disqualified from even attempting to answer the second. And certainly, we cannot claim true passion.

---

[123]David Wilkerson, "A Call to Anguish," YouTube Web site, Windows Media Player Video file, 7:25, http://www.youtube.com/watch?v=lGMG_PVaJoI, (accessed June 20, 2011). Uploaded on May 9, 2009 by http://ellerslie.com.

Conclusion

Passion—accurately defined, fully understood, and willingly undertaken—is a powerful thing. It is powerful because it is the most complete expression of obedience to the standard Jesus established for discipleship. True passion touches the heart of the Savior and results in the overwhelming blessings of God upon the passionate; blessings that are powerful within themselves for the value they bring to the church. Imagine for a moment the impact on your church and its ministry if the following short list of blessings overflowing from true passion were active in the Body right now.

True Passion Keeps the Focus of the Church's Greatest Love on Jesus

In extraordinary fashion, Jesus will be lifted up and maintained as the central object of the church's supreme affection. The church will continue to be a place where love abounds, but in comparison to its affection for Christ, all other loves will seem little more than disdain. Love will never be absent from the church, it will simply become the outflow of Christ loving through the Body.

True Passion Will Clarify the Church's Relationship with Jesus

While the Lord described His relationship with believers using a number of word images, the bottom line is, we are disciples and Jesus is the Master. It is in this disciple/master context that every follower of Jesus should hear the Master's words: "A disciple is not above his teacher, nor a slave above his master. It is enough for the disciple that he become like his teacher, and the slave like his master. If they have called the head of the house Beelzebul, how much more will they malign the members of his household!" (Matthew 10:24–25). The passionate church will accept and understand its relationship with the Master based on this truth. It will simultaneously rejoice in being called children and sheep, while accepting the difficult implications of being servant-disciples who must bear the reproaches leveled against their Master. Their passion will remain undiminished even when they are ridiculed, excluded, or made to suffer. Therefore, they are never ". . . surprised at the fiery ordeal among you, which comes upon you for your testing, as though some strange thing were happening to you" (1 Peter 4:12).

True Passion Will Help the Church Make Sense of the Struggles

It has been stressed repeatedly that in order for passion to be true passion, suffering must be included in its definition. For many believers, the concept of passion is an exciting one until suffering becomes part of the mix. Yet, if suffering is excluded from the meaning, passion is reduced to little more than mere excitement.

The difficulty with suffering is that it seems to make no sense, at least when our own circumstances make it personal. However, we all know (or at least know of) truly passionate saints of God who have endured intense sufferings and emerged with their faith intact, much stronger for the experience. Their faces light any room they enter; their stories are always shared with humble sensitivity, but nonetheless joyfully. We are blessed by them but, at the same time, wonder how it is possible that they retain such positive spirits despite the seeming injustice of it all.

Trust me; I too have raised the same question, along with multitudes of others. One such struggling seeker is Laura Story, a singer songwriter from Spartanburg, South Carolina. In 1996, Laura's husband, Martin, was diagnosed with a brain tumor. The months that followed his diagnosis were filled with suffering, anxiety, and uncertainty about his future. On several occasions, it seemed that Martin would not make it. During this period, Laura was flooded with questions as she struggled to make sense of Martin's disease and her own pain. In the end, Martin miraculously recovered. Today, both Laura and Martin attribute his victory over cancer to God's answers to multiple prayers, as He intervened through medical procedures enabled by divine power.

Laura's testimony speaks for many of us when she recounts, "I spent my whole life singing, 'Tis so sweet to trust in Jesus,' but until Jesus took me through something where my only option was to trust Him, I didn't really know that sweetness."[124] Further, she says, "Though I've doubted, His grasp has never released, never slipped. He's remained completely faithful to me. He has proven that He really is my foundation and my hope."[125]

At the end of her ordeal, Laura wrote a song entitled "Blessings." The song captures what passionate believers have known for ages. They help make sense of the struggles.

In beautifully penned lyrics, Laura speaks of the human tendency to pray for those things we believe will achieve the most immediate and comfortable results, convinced that what we ask God for is exactly what we need. Yet, very often, God's responses seem to include everything but the immediate and comfortable. In fact, sometimes the struggles only intensify.

Laura reminds us of two important things. First, God loves His children too much "to give us lesser things."[126] God's answers focus on meeting our needs in ways that sharpen our awareness of who He is and deepen our relationship with Him. While fulfilling our specific requests might provide some immediate relief, it is only in seeing God more clearly and knowing God more intimately that we will find relief and ultimately be able to make sense of our struggle. Any answer from God that simply relieves without deepening an

---

[124]Laura Story, interview, http://www.lyricshall.com/biography/Laura+Story/ (accessed July 6, 2011).
[125]Ibid.
[126] Laura Story, "Blessings," http://www.lyricshall.com/lyrics/Laura+Story/Blessings/ (accessed July 6, 2011).

understanding is a "lesser thing." And God loves us too much for that sort of partial answer. God's desire is that we come to know Him as the One who loves us so much that, while we may be faced with the consuming, "It is of the Lord's mercies that *we are not consumed,* because his compassions fail not" (Lamentations 3:22, KJV, italics added).

Second, Laura asks a profound and thought-provoking question: "What if trials of this life are Your mercies in disguise?"[127] I told you it was thought provoking. Perhaps this is a good time to reread Lamentations 3:22 within the context of the nine verses that follow. Do that now. Then, as the psalmist says, "Selah"—pause, lift the words up to God, and meditate on them.

"It is of the LORD'S mercies that we are not consumed, because his compassions fail not. They are new every morning: great is thy faithfulness. The LORD is my portion, saith my soul; therefore will I hope in him. The LORD is good unto them that wait for him, to the soul that seeketh him. It is good that a man should both hope and quietly wait for the salvation of the LORD. It is good for a man that he bear the yoke in his youth. He sitteth alone and keepeth silence, because he hath borne it upon him. He putteth his mouth in the dust; if so be there may be hope. He giveth his cheek to him that smiteth him: he is filled full with reproach. *For the LORD will not cast off for ever: But though he cause grief, yet will he have compassion according to the multitude of his mercies*" (Lamentations 3:22–32 KJV, italics added).

For all the reasons given, true passion is a powerful thing. There is, however, one last powerful benefit to be gained from true passion, one that makes all the others pale by comparison. It is this: a church where true passion exists would surely be a church Jesus would attend.

---

[127] Ibid.

Chapter 9

Two Closing Questions

Whether we fully realize it or not, nothing is more beloved by God and precious in this earth than the universal church of the Lord Jesus Christ. For the lost, it is the single venue through which God has designed to engage human beings in their lostness, bringing hope, light, and life. To the redeemed, the church is indispensable as family, fortress, and fraternity. Among all the institutions on the planet, the church alone bears the image of Christ, possesses the gospel of true salvation, and enjoys empowerment for living through the Holy Spirit. Only the universal church of Jesus Christ is assured of enduring strength, final victory, and eternal existence. In fact, the church alone can trace its roots back to Calvary and the atoning death of God's Son on the cross. Let it be shouted to the very foundations of existence, "The church is loved and precious!"

Even so, at the same time the universal Body of Christ is loved and precious, in its local and individual assemblies it can often be very frustrating. While the words *loved, precious*, and *frustrating* might sound like something of a paradox, it is nonetheless a reality. Parents, for instance, understand all too well the intertwining of love and frustration. They know that the children they love more than life itself can on occasion be the most frustrating creatures in their lives. This is precisely the case because parents *do* love their children, thus making some of the child's behaviors enormously frustrating. The parent does not cease to love because they are frustrated, nor do they view their children as any less precious. In fact, because of their love, parents seek to address the frustration by doing something about their children's actions. Sometimes, their well-intentioned actions only serve to deepen the frustration. They find themselves like the small-town newspaper that tried desperately to correct a typographical error it had made in a classified ad. It was in a "Dear Abby" column that the incident first gained broad attention, illustrating how good intentions can sometimes move things from bad to worse to horrible.

> Monday: FOR SALE—R. D. Jones has one sewing machine for sale. Phone 948-xxxx after 7 p.m. and ask for Mrs. Kelly who lives with him cheap.

> Tuesday: NOTICE—We regret having erred in R. D. Jones' ad yesterday. It should have read: One sewing machine for sale. Cheap. Phone 948-xxxx and ask for Mrs. Kelly who lives with him after 7 p.m.

> Wednesday: NOTICE—R. D. Jones has informed us that he has received several annoying phone calls because of the error we made in his classified ad yesterday. His ad stands corrected as follows: FOR SALE—R. D. Jones has one sewing machine for sale. Cheap. Phone 948-xxxx p.m. and ask for Mrs. Kelly who loves with him.

> Thursday: NOTICE—I, R. D. Jones, have no sewing machine for sale. I SMASHED IT. Don't call 948-xxxx, as the telephone has been disconnected. I have not been carrying on with Mrs. Kelly. Until yesterday, she was my housekeeper, but she quit.[128]

R. D. Jones notwithstanding, the analogy of parent and child fully capsulizes the motivation for and message of this

---

[128]Charles R. Swindoll, *Laugh Again: Experience Outrageous Joy*, (Waco, Texas: Word Books, 1992), 230. Quote taken from the California Newspaper Association.

book. That is, it has been my purpose to focus on the supreme love God has for the church, the precious and elevated place God has granted to the church while it remains on earth, and the deep devotion every part of the Body is called to give to the whole. I have sought to accomplish these things without denying the problems that often arise, and the frustrations they can cause. Hopefully, to some degree, this purpose has been achieved.

My overriding desire is that the content of this work will stimulate discussion. While I am certain that very little, if any, of what I have written can be construed as new information, I am hopeful that its presentation and the questions raised within it will cause the reader to ask more questions and dig a bit deeper. For example, what about my assertions regarding the *"what is?"* and *"what to do?"* questions? What are your thoughts related to the models of church order and structure as I proposed them? What are your thoughts regarding what I said concerning kingdom law and citizenship? Any questions there? How about the arguments regarding spiritual gifts as an avenue to ministry and worship, the place of the worship experience for teaching important spiritual truths, and the proper use of terms to honestly describe the reality of one's commitment to Christ? Whether you agree with my positions or not, it is the discussion that is important.

Because this book is designed as something of a think piece written to stimulate discussion, and because it is largely based on a single question—where would Jesus go to church?—I want to close it with two additional and final questions.

Would Jesus Go to My Church?

The first thing to note about this question is what I am *not* asking. I am not asking if Jesus would attend your church—*if.* You know what I mean. Would Jesus attend my church *if* this, that, or the other were changed or different? Of course He would attend if everything were properly in order. What I am asking is, would Jesus attend your church just like it is right now, with nothing altered, nothing changed?

Perhaps you are not sure just how to answer. Let me share with you a very practical and, I believe, effective way to know. If you have access to a copy of your church's budget, get one and look it over carefully, keeping in mind that all the church's financial resources are, in fact, God's. Note how the money is being distributed by categories and how it is being spent. Then recall the words of Jesus, "For where your treasure is, there your heart will be also" (Luke 12:34). Without doubt, money is part of what the church regards as treasure.

Next, take a long look at how the church's treasure—God's resources—is being expended. First, where is it being placed? Is it going into investment instruments designed to be left alone indefinitely for the sake of earning? Or is it being spent on missional ministry—what, in most cases, was it given to support? If you discover large interest-bearing accounts, ask yourself, at what point did the mission of the church change to include functioning as a financial institution? At what point did God start allowing us to call for giving that is intended only for building financial strength as opposed to doing ministry? Hear me clearly; there are numerous banking institutions designed to protect and increase financial security through investments. The church is not one of them! We are a missional ministry institution. The church is a repository for God's possessions, given by God's people, for the purpose of doing God's work. If your church has a building fund—build. If it has a benevolence fund—be benevolent. If it has an organ fund—buy the thing! Remember, saving and hoarding in the church, unless it is for a godly, God-directed purpose the church actually intends to accomplish, is not part of biblical revelation.

Second, check the evidence to see how the money in your church *is* being spent. In fact, simplify the process. Go immediately to the outreach categories in the budget. Once more, consider Scripture as you look. For example, Jesus said, "For the Son of Man has come to seek and to save that which was lost"

(Luke 19:10). Jesus further declared, "as the Father has sent Me, I also send you" (John 20:21b). The Lord's priority was and is seeking and saving the lost; He commissioned us, the church, as participants in this priority. With this truth in mind, determine what percentage of your church's budget has been allocated to the Lord's priorities, namely, missions and evangelism. Look at the other items being funded by God's resources. Which ones are receiving the lion's share? These are the things your church treasures. Where that treasure is, there the church's heart will remain, no matter what it may claim to the contrary. Be assured, a church that does not share the priorities of its Head and holds as treasure anything other than what matches His heart will be devoid of His presence.

There is one other issue to be addressed when answering the question, would Jesus attend my church? It may sound strange, but it is important. Ask yourself, would Jesus be *allowed* in my church? I told you it would sound strange.

Perhaps you are familiar with the account of a man who seated himself on the front steps of a large suburban church early one Sunday morning. As the story goes, a dirty, disheveled, and obviously homeless man was discovered on the front steps of a large church just as the members were entering for worship. He made no fuss or overt spectacle of himself. Only occasionally did he ask a passerby for coins, water, or a bite to eat. Everyone pushed past him. Most people ignored him; some, however, voiced their disgust in tones they no doubt intended for him to hear. After a while, a delegation of men from the church came to remove him from the premises, forcibly if necessary. The man quietly surrendered to them and left.

Inside the church, worship began. All progressed as normal until, at the front entrance to the sanctuary, a door opened and the homeless man entered. The instrumentalists hit wrong notes, the choir stumbled in their singing, and the congregation sucked in a collective breath. Then all went tensely silent as the man turned and quietly walked toward the platform. The people were too stunned to react. But nothing could match the electricity that shocked the crowd when the man began to remove his hat, his coat, his wig, and his makeup. It was the pastor! He stepped to the pulpit and quoted the following verse of Scripture from Matthew 25:40: "The King will answer and say to them, 'Truly I say to you, *to the extent that you did it to one of these brothers of Mine, even the least of them, you did it to Me*'" (italics added).

While I know that the broad lesson intended by Jesus was offered within the context of commending faithful saints who had treated others well, the reverse imagery used by the pastor was spot on. It drives home the sad truth that there are those churches where Jesus would not be truly welcome were He to walk in next Sunday.

The point is this: as a body of disciples the church is fundamentally called to follow Jesus—wherever He goes. The words of Jesus are unambiguous regarding this fact: "Then Jesus said *to His disciples,* 'If anyone wishes to come after Me, he must deny himself, and take up his cross and *follow Me*'" (Matthew 16:24, italics added). To obey the call to follow Jesus means that His disciples will go where He goes. Further, they will love those He loves and touch those He touches, always seeking to retrieve them for the Kingdom of God, no matter their state or appearance.

Disciples are encouraged to count the costs before undertaking to follow Jesus. So, it is important to be familiar with where Jesus' journey took Him, realizing that this will be the disciple's journey as well. Jesus traveled through towns, villages, and rural byways. He moved with equal fluidity among the religious and social elite, as well as the outcast and downtrodden who were most scared and soiled by life. Along the way, Jesus did the unpopular, embraced the untouchable, advocated for the voiceless, and included the excluded. All of this He did while cloaked in human flesh in order to fully identify with those He encountered, and assuming the appearance of a servant so as to make clear His purpose among humanity. This is to be the disciple's life as well, for following Jesus demands more than simply making the journey; it requires joint participation with Christ in the lives and experiences along the way.

When disciples truly follow Christ, lives are changed. Interestingly, it is often the lives of the disciples that are most changed. As these Christ followers participate in the journey, they see their Lord as they have never seen Him before. They witness His power, compassion, and love in practical expressions they never dreamed possible. As they witness human transformation when the gospel of Jesus is preached to the poor, when captives are released by holy decree, when blindness from sin and darkness is turned to sight by the illumination of the Holy Spirit, and when prisoners are set free by the power of God (Luke 4:18), these folk are changed forever. Suddenly, lonely hospital rooms, sad mortuaries, dingy village huts, halfway houses, and rescue missions become cathedrals of praise, places where God is met and worshiped. Dirty hands and faces, diseased bodies, and impoverished people are turned to objects of affection instead of sad specimens to be avoided lest the dirt rub off. Definitions of ministry, sacrifice, surrender, and discipleship are changed forever. The supposed "radical" expressions of faith become the normal state of affairs.

As much as anything else, people who follow Jesus as participants in His journey will gain a completely different perspective on beauty. It is not that the ugliness of sin will become any less ugly to them; instead, these folk will be illumined to see the potential for beauty that lies beneath the ugly outer appearance. You see, one of the miracles of the journey is that it not only develops the heart and mind of Christ in His followers, it also produces in them His eyes and ears. These followers begin to see and hear what Jesus sees and hears. When they see a filthy, destitute person on the steps, they do not miss the reality of his or her condition. They simply view it as an ugliness covering from view the beauty of what is yet to be created when Jesus passes by. Then they are drawn to action as participants in Christ's journey. After all, that's what it means to follow Jesus.

So, here is the question. Would the Jesus I have described be welcome in your church? Remember, if He were to appear for a visit, He might very well bring with Him the ragged and ruff, the broken and destitute, or perhaps even the social elite who formerly preyed on some of those in the congregation. You know He will demand that they be received and that all in the church who claim to be His followers welcome them and join alongside them on the journey. Again, I ask, would He be welcome?

Would Jesus Be Comfortable Going to Church with Me?

It should surprise no one that the discussion ultimately comes down to this question. Asking it is unavoidable because, as has been stated time and again throughout this book, the church is a single body comprised of multiple parts. Therefore, any question related to the church as a whole is essentially an issue that includes each individual member. So, what is the best way to go about answering the question? As I did in the previous section, allow me to suggest a simple place to start. Look back at the previous section and make all the things said there about the church as a whole specific to yourself.

First, recall that the question is not framed with the conjunction, *if*. The question should be asked based on your life right now, without regard for the presupposed, hypothetical, *if* this or that were different. In other words, would Jesus feel comfortable attending church with you just as you are right now, with nothing altered, nothing changed?

Now, take a close look at your heart as it reflects your treasure. Little speaks as plainly about your true spiritual heart condition as the proximity between your treasure and what the Lord Jesus holds dear. Honestly and biblically consider whether or not what you treasure aligns your heart with the priorities of the Church's Head. Is there a difference there, even a minor one? Do you treasure pride of position and material possessions? Compare those things with Jesus' heart priorities as evidenced by His actions: "who, although He existed in the form of God, did not regard equality with God a thing to be grasped, but emptied Himself, taking the form of a bond-servant, and being made in the likeness of men. Being found in appearance as a man, He humbled Himself by becoming obedient to the point of death, even death on a cross" (Philippians 2:6–8). Do you treasure security and personal comforts? Take a look at Jesus' description of His earthly conditions. "And Jesus said to him, 'The foxes have holes and the birds of the air have nests, but the Son of Man has nowhere to lay His head'" (Luke 9:58). Do you treasure a degree of authority, recognition, and status? Pay attention to Isaiah's prophetic description of the Messiah in regard to such things. "He has no stately form or majesty that we should look upon Him, nor appearance that we should be attracted to Him. He was despised and forsaken of men, a man of sorrows and acquainted with grief; and like one from whom men hide their face He was despised, and we did not esteem Him" (Isaiah 53:2b–3).

Now it's time to assess the proximity of your heart to Christ's by honestly comparing your treasures with those of the Lord Jesus, knowing that any and all gaps discovered *must* be closed. Nearness and approximations are not enough, for they are insufficient to please the Lord. One may narrow the gap, but until it is closed, it is still a separation. The only thing that is sufficient was made plain by Jesus: "It is *enough* for the disciple that he become like his teacher, and the slave like his master" (Matthew 10:25a, italics added). The Greek word translated "enough" can also be rendered "sufficient." The phrase "become like his teacher (master)" implies the added phrase "in every way." The result is a statement from Jesus to His disciples to this effect: "It is sufficient (the only thing sufficient) for the disciple that he become like his teacher/master in every way." In other words, anything less than becoming completely like the master is insufficient. The gaps must be closed.

The gap-closing process is often a long and difficult one, but it is never an impossible one. Jesus said, "A pupil is not above his teacher; but everyone, after he has been fully trained, will be like his teacher" (Luke 6:40). The promise of our Lord—the Head of the church—stands as true: every disciple, when he or she is trained to maturity, will become like the Master. Perhaps this is a good time to ask, what part of "everyone" and "will be" is difficult to understand? The promise is made, the Master is able, the gap can and must be closed. It is now up to you to admit and yield.

Finally, if you consider and call yourself a true Christ follower, are you willingly following Him wherever He goes? Have you balked at certain destinations? Have you detoured from the obvious paths of Christ's travels in order to avoid particular places and peoples? Do you look for a course to follow that is less costly, a bit more secure, and far more comfortable than the route Jesus takes? Do you somehow imagine that as long you and the Lord wind up at the same destination it is unimportant just how you got there?

Follow means follow, step for step. Jesus used the word *follow* as a command several times in the New Testament. Each usage comes from the Greek word, *akoloutheō*, generally translated, "to be in the same way with," "to follow one who precedes," or "to accompany." However, to these meanings can be added another rather enlightening definition. Namely, "to join another as his attendant." Look over each of these definitions of "follow" and ask yourself, how is it possible to obey the elements of the command without always being with Jesus on the journey? Can you be "in the same way" or "accompany" Jesus unless you are there with Him? Can you attend to Him without being in His company? The answers are obvious, and so is the bottom line. To follow Jesus is to be right behind Him, making every step He makes, no matter where those steps may take you. His journey is your journey, no matter how He maps it out. If you are not in step, get back on track.

Debating whether or not Christ would go to church with you may seem rather foolish. My intention has not been to encourage a waste of time but to provide an object lesson regarding the importance of evaluating our own contributions to the frustrations often encountered within the church. It has been to help us never lose sight of the fact that any discussion of the frustrations with the church must begin with an honest appraisal of our own, individual spiritual condition. Let's face it, we all bring things to church. Sometimes, as I have heard it said, the devil himself rides in on the shoulders of believers. Why not be assured that we are not contributing to potential frustration within the Body? Let's know for certain that Jesus alone accompanies us when we enter His house.

Conclusion

As a university professor, I quite often hear students complain about writing papers. Most of the time their complaints center around the difficulty of getting started: writing that first sentence or paragraph. I, on the other hand, find the greatest struggle to be in concluding, especially closing the work altogether. It is important to me to find just the right words to capture the essence of all that has been written, and what is true for a paper is equally true for a book.

As I considered how to close this book, I came across a statement used as a creed by the Fusion[129] program of the International Mission Board, SBC. It is a powerful declaration that captures everything this book has sought to set forth. With it, I bring my thoughts to a close. I ask that you read it closely and carefully. As you do, frame them within the context of these familiar words from Jesus, the Head of the church. Then Jesus said to His disciples, "If anyone wishes to come after Me, he must deny himself, and take up his cross and follow Me. For whoever wishes to save his life will lose it; but whoever loses his life for My sake will find it. For what will it profit a man if he

---

[129]Fusion is a student ministry that blends personal and spiritual disciplines with challenging global opportunities for ministry leadership and practice.

gains the whole world and forfeits his soul? Or what will a man give in exchange for his soul?" (Matthew 16:24–26).

FUSION CREED

As a follower of Christ, I am called
not to comfort or success but to obedience.

Consequently my life is to be defined
not by what I do but by who I am.

Henceforth, I will proclaim His name without fear,
follow Him without regret, and serve Him
without compromise.

Thus to obey is my objective, to suffer is expected,
His glory is my reward.

To Christ Alone, be all power, all honor, and glory
that the world may know.

Amen.

Afterword

You are at the end of the book, which actually brings you back to the initial question: where would Jesus go to church? Perhaps you have already framed your answer. If so, good for you. On the other hand, you may be waiting on me to do that for you. I believe, however, it will prove most beneficial if you think through the material and craft your own response (sorry, I can't avoid the professor in me). To help you do that, take a look back at a handful of closing statements from each of the book's chapters. Then, in the space below those statements, write your own composite answer to the question.

Chapter 1

If Jesus were walking the earth in flesh today and seeking a church to attend, He would be most comfortable worshiping with people whose understanding of church is undergirded by a clear knowledge of what and who they are, as the determining basis for all they do. In this environment, Jesus would enjoy the highest likelihood of being the sole object of worship.

Chapter 2

Ministry is still the heartbeat of the Savior. A church that is focused on engaging God in Spirit-led worship, and is singular in its purpose to be a biblical "house of prayer," can expect the spontaneous expressions of God's presence evidenced in genuine worship for those within the Body, and meaningful ministry to those without.

Chapter 3

The church in Acts lived out two primary ministry functions. These two functions were enough to produce the extraordinary church of the first century. First, the church called out God's people to public identity with Jesus Christ, His teachings, and His church through the full and faithful exposition of Scripture. Second, the church was a place where changed people were led to develop new allegiances and devotions, such as consistent growth in biblical truth, commitment to unimpaired Body unity, maturity in spiritual disciplines, and a worshiping relationship with God that exalts and glorifies Jesus Christ as Lord.

Chapter 4

The church is intended by Christ to facilitate ministry that accomplishes the will and desires of God. This is seen in at least three ways:

- The Body is interconnected—Body to Head and each member to every other member—and in this interconnectedness it matures as individual members provide ministry to one another through their spiritual gifts.
- The Body is called and fashioned to accomplish the great desire of God to be made known to the entire world.
- The Body is to be led by individuals whose lives exemplify the highest ideals of holiness as set forth in Scripture. The great truth overarching all of this is: Jesus is supreme as Lord of His church.

Because He is a sovereign Lord and fully deserving of the honors of royalty, Jesus cannot help but feel most at home among people who realize His supremacy, not only by celebrating His deity but by submitting to His full control over every detail of the church's life and function.

Chapter 5

The church must be constantly vigilant to assess honestly its fidelity to kingdom principles (laws) and judge with equal candor any possible deviations from them, as well as the motivation for those deviations. Three principles should be kept in mind as a basis for this assessment.

- When the church gathers it does so as a kingdom family.
- The laws of the kingdom are never to be preempted in our corporate assemblies—including worship—for the sake of personal preferences or on the basis of cultural counsel.
- God has purposes for worship that reach far beyond singing and preaching, purposes that include the expectation of actually practicing the things we preach.

Chapter 6

The most effective way to reach the unreached is with a missionary commitment and methodology guided by a missional mindset. Congregations with a missional mindset discover that local ministry and global missions do not compete with one another, simply because the two things are, in both nature and practice, one and the same. These churches have learned that God blesses an Acts 1:8 vision. Label such churches what you will; the truth is they are relational mission outposts. Their testimonies provide compelling evidence that the only mindset equal to the church's task on the single global mission field of the twenty-first century is one that is fully missional.

Chapter 7

The task of making mature, missional disciples is the most effective method for accomplishing church growth and/or revitalization. When the church has a missional mindset, missional thinking and ministry will flow as a natural consequence, and so too will the benefits. The missionary heart of God will show itself to the world around as God's people, without the need for continued prodding, reflect the example of the church's Head—"the Word [who] became flesh, and dwelt among us, and we saw His glory, glory as of the only begotten from the Father, full of grace and truth" (John 1:14).

Chapter 8

True passion is powerful. It yields extraordinary fruit for the individual believer and the church corporately. The reason is not so much because of heightened emotion; rather, it is because of heightened "Jesus awareness." Those truly passionate about Christ are passionate about the things that touch the heart of God. They love what He loves, hate what He Hates, and share His heartbreak over those who continue to reject Him. These folk tend to see with the eyes of God and react with the heart of God. They not only see the sin around them, they feel its consequences and are driven by what they experience, compelled to sacrificial service out of passion for the Savior.

Chapter 9

Disciples are commanded to follow the Master. By follow, I mean follow, step for step. Jesus used the word *follow* as a command several times in the New Testament. Each usage comes from the Greek word, *akoloutheō*, generally translated, "to be in the same way with," "to follow one who precedes," or "to accompany." To these meanings can be added another rather enlightening definition, namely, "to join another as his attendant." Look over each of these definitions of "follow" and ask yourself, how is it possible to obey the elements of the command without always being with Jesus on the journey? To follow Jesus is to be right behind Him, making every step He makes, no matter where those steps may take you. His journey is your journey, no matter how He maps it out.

Your turn: where would Jesus go to church?

_____

_____

_____

_____

_____

_____

_____

_____

_____

_____

One Last Important Matter

It would be interesting to see your answers to where Jesus would go to church. One thing is for certain, however, Jesus will build His church—*the kind He would attend*—with or without you or me. Now before that statement sounds too anticlimactic, let me hasten to add, the fact of the matter is, He intends to do it with us as co-laboring partners. However, being a partner with God in building His church requires full cooperation on our part. And I am not just talking about cooperating with God in developing the skills to lead and build Christ's church. What I speak of is far more important. I believe full cooperation with God calls for continued personal, spiritual revitalization. You see, you will never be able to revitalize anything without yourself being vital, invigorated, and energized enough to cooperate as a leader in the building process.

You may as well face it now; sometimes the nitty-gritty reality of real time, day-to-day ministry and the struggles that accompany those efforts often has a way of making you feel less like a key actor and more like a bit player in a major production for which you will ultimately be held responsible. If you are not constantly "sober" and "alert" "your adversary, the devil," will devour you (1 Peter 5:8) and all the vitality you possess! Remember, no one should ever be able to say with any degree of truth that the greatest impediment to your ministry was your lack of enthusiasm and spiritual vitality for the task.

It is with this in mind that I want to close by offering you four steps to full cooperation with God as you seek, despite the struggles, to be faithful to Christ in building a church Jesus would attend. Again, I will simply state them and urge you to meditate on them and draw your own conclusions.

- Reacquaint yourself with Jesus, your "first love."
  There is simply no substitute for intimacy with Jesus.
- Reaffirm your call.
  Assurance of God's call is a powerful motivation to faithfulness.
- Reclaim your vision.
  Ask God to let you see again the picture He gave you of your future.
- Regain your purpose.
  Ask God to once more set your life in the context of who and what He called you to be.

I am sure you will agree, enough has been said. It is now time to prove what has been written by putting these truths into practice. As you do, keep in mind what has been affirmed throughout the text: Jesus is the undisputed, single Head of the church. While it is true that Jesus uses us as leadership partners, we remain Body parts. As you hammer out these or any other principles on the anvil of ministry, stay vital and remember: "The lot is cast into the lap, But its every decision is from the LORD" (Proverbs 16:33).

Bibliography

Arends, Carolyn. "Hospitality Sweet: One of the Forgotten Keys to the Dynamic Worship of God." *Christianity Today*. October 2010.

Barth, Karl. *Sermon Illustrations*. http://www.sermon illustrations.com/a-z/d/discipleship.htm (accessed May 30, 2011).

Berstecher, John. *Sermon Illustrations*. http://www.sermon illustrations.com/a-z/c/church.htm. (accessed January 30, 2010).

Bruce, F. F. *The Spreading Flame: The Rise and Progress of Christianity from its First Beginnings to the Conversion of the English*. Grand Rapids: Eerdmans.

Callahan, Kennon L. *Effective Church Leadership*. San Francisco: HarperSanFrancisco.

Chaney, Charles L. *Church Planting at the End of the Twentieth Century*. Wheaton, IL: Tyndale House Publishers, Inc.

Collins English Dictionary: Complete & Unabridged, 10th Edition. HarperCollins Publishers. http://dictionary.reference.com/browse/passion (accessed: June 02, 2011).

Colson, Charles W. *The Body*. Nashville: Word Publishing.

Dweck, Carol. "Mindset," http://mindsetonline.com/changeyourmindset/natureofchange/index.html (accessed April 23, 2010).

Dyck, Drew. "The Leavers." *Christianity Today.* November 2010.

Elder, George P. *Sermon Illustrations.* http://www.sermon illustrations.com/a-z/c/church.htm (accessed December 14, 2010).

Eusebius. *Ecclesiastical History.* III, 37, 2–3.

Goldsworthy, G., "The Great Indicative: An Aspect of a Biblical Theology of Mission." RTR 55 (1996), 2-13. quoted in Andreas J. Köstenberger and Peter T. O'Brien, *Salvation to the Ends of the Earth: A Biblical Theology of Mission.* Downers Grove, IL: InterVarsity Press, 2001.

Gonzalez, Justo L. *The Early Church to the Dawn of the Reformation: The Early Church,* vol. 1. San Francisco: HarperSanFrancisco.

Hammond, Jeoff. "Innovative Church Planting: Re-potting underway in California." North American Mission Board Web site. http://www.namb.net/Innovative_church_planting_re-potting_under_way_in_California (accessed July 10, 2010).

Harris, Richard H. "A 20/20 Vision for the Twenty-First Century." 1.1 [on-line] http://www.namb.net/cp.NAMB.html (accessed 6 June 2002).

Hein, S. *Emotional Intelligence.* "Showing Empathy." http://eqi.org/empathy.htm#Showing Empathy (accessed July 3, 2011).

Hoefer, Herbert E. *Churchless Christianity.* Pasadena, CA: William Carey Library.

Hodges, Melvin. *Build My Church.* Chicago: Moody Press.

Holmes, Michael W., ed. *The Apostolic Fathers*, 2nd ed. Translated by J. B. Lightfoot and J. R. Harmer. "The Epistle to Diognetus." Grand Rapids; Baker Book House.

Hughes, Kent and Barbara. *Liberating Ministry from the Success Syndrome.* Carol Stream, IL: Tyndale House Publishers.

King, Martin Luther. "1963 WMU Speech." Western Michigan University Libraries, Archives and Regional History Collections. http://www.wmich.edu/library/archives/mlk/q-a.html, (accessed March 1, 2011).

Köstenberger, Andreas J. and Peter T. O'Brien. *Salvation to the Ends of the Earth: A Biblical Theology of Mission.* Downers Grove, IL: InterVarsity Press, 2001.

Leonard, Bill J. "Analysis: Southern Baptists Face the Future—and an Identity Crisis." Associated Baptist Press Web Site. http://www.abpnews.com/content/view/5341/53/ (accessed 14 July 2010).

Littel, Franklin H. *From State Church to Pluralism.* Garden City, NY: Anchor Books, Doubleday and Company.

MacGorman, Jack W. *The Gifts of the Spirit.* Nashville: Broadman Press.

McGowan, Michael. "The Heart Has Reasons: Rational Proofs Alone do Not A Christian Make." *Christianity Today.* review of Clifford Williams, *Existential Reasons for Belief in God: A Defense of Desires and Emotions for Faith.* June 2011.

Moody, Dwight L. *Sermon Illustrations.* http://www.sermon illustrations.com/a-z/d/discipleship.htm (accessed May 27, 2011).

Moring, Mark. "Pop Goes the Worship." *Christianity Today.* March 2011.

Nee, Watchman. Private letter quoted in, Bob Finley, *Reformation in Foreign Missions* Charlottesville, VA: Christian Aid Mission.

Neill, Stephen. *A History of Christian Missions*, 2nd ed. New York, NY: Penguin Books.

Niebuhr, Richard. *The Purpose of the Church and Its Ministry.* New York: Harper & Brothers.

Noll, Mark A. *Turning Points: Decisive Moments in the History of Christianity.* Grand Rapids: Baker Books.

North American Mission Board, Nehemiah Project site menu. http://www.namb.net/nehemiah/whatis.html.menu.html; Internet (accessed 17 June 2002).

_____. "Nehemiah Project: Introduction." http://www.namb.net/root/nehemiah/intro.html.NAMB.html (accessed 24 June 2002).

Oxford English Dictionary. http://www.oed.com/view/Entry/90999?redirectedFrom=identify (accessed, July 4, 2011).

Penner, Glenn. "The Limits of Statistics." *The Voice of the Martyrs Persecuted Church Weblog.* http://persecuted church.blogspot.com/2009/04/limits-of-statistics.html (accessed June 26, 2011).

Pocock, Michael, Gailyn Van Rheenen, and Douglas McConnell. *The Changing Face of World Missions: Engaging Contemporary Issues and Trends.* Grand Rapids: MI, 2005.

Purkiser, W.T. *The Gifts of the Spirit.* Kansas City, MO: Beacon Hill Press.

Rainer, Thom S. *Effective Evangelistic Churches: Successful Churches Reveal What Works and What Doesn't.* Nashville: Broadman & Holeman.

Story, Laura. "Blessings." http://www.lyricshall.com/lyrics/Laura+Story/Blessings/ (accessed July 6, 2011).

Swindoll, Charles R. *Laugh Again: Experience Outrageous Joy.* Waco, Texas: Word Books.

Thomas, Norman F., ed. *Classic Texts in Mission and World Christianity: A Reader's Companion to David Bosch's Transforming Mission,* American Society of Missiology Series, No. 20. Maryknoll, NY: Orbis Books.

Tozer, A. W. "The Old Cross and the New," *The Alliance Witness* 12. September, 2000. http://www.christian-witness.org/archives/van2000/tozer.html (accessed July 7, 2011).

Vincent, Marvin R. *Word Studies in the New Testament.* e-Sword freeware. http://www.sword.net (accessed January 14, 2011).

Wagner, C. Peter. *Your Spiritual Gifts Can Help Your Church Grow.* Ventura, CA: Regal Books.

Wikipedia. "Mindset." http://en.wikipedia.org/wiki/Mindset (accessed April 23, 2010).

Wilkerson, David. "A Call to Anguish." YouTube Web site. http://www.youtube.com/watch?v=lGMG_PVaJoI (accessed June 20, 2011).

Zodhiates, Spiros, ed. *The Hebrew-Greek Key Study Bible.* Chattanooga, TN: AMG Publishers.

Zwicky, Arnold. "No Pain, No Gain?" *Language Log.* http://itre.cis.upenn.edu/~myl/languagelog/archives/002454.ht ml (accessed: June 4, 2011).

CPSIA information can be obtained at www.ICGtesting.com
Printed in the USA
LVOW11s1319141214

418773LV00002B/293/P